INDIRA

ALSO BY KRISHAN BHATIA

*The Ordeal of Nationhood: A Social
Study of India Since Independence* (1971)

INDIRA

A BIOGRAPHY
OF PRIME MINISTER GANDHI

Krishan Bhatia

PRAEGER PUBLISHERS
New York • Washington

Photographs on pages 56, 58, 59, 63, and 65 courtesy the Nehru Memorial Library, New Delhi, India. Photographs on pages 158 and 218 courtesy the *Illustrated Weekly of India*. Photograph bottom of page 213 courtesy Rajan Devadas. All other photographs courtesy the Press Information Bureau, the Government of India.

Published in the United States of America in 1974
by Praeger Publishers, Inc.
111 Fourth Avenue, New York, N.Y. 10003

Library of Congress Cataloging in Publication Data

Bhatia, Krishan, 1925–
    Indira: a biography of Prime Minister Gandhi.
    Bibliography: p. 283
    1. Gandhi, Indira Nehru, 1917– 2. India—
Politics and government—1947– I. Title.
DS481.G23B48   954.04'092'4 [B]   72-92880
ISBN 0-275-19900-2

Printed in the United States of America

TO KANTA

ONCE AGAIN WITH LOVE

Contents

Preface

Writing the biography of a political leader who is still in power is always difficult. It is a particularly sensitive task when the subject is a person like Indira Gandhi, who is notably jealous of her privacy and permits others to pry into her mind only to the extent to which performance of her duties as Prime Minister justifies such sharing.

I came to Delhi from Lahore as a journalist in 1946, about the same time Mrs. Gandhi arrived there with her already illustrious father, the year before he became Prime Minister. One of my earliest reporting assignments was to follow Jawaharlal Nehru as he guided the Constituent Assembly in Delhi in the task of framing free India's Constitution or traveled to various parts of the country coping with the diverse and complex new problems of national independence. As I look back to that period, I am surprised to realize how little one noticed Jawaharlal's daughter then. Her proximity to her father seemed to shroud her in obscurity the way a circle of darkness covers the base of a candle. In my later years in Delhi, I covered or analyzed most major political developments of the time. With many of those events Mrs. Gandhi was associated either directly or indirectly as her father's conscience-keeper and unofficial adviser. But even then one had always to make a special effort to identify her specific role. She has always been, as she herself says, and this book concludes, a very private person.

Besides drawing upon my own understanding of personalities and events, past and present, in the course of writing this biography I interviewed a number of people who worked with Mrs. Gandhi or her father, or were close to the Nehru family, or played a part in the events to which I make reference. In selecting people for such interviews,

their integrity and reputation for veracity was as important a consideration as their possession of important information. I also met with Mrs.
Gandhi a few times, but reliance on direct interviews with her was
limited by my own choice and for two reasons: First, I did not wish
the book to be only or essentially an account of the Prime Minister's
life as she herself sees it. Second, I believe that, beyond a certain point,
dependence on direct interviews restricts an author's scope for independent assessments.

My concern with events and those who shaped them grew out of
my years as a political columnist in India and later as editor of a leading English-language daily. In these capacities, I had access to the most
exclusive political circles in Delhi. But I have always been anxious to
maintain a certain distance between myself and top politicians and in
nearly thirty years as a journalist have guarded strenuously against getting too close to a leader or becoming the "trusted friend" of someone
in power. I find that, whatever special insights into events such proximity to the seat of power might bring, a journalist always pays dearly
in terms of lessened professional independence. As I wrote this book
I watched over myself with sternness born of old habit. In collecting
material for it, I met Mrs. Gandhi's opponents as well as her supporters. In assessing the material I endeavored consciously to try to see that
her successes—and they have been many—did not influence my judgment about her failures. And vice versa. I hope the fact that for the last
seven years I have lived in the United States (though I have made frequent trips home during that time) has lent my narrative additional
perspective. My aim has been to provide as objective an account as possible of the Indian Prime Minister's life.

I regret that I cannot thank individually all those who contributed
in various ways to the writing of this book. I would, however, like to
express my appreciation for the help I received from Lois Decker
O'Neill, senior editor and director of the Washington office of Praeger
Publishers. Mrs. O'Neill, who herself lived in India with her husband
and family for many years, offered valuable suggestions, asked perti-
nent questions, and generally made my work go happily.

Washington, D.C.
February, 1974

PART I

Confluences

1

Daughter for the Nehrus

As those who were present at the time remember it, the day she was born was bright and sunny and pleasantly cool. The morning mist that floated over Allahabad from the nearby Ganges had disappeared to leave behind a clear, cloudless sky. It was that brisk, welcome time of the north-Indian year when men and women like to spend the best part of the day outside their houses, basking in the gentle sunshine.

The gardens of Anand Bhavan, the "House of Joy," as the sprawling bungalow of the Nehru family was named, were, as always, especially inviting. The *malis* who tended them had only a few weeks earlier severely pruned the extensive beds of hybrid tea roses and given the carefully nurtured prize bushes their first feed of organic manure. There would not be an abundance of blooms until the Christmas holidays, but the beds looked beautifully kept, and already many kinds of perennials and creepers were in flower. The lemon trees that flanked the front lawn were covered with fragrant blossoms mixed in with young fruit. Towards the rear of the house, by a servants' quarters, rows of papayas were ripening, and from the dark, shiny foliage of the massive mango trees quarrelsome yellow-green parrots darted to plunder the fresh crop of guavas for which Allahabad was famed.

But that day, the nineteenth of November, 1917, the gardens of Anand Bhavan were empty of people save for the *malis* watering the vegetable beds and the rose garden from their supple goatskin bags.

There was no one strolling on the close-clipped lawn, no one on the grass tennis court.

Indoors, the household had an atmosphere of tense expectancy. Besides the members of the immediate family, a number of cousins, aunts, and even more distant relatives had assembled for the birth of the child. They sat around nervously, anxious to appear to be involved in the event yet not knowing what they might do. They flitted about attending to needless chores with feverish energy, thereby demonstrating their presence and their concern. The expectant father, Jawaharlal, then twenty-eight, stood on one side of the large living room. His face showed a studied expression of nonchalance, yet he was conspicuously self-conscious and worried. His father, Motilal Nehru, whose house it was, also waited at home as anxiously as everyone else. This was the first child to be born to his only son, whom he loved beyond measure. But Motilal, unlike "Jawahar," as the family called him, was composed and cheerful, joking with people around him, in charge of himself and the occasion, as he always was. He had, after all, made the arrangements, and, as usual in his household, no thought or cost had been spared.

Across the bungalow's central courtyard, doctors and nurses were assembled to deliver the child. As was customary the delivery was to take place at home and not in the local civil hospital. But there was one thing about the arrangements that was decidedly not customary. Ordinarily, Hindu girls go to their parents' home for the birth of their first child. Their own families look after them in the later months of pregnancy, bear the expenses involved in the delivery, and then send them back to their in-laws. This social obligation, next in importance only to the provision of a suitable dowry at the time of marriage, springs from a general belief that a bride may not have established her position in the new household by the time the first child is expected. By all accounts, nearly twenty months after her wedding, the barely eighteen years old Kamala was still something of an alien in the Nehru family and would probably have been happier having her first child in Delhi, where her parents lived. But Motilal, whose affection for his young daughter-in-law was deep and genuine, had insisted that she stay in Allahabad, where he could command the services of the best of the British doctors then available.

It was a Scotsman who delivered the child and brought the awaited

news. He trundled across the courtyard to where Jawaharlal was standing and announced, "It's a bonny lassie, sir."

Indira's grandmother, Swarup Rani, could not conceal her disappointment. She blurted out, "Oh, but it should have been a boy."

Despite the family's European life style, Swarup Rani remained set
in her orthodox ideas. Within Anand Bhavan she preserved a small
world of her own where she read the Hindu scriptures, offered prayers
to various deities, and followed the rituals of the ancient religion. Her
husband's unbounded admiration for Western culture and her own
several visits to Europe in his company had not changed her basic
attitudes and beliefs. As for her preference for a grandson, her sentiments on the point were seemingly given a touch of tragic intensity by
the fact that she herself had lost two sons soon after their birth. Only
Jawahar and his two sisters had survived.

Motilal was angered by this display of prejudice on the part of his
wife. She must not say such a thing or even think it, he sternly told
her. "Have we made any distinction between our son and daughters
in their upbringing? Do you not love them equally? This daughter of
Jawahar, for all you know, may prove better than a thousand sons," he
is supposed to have said before walking away to emphasize his
annoyance.

Possibly history's subsequent course affected the memory of the
member of the household who later recorded those words, but that
Jawaharlal had had a daughter, not a son, obviously caused a certain
disappointment. It created a situation of some delicacy a few days after
the birth. An old Muslim family servant, who was dying of cancer,
asked to see Jawaharlal's child and give it his blessings. Munshi Mubarak Ali, or Munshiji, as he was respectfully called, had spent virtually
his entire life serving the Nehru family. In his later years he had
risen to be chief of a staff comprising nearly fifty servants from sweepers and scullery boys to expert cooks and hunting guides. As Munshiji
fought a losing battle with his incurable ailment, Motilal and his wife
frequently visited him in his cottage on the grounds of Anand Bhavan.
During one such call the old servant had asserted his determination to
cling to life until he had seen young Jawaharlal's child. Motilal therefore proposed a formal visit to Munshiji's deathbed to show him the
child. A few days after birth she looked like a porcelain doll with an
unusually thick mop of black hair. Bundled in a fine Kashmir shawl,

she was carried to the cottage by her grandmother. As he held the child in his arms, Mubarak Ali took it for granted that he was seeing Jawaharlal's son, and he showered on the tiny girl the prayers and blessings customarily reserved for the male heir of a dear friend. No one pointed out his mistaken assumption, for fear of causing him disappointment. A few days later, when he died, he carried with him the belief that the family name of his employer and benefactor had been assured continuance for another generation.

Probably Motilal himself, his European orientation and rebuke to his wife notwithstanding, was not entirely free from a sense of disappointment over being denied a grandson. On the day of the birth those who came to felicitate Motilal on the happy event were offered Scotch whiskey, a routine drink for visitors to the Nehru house that did not suggest anything special or festive. The elder Nehru's large cellar was well stocked, but he did not bring out his vintage champagne that evening in a spontaneous display of his happiness. It was not until a few days later, by which time he probably had admonished himself for any inadequacy in his enthusiasm, that Motilal brought out champagne to celebrate the birth of the child he named Indira, after his mother.

Her parents added Priyadarshini or "dear to behold" to this name. Later her family often called her "Indu." But it was Indira, the name her grandfather chose, by which she would be known to Allahabad, to India, and, in time, after she became Prime Minister governing a country of over 550 million people, to the world.

Across the street from the house in which Indira was born is the famous Bharadwaj Ashram. This place of religious retreat and instruction is named after the legendary sage revered for his piety and learning who figures in the Hindu epic the Ramayana, and it was at the spot where the Ashram is now located that Rama, the god-hero of the epic, is said to have met the saint before crossing the river to extend his wanderings to the southern parts of India. Allahabad, among the oldest cities of India, is also, for Hindus, among the most sacred. It is mentioned in the Puranas, or the Hindu scriptures belonging to a period well before the beginning of the Christian era. According to Hindu mythology, when Vishnu the creator had the seas of the universe churned for nectar, a few drops fell where Allahabad now stands. The Hindus called the city Prayag, or the place of a thousand *yagnas* (ritual fires). Another ancient name by which the city was known was Triveni, from its situation at the confluence of three rivers, the Ganga (or the Ganges, to give it its Anglicized name), the Jamuna, and the mythical Saraswati. Because the Aryan settlers who gave India its dominant religion and philosophy lived mainly along the river banks, all streams and waterways assumed special importance in Hindu ritual. A point where three rivers joined together, as they did at Prayag, inevitably became sanctified, and thousands have visited Allahabad every year for untold years for a dip at the confluence to cleanse themselves of past sins. The city acquired its present name, meaning the abode of Allah, in the fifteenth century, when Akbar, the Moghul Emperor, built a fort at Triveni to mark what was then the eastern extremity of his empire.

Allahabad is still sacred for millions of Hindus. But no longer is it either the frontier of a medieval empire or, as it was for a long time under the British, the capital of an important province. Today it shows unmistakable signs of physical decay and economic decline and is hardly distinguishable from numerous other district headquarters and military cantonments that the British left behind them. The old city, with its traditional markets and bazaars, its narrow winding lanes and cramped houses, is on one side of the railway track, while on the other side is the area known as Civil Lines, where the British ruling class lived in large colonial bungalows, sometimes even palace like residences, each set in the center of a 3- to 4-acre plot of land. Many of these houses still stand and are occupied, but no attempt is made to hide their state of neglect. The gardens are overgrown with weeds, flowering shrubs have given place to tangled undergrowth, the fruit trees are being strangled by vigorous and merciless climbers. The magnificent porches where former residents and their visitors alighted from their carriages are crumbling, as are the canopied structures built on decorative pillars in the middle of the garden for people to sit and enjoy the cool breeze during the rainy season. Inside these bungalows are reminders of former glory—large gilt-framed mirrors, life-size portraits, the annual group photographs of the local gymkhana club, often covered with grime. What might have been the house of a general or a senior British administrator may now be a local government office, a complex of diverse small stores, or even a gas station. Anand Bhavan itself, the house of the Nehrus, is a museum.

In 1917, when Indira was born, Allahabad—or at least its Civil Lines—had an air of elegant aloofness. It was the capital of the United Provinces, one of the largest administrative units of British India, and the seat of the provincial High Court. (The provincial capital shifted to Lucknow in 1922, but the High Court has stayed in Allahabad.) The British had built not only large residences but also numerous beautiful churches with sleek steeples and an abundance of stained glass. Allahabad probably has more churches than any other former provincial capital, and their construction may well have been intended to de-emphasize the city's unmistakable, perhaps overwhelming, Hindu character for the benefit of its foreign elite.

That elite scrupulously avoided fraternizing with almost all Indians, regarding them as socially inferior. It admitted into its small, exclusive, social circle only a few "natives" who, in its estimate, had adequately imbibed Western culture. On the Civil Lines' paved streets there moved only the two-horse victorias and an occasional motor car; the lowly single-horse *ikka,* which provided local transportation for the ordinary Indian, was banished to the rutted streets of the old city. The shopping center in the area, designed to serve patrician needs, and Alfred Park with its imposing statue of Queen Victoria were virtually out of bounds to the common man. A contemporary of Indira Gandhi, who is now a judge of Allahabad High Court, recalls how many a time he was chased away by angry guards if he ventured into the park in non-European clothes.

The Nehru family, of course, had gained social acceptance in the city's European community long before Indira's birth. Anand Bhavan into which Motilal, the hugely successful barrister, had moved in 1900 was not strictly part of the Civil Lines, but it was far enough from Karimganj, the old, congested city where the family had lived for many years earlier and where Indira's father, Jawaharlal, was born, to be another world.

It was Motilal who built the family fortune and achieved something like social equality with the British—and national prominence. But the Nehrus, Kashmiri Brahmins or Pandits who had left their ancestral homes in the snowy, lake-studded Vale in Northern India several generations ago and settled down in a few urban centers like Allahabad, had already produced other distinguished lawyers. They had also had their share of the trials and tribulations usually suffered by people in search of a new place to grow roots.

The Kashmiri Pandits constitute what was and still is one of the smallest and culturally closest-knit communities in India. Yet its cohesiveness and strong sense of communal belonging may be among the less important of its characteristics. Also typical of the Kashmiri Brahmins are such traits as shrewdness, adaptability, an uncanny capacity to judge friends and foes, and a remarkable instinct for survival. (Significantly, these were the very qualities that enabled Indira Gandhi to turn herself from a weak leader of a dilapidated party constantly plagued by ambitious rivals and powerful enemies into a Prime Minister with almost awesome, unchallenged authority.) It is commonly believed that several centuries ago a number of Brahmins fled from the valley of Kashmir into the plains of the Punjab and beyond to escape the tyranny of the Vale's Muslim rulers. These Pandits apparently had exercised, as they do in modern Kashmir, political and economic influence far out of proportion to their numerical strength and had thus invited upon themselves the wrath of the Muslim administrators, who were not known for religious tolerance and broadmindedness. On other occasions in the past, many Kashmiri Pandits presumably left their cramped homeland for the big cities and princely courts of India in search of jobs and personal advancement. But the total number of migrants was small. According to one estimate, Kashmiri Brahmins settled outside Kashmir numbered no more than about 5,000 at the beginning of the present century when India's total population was nearly 300 million.

It is a measure of their unusual capacity to adjust themselves to their surroundings and circumstances that once they left their homeland Kashmiri Pandits seldom looked back. Neither the heat and dust of the Punjab and Uttar Pradesh nor the sandy flatness of Rajasthan made them yearn unduly for Kashmir's massive mountain ranges, magnificent cherry blossoms, and snow-fed streams. When they took up abode in Lahore, Jaipur, Delhi, Agra, or Allahabad, theirs was not a Diaspora that must end in a Return. The Kashmiri expatriates would often visit relatives and friends they had left behind, but if time inexorably caused their emotional ties with the homeland to weaken and wither away, few Kashmiris put up any resistance. Jawaharlal often visited Kashmir, but less because Kashmir appealed to some ancestral attachments buried deep in his mind than because he loved mountains and glaciers. He admired the Himalayan ranges of Assam with equal fervor and would probably have visited them oftener had they been more easily accessible from where he lived. His daughter's attachment to Kashmir was to be even more tenuous and less noticeable. Like the Nehrus, other Kashmiri Brahmins who migrated to the plains readily came to terms with their new environs, but despite their being a tiny minority and despite a willingness in certain respects to blend with the surrounding scenery, they preserved their distinctive identity. Perhaps the very smallness of their community enabled it to maintain its exclusive character. Even in a city of Allahabad's size, there were no more than a few hundred Kashmiri Pandits. Each of them was known to the others. All would be invited to a wedding or any other comparable social event, and most marriages were arranged within the community. Thus, although Motilal had adopted many Western values and practices and his son had studied in Britain, when time came to look for a bride for Jawahar, the search never went beyond the small, restricted circle of Kashmiri Brahmins. (A quarter of a century later, when Indira wanted to marry a Parsi from Bombay, it would require a tremendous intellectual and emotional effort on Nehru's part to cross the caste barrier involved in the proposed wedding.) That most Kashmiris are fair complexioned, with facial characteristics denoting their Central Asian origin, also helped them retain their separate identity and won them ready social acceptance from the British. Their pale, Occidental complexions prompted many other Indians, with their notorious weakness for fair skin, notwithstanding frequent protestations to the contrary, to regard Kashmiri Pandits with special deference. For their part, most Kashmiris expected to be considered members of a somewhat superior community. As they often justifiably reminded themselves, there was almost no illiteracy among them, their women disdained *purdah,* and they had produced from amongst them an unusually large number of *dewans* (prime ministers of former princely states) and distinguished scholars.

Indira's ancestors left Kashmir in the beginning of the eighteenth century "to seek fame and fortune in the rich plains below," as Jawaharlal Nehru later wrote. One of them, Raj Kaul, was a noted Sanskrit and Persian scholar who had attracted the attention of the then Moghul Emperor, Farruksiar, during the latter's visit to the beauteous valley. It was probably at the invitation of the Moghul ruler that Raj Kaul joined the Delhi court. As a mark of imperial favor he was given a house on the bank of a canal and a *jagir,* or rights of overlordship, for a number of villages. The location of the house gave the family the name by which it later came to be known—Nehru is a corrupted version of *nehar,* which means canal. For a period, Indira's distant forefathers sported the hyphenated family name of Kaul-Nehru. Later, the Kaul was dropped.

Raj Kaul's good fortune did not last long. In 1719, when he had barely started enjoying the financial fruits of the *jagir,* his patron, Farruksiar, was deposed and later put to death by the order of his own ministers. The disintegration of the Moghul Empire had already started, and in the following century or so its size and authority dwindled steadily under the relentless pressure of the expanding political power of the British East India Company. The decline in the fortunes of the Kaul-Nehrus virtually corresponded with the contraction of the prestige and position of the Moghul court. By the middle of the next century, when Indian soldiers rose in revolt against the company's control, Indira's great-grandfather, Ganga Dhar, was Delhi's *kotwal.* This post was a senior one in the city's police hierarchy and probably fairly important, but it was obviously a far cry from the position of feudal nobility that the family had originally occupied.

The so-called Mutiny of 1857 was put down with a firm and bloody hand. In punishment for the Indian soldiers' action in raising the standard of revolt and killing a number of European residents of Delhi and the nearby city of Meerut, the British deposed and exiled the last of the Moghul emperors, Bahadur Shah, a figure straight out of a Greek tragedy. They also executed by shooting or hanging over twenty princes and allowed their troops to run amuck in Delhi. British soldiers killed able-bodied men indiscriminately as possible rebels and continued looting and plundering shops and private homes for weeks after the uprising had collapsed. Thousands of terror-stricken residents camped temporarily some miles outside the city in the hope of returning when the orgy of killing and looting ended. But many others left the city for good—among them Ganga Dhar and his family. They headed towards Agra, 120 miles to the south of Delhi, and they very nearly lost their lives on the way. As Jawaharlal tells it in his *Autobiography,* the family was stopped by a posse of British soldiers, who suspected that a baby daughter, very fair in complexion, was an English child whom the family had somehow kidnapped. In the venomous mood of those days this suspicion could have been enough to cause the entire family to be hanged from the nearest tree, and the soldiers almost proceeded to administer such summary "justice." Ganga Dhar knew no English, but fortunately one of his young sons could speak it well enough to explain the truth to the soldiers and convince them of the family's innocence.

Ganga Dhar died three months before his son Motilal was born in Agra in 1861, leaving the responsibility of bringing up the child and looking after the rest of the sizable family on his two older sons, Bansi Dhar and Nand Lal. The latter studied law and built a big practice first in Agra and later in Allahabad when the provincial High Court moved there. It was he who took young Motilal under his protective wing and established with him a bond of deep affection.

Motilal was known in his boyhood for his high spirits and irresistible fascination for pranks and practical jokes. Until he was twelve, he studied no English, only Arabic and Persian. But once he realized the importance of English in making a successful career under the British Raj, he learned it quickly and well. In Muir Central College, which later grew into Allahabad University, his British professors not only regarded his escapades with indulgence but many of them developed much affection for him. He, on his part, idolized some of them, particularly the principal, Mr. Harrison, who often rode through the college on a high-wheeled bicycle. These bonds of mutual admiration frequently saved Motilal from the punishment that he might normally have received for his acts of exuberance and seeming indiscipline. But, what was more important, they created in him much fondness for European, particularly British, culture—a fondness that was to determine the way of life of the Nehrus and to help shape the political outlook of Jawaharlal and later, though to a lesser extent, of Indira.

Influenced apparently by the example of his elder brother and possibly because the bar was the only field in which Indians at the time could expect social advancement and adequate financial rewards, Motilal took to law as a profession. After a 3-year apprenticeship in a lower court in Kanpur, he moved to Allahabad, which offered a considerably larger professional pasture. Soon after his arrival in Allahabad, however, he lost his elder brother, Nand Lal, and at twenty-five became the head of and the only breadwinner for a large joint family comprising, among others, seven nephews and nieces. He himself was married when he was only eighteen but lost his wife as well as a son born to her. His second wife, Swarup Rani, a girl with features and complexion described as of "Dresden China perfection" lost her first son but in 1889 gave birth to a second, who was called Jawaharlal (a name that he, as he confessed many years later, disliked intensely).

Motilal, by all accounts, worked exceedingly hard to establish himself as a successful lawyer. His first brief brought him only five rupees, a fact he once mentioned to his son to emphasize the uphill task he had had to tackle at that stage of his career. Within a few years, however, he was earning 2,000 rupees per month, which in India of the 1890s was a veritable fortune. It enabled him to fulfill his family obligations—he spent generously on his nephews' education and the maintenance of numerous other relations—and also to live in a style that was the envy of many a senior British administrator. That his late brother had had an extensive legal practice undoubtedly helped Motilal, but he would not have been able to hold on to the former's clients and briefs if he had not had professional competence of his own. His grasp of the Indian civil law—he usually disdained briefs involving criminal violations—was stupendous. The civil law then was a confusing mass of jurisprudence in which many British concepts had been superimposed on traditional Hindu and Muslim laws relating to property and inheritance. More experienced lawyers were often daunted by its complexities, but Motilal's understanding of it was truly impressive. Additionally, he was a forceful speaker with complete mastery over English, then the language of the courts.

In the British system of justice the laws of contempt are so severe that judges often tend to treat lawyers brusquely and sometimes even insult them, in the knowledge that most will accept everything meekly. Not so Motilal, who gave the bench the deference to which its members were entitled but would tolerate no undeserved rebuke or even seeming lack of courtesy on the part of the judges. On one occasion, when a senior and widely respected member of the bar, who was later knighted, was insulted unjustifiably by a haughty British judge in an open court, Motilal was bitter that the lawyer had accepted the humiliation without protest. He wrote about the incident to his son, who was then studying in England, and remarked angrily that the judge would not have got away with it if he had "dared talk to me in that manner."

Such strong personal pride was an important trait in Motilal's character—a trait that Jawaharlal, and Indira after him, inherited. Another legacy from Motilal was his volatile temper. Jawaharlal could lose his temper almost instantaneously over something as routine and minor as a momentary failure of a loudspeaker system at a political rally he was addressing, just as his father often worked himself into a towering rage over trivial matters.

Servants as well as members of the family scrupulously avoided giving Motilal cause to be angry. Swarup Rani herself was a strong-willed person and in domestic matters a bit of a Tartar, but she always took care not to cross her husband's path. Motilal's wrath was like a flash flood, however, for it developed suddenly, sweeping away whatever happened to be in its path, but spending itself quickly. On one occasion when he was dining with Jawaharlal and some others, Motilal recited a Persian couplet and asked his son if he followed the rather subtle thought it contained. Jawaharlal, whose knowledge of Persian did not match his father's, avoided giving a direct answer and tried to change the subject. The father, however, persisted and in the process needled Jawaharlal for not understanding fine Persian poetry. This occurred at a time when father and son had been arguing about the political goal of the Indian independence movement. Young Nehru believed that complete independence would come only through severence of all political links with Britain. His father reasoned that Dominion status within the British Commonwealth would bring the country the freedom it sought. When Motilal continued to tease young Jawaharlal about his inability to appreciate poetry, the son finally remarked with unconcealed testiness that he, at least, understood the difference between independence and Dominion status, which his father did not. Motilal seemed stunned that his son would fling this insult at him when others were present. Next moment, he was seized by such a fit of anger that he grabbed the edge of the dining table and upturned it, throwing all the silver and china dishes on the floor.

"His temper was indeed an awful thing and even in after years I do not think I ever came across anything to match it in its own line," Jawaharlal wrote in his *Autobiography*. But if Motilal made it abundantly clear that he was the master in the house, whose wishes must be respected and orders obeyed, he was by no means parsimonious in giving of his love and affection to his family. Jawaharlal bore no resentiment or ill will towards his father, and his "admiration and affection for him remained as strong as ever." As for Indira, she has nothing but the warmest of feelings for her grandfather, who doted on her and indulged her to the point of spoiling her.

A relative of Indira's on her mother's side once referred to Motilal with a touch of contempt as *nouveau riche.* Motilal had undoubtedly greatly enlarged the family fortune and some aspects of his life style were rather *parvenu,* but the suggestion is uncharitable. He lived well, in fact ostentatiously, because he genuinely enjoyed the pleasures of life. In the words of his son, "The idea of hoarding money seemed to my father a slight on his own capacity to earn whenever he liked and as much as he desired. Full of the spirit of play and fond of good living in every way, he found no difficulty in spending what he earned. And gradually our ways became more and more Westernized."

Motilal built Anand Bhavan, the house in which Indira was born, large enough to accommodate not only his own family but also numerous guests who came to stay for long periods. A sprawling structure with massive thick walls and a wide verandah running all round it, the bungalow had an indoor swimming pool with a row of dressing rooms for men on one side and for women on the other. It also housed a retinue of servants, and there was provision for several magnificent riding horses and ponies and numerous dogs. Many years later, in a corner of the extensive grounds attached to the bungalow, Motilal built a more modern and somewhat smaller house and transferred the name Anand Bhavan to it. The new 2-story house looked curiously like a wedding cake crowned with a dome-like structure for which the designer seemingly got his inspiration from the round pith helmet that nineteenth-century European soldiers and explorers wore in the tropics. The older bungalow, renamed Swaraj Bhavan, or "House of Independence," was bequeathed to the Indian National Congress, the political party with which the Nehrus had become closely associated by then.

In later years, particularly after Jawaharlal cast his charismatic spell on it, a doting public told many a fanciful story about the Nehru family's wealth and the magnificence of their standard of living. Some would say the Governor of the United Provinces wanted to hire Motilal's cook but could not afford to pay his wages. Their clothes, it was said, were sent to Paris for laundering. The grain of fact on which such a story was elaborately built was usually quite small and not unreasonable. The tale about clothes being sent to Paris for washing, for example, started when, during a visit to Europe, Motilal left a suit of clothes with the cleaners, who later sent it to him in India. Exaggerated though they were, these stories effectively suggest the extent to which the high-spending existence of the Nehrus fascinated others.

Many Indian families, some whose heads were considerably wealthier than Motilal, lived extravagantly. But the Nehrus had a style all their own. They consciously chose to live like *sahibs*—and yet did not appear to be mindlessly aping the British. The reason for this was simple. When he left Karimganj to live in Civil Lines, Motilal was not trying to ingratiate himself with the foreign rulers in the hope of personal favors so much as he was escaping from the backward-looking, tradition-bound society into which the urban middle class had then grown. But the Nehrus revolted against the narrowmindedness and insularity of Indian society, not against its fundamental values, and thus, although Anand Bhavan adopted the modern conveniences of a British home, it retained the atmosphere of graciousness and ebullience traditionally associated with Indian families of social standing.

Theirs was the first house in Allahabad to be equipped with electricity and running water. New household appliances and gadgets then making their appearance in Britain and the United States fascinated Motilal, and he hastened to acquire them. During his several visits to Europe in the first decade of the century, he spent a small fortune on the finest of furnishings and draperies for his house. In 1904 he bought his first motor car, even before the Governor of the United Provinces had one. Later, while traveling in Europe, he purchased a Fiat and a Lancia and imported them into India. One of the favorite photographs in the Nehru family album is of a large automobile, with a forbidding tool box on the side and an ornate luggage rack on top, parked in front of the original Anand Bhavan. A little girl dressed in European clothes is framed in the rear-seat windows. At the wheel is Motilal wearing a cap and a cavalry mustache, every inch the would-be English country squire.

Only one aspect of the life in Anand Bhavan is represented in that photograph, however. There were, of course, tea parties on the spacious lawns and some social tennis—the favorite pastimes of India's colonial ruling class. Motilal also rode and hunted and encouraged his children to do the same. But, thanks largely to his encompassing zest

for life, Anand Bhavan was conspicuously devoid of the starchy stiffness and cold aloofness commonly associated with the British upper
classes of the time. If he played tennis occasionally, Motilal also always
remained fond of wrestling or *dangal,* as it was called in Hindustani.
As a young man, he often wrestled himself. (Indian wrestling with its
elaborate rules is a much more civilized sport than the no-holds-barred
version popular in the West.) In later years he frequently watched
good wrestling bouts, and, when his preoccupation with work denied
him the time for such shows, he would sometimes encourage the young
from amongst the household staff to organize a brief contest for his
enjoyment. The family usually ate in Western style sitting around a
dining table large enough to seat twenty-four and using expensive egg-
shell china and silver cutlery. But every so often Motilal and others in
the house would revert to the customary Indian method and eat squatting on the ground and with their fingers out of silver trays ceremoniously placed before them on low wooden tables. He himself had little
interest in Hindu religion or any care for the various taboos it pre-
scribes for believers. But he respected the right of others in the house
to follow their consciences in the matter. Swarup Rani, like most
Hindu women of the time, stuck to her orthodox way of life, and so
did Rajvati, a widowed sister of hers who lived with them. They both
maintained their own *puja* rooms, where they spent long hours daily
reading the Hindu scriptures and offering prayers.

Perhaps the most important element in the atmosphere in Anand
Bhavan was the scale and warmth of its hospitality. It was perpetually
an open house. Members of the Kashmiri community, professional associates, and friends from various parts of India or abroad arrived there
in large numbers and were always welcome. Anand Bhavan maintained two separate kitchens: one with Christian and Muslim cooks
catering exclusively European-style dishes, the other manned by Hindu
cooks responsible for producing Indian food. Whatever the style, the
menus were always elaborate and the food delicious. Motilal was himself fond of good food and wine—his wine cellar in those days was believed to be one of the finest in India—and enjoyed good company.
When he left Allahabad for even a brief visit to a hill station, his cook
and other staff would precede him, and provisions would arrive at the
temporary kitchen on the backs of several mules. While in Allahabad,
however pressing the brief in hand, he would shut his law books at

about 7 P.M. and be ready to receive friends. Over a glass of wine or a Scotch and soda there would be pleasant discussions on subjects ranging from the latest order of the British Viceroy to the philosophic basis for the medieval cult of Sufi-ism. The host himself joined in the debate with enthusiasm and punctuated it with appropriate quotations from Persian and Arabic poetry or relieved dull moments with his witty remarks. His capacity for genuinely mirthful laughter was enormous. St. Nihal Singh, an Indian journalist who spent the best part of his life in Europe, stayed in Anand Bhavan in 1910 and found the "intellectual feasts served in the evening stimulating." He also left the following account of the hospitality he received there:

> The meals were good enough to be placed before royalty. Wine flowed liberally—wine of many kinds. With the dessert were brought boxes of cigars and cigarettes and liqueurs. A fair-sized bar could have been opened with the decanters placed in front of us.

At the time St. Nihal Singh visited Allahabad and wrote this account, Motilal's involvement in politics was confined by and large to an occasional verbal probe into the actions of the British Government and its representatives in India. Of his father's political inclinations then, Jawaharlal wrote in his *Autobiography*:

> He was, of course, a nationalist in a vague sense of the word, but he admired Englishmen and their ways. He had a feeling that his own countrymen had fallen low and almost deserved what they had got. And there was a trace of contempt in his mind for the politicians who talked without doing anything, though he had no idea at all as to what else they could do.

The Nehru family's first exposure to the West had occurred in 1897, when Motilal's eldest brother, Bansi Dhar, undertook a round-the-world voyage, the highlights of which included watching the diamond jubilee celebrations of Queen Victoria's reign in London and an audience with President McKinley in Washington. Motilal himself visited Europe two years later, invoking as had his brother the wrath of the orthodox community. On his return he angrily refused to do *praiyashchit* or religious penitence to "purify" himself after his "sinful" act in crossing the sea and eating with the "unclean foreigners." When he dismissed the demand as "tomfoolery," the priests excommunicated him and ordered a social boycott of him. In the decade that followed, undeterred by the communal sanctions, he crossed the sea several more times to visit Europe.

That he turned to Britain so often and with such zest was not merely an angry reaction to the tyranny of the foolish and narrowminded section of the Kashmiri community. His admiration for British culture was genuine and deep-seated. He engaged a European governess for his two daughters and an Englishman to tutor Jawaharlal not because he wanted to cock a snook at his social tormentors but because he was convinced of the superiority of British education. He sent his son to Harrow and Cambridge after preliminary tutoring at home and would have done so even if he had had no provocation from the Kashmiri community. In a speech in 1907 he said of Britain:

> England has fed us with the best food that her language, her literature, her science, her art and, above all, her free institutions could supply. We have learned and grown on that wholesome food for a century and are fast approaching the age of maturity.

To those in India who were even then getting impatient with Britain's niggardliness in responding to the country's demand for self-government, Motilal spoke reassuringly. He firmly believed, he told them, that "John Bull means well—it is not in his nature to mean ill."

Any void in the Nehru family's life about the time of Indira's birth that might have been caused by the aloofness of the more orthodox in the Kashmiri community or of the extremists in Indian politics was entirely filled by Motilal's European friends. The Nehrus had numerous close acquaintances among top British administrators, and the circle of Motilal's personal friends included the governor of the province. The governor sometimes visited Anand Bhavan and invited the Nehrus to Government House for dinner and garden parties. The high-water mark of the family's social acceptability had probably come in 1911, when Motilal and his wife were invited to attend the *durbar,* or public audience, that King George V, Emperor of India, held in Delhi during the royal visit to the Empire. Motilal was duly impressed and flattered and cabled excitedly to Jawaharlal, who was then studying in Britain, to get the court dress prescribed for the occasion. Confirming that he had ordered the dress, Jawaharlal wrote:

> I suppose you want the ordinary levee dress with sword and everything complete. The shoes for the court dress will be made at Knighton's and the

gloves at Travellette's. . . . the hats I am sending ought to fit you. Heath's man has managed to fish out your old measures and cast, and he will shape your hats accordingly.

At that Delhi *durbar,* the Nehrus were accorded tremendous personal courtesy. They were accommodated in the special camp of the Lieutenant Governor (principal official) of the United Provinces, and Motilal noted with satisfaction that his wife was one of the two Indian women in the United Provinces camp. They were invited to all important functions and given the most prominent places and, as he gushingly wrote to his son later, "received special bows from the King and Queen."

Things were to change, and change rapidly. As Allahabad had been built at a confluence of rivers, so Anand Bhavan had been built at a confluence of historical currents. Unlike the waters of the Ganges, the Jamuna, and mythical Saraswati, they did not blend—though inside the walls of Motilal's mansion it had seemed for a time that they might.

On that sparkling November day in 1917 when Indira was born to the Nehrus, Anand Bhavan belonged to the Empire. The household had begun to feel faint stirrings of unease about this allegiance, but it belonged. By the time Indu was a bright-eyed, curly-haired little girl of two, her grandfather Motilal had lost his faith in the good intentions of John Bull and, led more and more by his son, was turning towards Mahatma Gandhi. The elder Nehru's love for Britain and its traditions remained unaffected, but his friends among the bureaucrats and senior administrators of the Raj had begun to regret their jovial past associations with the Nehrus.

The lawns of Anand Bhavan were beautifully kept as always. The mangoes ripened in the heat. The house resounded with Motilal's uproarious laughter as before. But all entrances to the grounds were under constant police surveillance. Indira was to grow up in a setting totally different from the one in which her father and her two aunts had lived as children.

2

"New Soul"

THE year of Indira's birth was, as her father frequently reminded her later, the year of the Russian revolution. For India, too, it was a time of turmoil and anguish. The changes taking place in the country were less abrupt and bloody than those in Czarist Russia but in their way as significant.

Looking back, 1917 can also be seen as a watershed for Indira's family. Some years earlier Motilal had longed for his son to join the Indian Civil Service, at the time often described admiringly as the "steelframe of the British Raj." His own pride in the Raj's acceptance of him and his family was such that on one occasion he had beamingly written to Jawaharlal of how, during a visit to Nainital, the Lieutenant Governor of the United Provinces had done him the honor of treating him as the chief guest at a dinner ("he taking in your mother and I, Mrs. Porter"). But his attitude and values had undergone a sea change. Motilal and Jawaharlal had long wrangled over the degree of trust that could be placed in Britain's good faith and the methods that might be employed to win national freedom. The son had often sharply criticized the father for being "immoderately moderate" in his approach. By 1917 circumstances had proved the younger Nehru right, and Motilal was rapidly moving towards greater political militancy. His faith in the good intentions of the British Government had been badly shaken. A few months before Indira's birth he was sending cables to the British Prime Minister, Lloyd

George, angrily protesting against Britain's "unconstitutional methods of repression in India."

Outside Anand Bhavan, the change was even more pronounced. At its Allahabad session held during the Christmas week of 1910 the Indian National Congress had formally passed a resolution recording its "deep and heartfelt joy" at the impending visit to India of King George and Queen Mary and offering them its "humble homage." It had retained the loyal-subject approach to politics well beyond that year, but by 1917 memories of such professions of loyalty to the British Crown had begun to embarrass most Congress Party leaders. The moderates had lost the battle in the party the way Motilal had at home and Mohandas Karamchand Gandhi, whom Winston Churchill many years later described as "the naked fakir," had arrived from South Africa to assume leadership of the freedom movement. The stage was set for the start of what proved to be one of the most extraordinary struggles that a subject people ever launched against their foreign rulers.

A few weeks after Indira's birth, in a brief, hurried note of congratulations to her parents, poetess Sarojini Naidu referred to Jawaharlal's daughter as "the new soul of India." Considering the enormous following that Indira later built for herself as Prime Minister, Mrs. Naidu's remark can be taken as almost prophetic. However, when she wrote that letter, she was simply using the child as a symbol in acknowledging the emergence of an India that, after centuries of stoic acceptance of humiliation and foreign oppression, was in a different and unusual mood of deep indignation.

The new India that Mrs. Naidu perceived had spent over three decades groping for a sense of purpose and acquiring a "soul." The Indian National Congress, later interchangeably called the Congress Party or simply the Congress, had been formed in 1885. Its origins were humble and unpretentious. At the time of its formation and for many years later it made no claim to be working for India's independence. Patriotic sentiments and a desire for freedom from undue foreign domination had existed even before its creation, but Indian nationalism was like a number of tiny seasonal streams that came to life briefly every now and then, tended to run along some unchanneled course, and often disappeared into the sandy vastness of apathy.

In the Congress the various small rivulets coalesced into a mighty river, which in time swept even massive rocks and boulders out of its path. But the process was gradual.

Ironically, it was a retired British civil servant, Allan Octavian Hume, and not some Indian political firebrand, who organized the Congress. Seventy-two Indians from various parts of the country responded to Hume's invitation and assembled in the auditorium of a Bombay college appropriately garbed in morning coats, striped trousers, and top hats, the prescribed dress for formal occasions (some made a small concession to their orthodoxy and wore silk turbans instead of top hats). To most of those invited, the first meeting of the Congress was no more revolutionary than the annual meeting of the Red Cross or an investiture ceremony in the governor's palace. In fact, the Governor of Bombay very nearly agreed to preside over it. Lord Dufferin, the then Viceroy, looked on the organization benignly, expecting it to function something like a docile and humble version of the Loyal Opposition in his own country.

For many years after its formation the Congress continued to affirm its undying loyalty to the British Crown, but gradually its pronouncements and resolutions began acquiring an abrasive, challenging note. Often what its leaders said was empty rhetoric. Hume, for example, talked of approaching "the great English nation" directly if the Raj failed to redress the people's grievances. At times, however, demands were concrete and the tone, as it sounded to British ears, even arrogant. The Congress criticized British authorities for denying Indians the right to bear arms and clamored for a share in senior administrative posts. It also urged reform of the legislative councils to make them more representative of the people. To British rulers who had put down the bloody rebellion of 1857 only a couple of generations earlier, such talk was not merely offensive but almost seditious; they thought it might, if not curbed, lead to another rebellion. Had it not been for the presence at its helm of a Briton of proved loyalty, the government would probably have extinguished the Congress Party during its infancy. Lord Dufferin regretted his misjudgment of the real nature and purpose of the organization, but the fact that he himself had encouraged its creation made an official attempt to liquidate it embarrassing. By the time the founding fathers of modern India, men like Bal Gangadhar Tilak and Gopal Krishna Gokhale, came to dominate it, the party had developed enough strength of its own to survive British displeasure.

The leadership for the growing party came largely from the new, Western-educated middle class, which at the time was acquiring an identity of its own, distinct from the feudal elements who until then had led the Indian people. Indians were among the first in Asia to take to Western education and the quickest to absorb the concepts of nationalism and democracy. By the end of the century the country had over 300 newspapers published in English and various Indian languages, which gave those concepts wide currency and secured them extensive public support. Some of the actions and attitudes of the British rulers only added to the Indian sense of humiliation and strengthened the movement for freedom. Unlike the Portuguese, who lacked any pronounced race prejudice and mixed freely with the people in their Indian colonies, the British held themselves aloof from the "natives" whom they treated, at best, patronizingly.

Most British civil servants of that period sincerely subscribed to the philosophy of Asians and Africans being the White Man's Burden. They considered the people over whom they ruled not only a subject race but also an inferior one. The natives, they believed, were entitled to kindness and consideration but occasionally must get a firm disciplining hand for their own good. In return they must offer those who had brought them the blessings of the Raj unreserved loyalty and abject submission. In the presence of a Briton, an Indian must speak softly and only when spoken to, fold his hands in a gesture of servility, and keep his eyes on the ground. He must approach his ruler barefoot. He must promptly close his umbrella, habitually used against the Indian sun, for an open umbrella might suggest a claim of equality on his part. It was not only the top-ranking British official who expected such demonstrations of meekness and self-abasement. Even the young, junior recruit to the administrative service or the armed forces whose own family and social background was often pretty humble would consider himself entitled to it. In railway trains, for example, there was no formal racial segregation, but should an Englishman enter the first-class compartment—and he seldom traveled in any other class— any Indian occupant who might already be there was expected to volunteer to move elsewhere. If the British traveler was in a gracious, friendly mood, he might permit the Indian to stay where he was.

To Indians who "knew their place," the British could be kind, even generous, but with those who considered themselves as their equals they were most often harsh and insulting. Only a small segment of Indians were sufficiently Westernized in their outlook and behavior to earn British cordiality. Even for these few, the friendship of the ruling class was not entirely free from an element of condescension. Motilal Nehru's success as a lawyer and the high standard of living that he maintained so impressed the Chief Justice of the Allahabad High Court that he offered to propose him for membership in the exclusively European Allahabad Club; Motilal politely declined. In the words of his biographer, "he sensed the width of the racial gulf and did not want to risk being 'black-balled' by the newest subaltern from England."

Despite the haughtiness that the British generally displayed towards them, however, a sizable section of the educated Indians had long believed that their country could attain its political aspirations with Britain's cooperation and good will. Like Motilal, they reposed tremendous faith in the British sense of fairness. How could the British who were so jealous of their personal freedoms and who watched over their democratic institutions with such tender care deny the same privileges and liberty to another people who were ready for them? they would ask rhetorically. Twelve years after the formation of the Congress Party one of its leaders argued at its annual session that "to deny us the freedom of the Press, to deny us representative institutions, England will have to ignore those very principles for which the noblest names in her history toiled and bled." Other moderate leaders in the Congress—Gokhale being the most notable among them—used their extensive command of the English language and their eloquence to appeal to Britain to see the strength and genuineness of India's longing to be its own master. They believed that peaceful, constitutional agitation on their part would enable them to attain their objective. If anyone argued that there was no instance in world history of a people's attaining independence without conflict with their rulers, Gokhale would stubbornly remind him that history was still in the process of being made and that India might provide the first example.

Those in the party who were unimpressed by this reasoning included among them some towering personalities. Bal Gangadhar Tilak, Bipin Chandra Pal, and Lajpat Rai firmly believed that the country could not expect to reach the distant goal of freedom by moving towards it in a series of tiny steps, each of which first must be approved by an unsympathetic, uncomprehending foreign power. Moreover, in their view freedom from British rule should mark the entrance to the arduous path of self-realization, not the end of a long and tortuous road of constitutional advancement.

The internal battle between the moderates and the extremists in the Indian National Congress continued for several years, with periodic fluctuations in their relative strength. The public mood, too, changed with events. During Lord Curzon's viceroyalty (1899–1905), noted for its arrogance and disregard of Indian sentiments, the public shared the extremists' despair and rationale for confrontation. At other times, as for example under Lord Ripon (1880–84), whose leniency earned him from his fellow countrymen the derisive description of "white *babu*" (clerk), many among the educated Indians were encouraged to hope that the basic goodness and humanity of the British would triumph over their imperialist predilections and that a serious conflict with the foreign rulers would be unnecessary. The beginning of World War I in 1914 strengthened such hopes and expectations. If Britain, as it claimed, was fighting to preserve freedom, how could it deny that freedom to a people who were fully qualified to be their own masters? Indian leaders asked one another. Indian soldiers had traveled thousands of miles from home to fight bravely in distant war theaters to defend people they knew nothing about. Even as committed a Tory as Lord Curzon, who had by then moved from the viceroyalty to a position of even greater eminence and influence in the British Government, acknowledged that the East was "sending out civilized soldiers to save Europe from the modern Huns." This partnership with Britain in spirit and on the battlefield was expected to bring concrete and substantial political rewards after the war. In that mood of buoyant optimism the Indian members of the Imperial Council readily voted grants for the conduct of war and even accepted without demur the Defense of India Act, which further limited personal freedoms and placed Draconian powers in the hands of the government.

Frustration and cynicism, however, set in long before the war appeared to be ending. As the conflict in Europe dragged on, the British tendency to regard India as a partner facing a common peril disappeared, and the old colonial attitudes began reasserting themselves. Instead of being praised for volunteering to fight on the Allies' side, Indian soldiers were criticized for their inability to adjust themselves to Europe's winters. The Defense of India Act was used not merely to remove impediments in the way of the war effort but to discourage Indian aspirations for independence and even to settle some petty, past political scores. The Raj was headed by Lord Chelmsford, whom an exasperated Secretary of State, Lord Montagu, described as "cold, aloof, reserved, strongly holding views collected from his surroundings." His surroundings at the time included senior members of the British bureaucracy of the type who believed that for many years to come Indians should aspire to nothing beyond autonomy in "municipal work." In London liberal members of the British Government had to contend with stern defenders of the Empire like Lord Curzon, who angrily demanded to know why Montagu was proposing to introduce constitutional reforms in India "at a break-neck speed."

What appeared to Curzon as virtual revolution was merely a modest offer of reform made jointly by Montagu and Chelmsford to the Indians in 1918. It divided the governments in the provinces into two sections and established a group of relatively innocuous departments, proposed to be answerable to a legislature elected on the basis of a markedly restricted franchise. To an extremist like Tilak the offer was "entirely unacceptable." Even Motilal Nehru, who until then had not abandoned his strong moderate moorings, was so disappointed by the limited nature of the proposal and the number of reservations it contained that he thought what the reforms "gave with one hand they took away with the other."

That the Montagu-Chelmsford reforms were niggardly did not come as a shock to most Indian leaders. For some years, distrust of the British Government and political disgruntlement had been engulfing these men steadily and inexorably. By now they felt trapped in the old quicksand of racial arrogance. Unaffected by their countries' sharing of a war, prejudice was so strong that even Lord Baden Powell's Boy Scout organization barred the entry of Indian school children.

In the years before Indira was born to Kamala and Jawaharlal Nehru, Indian resentment had been finding new expression in Annie Besant's movement for "Home Rule." A British subject of Irish descent who had adopted India as her home, Mrs. Besant had come to politics after spending many long years as an active Theosophist. She was approaching seventy when she founded her Home Rule League. Because she was a tireless worker and a magnificent organizer—but even more because the Indian people's disenchantment with the British needed an outlet—the message of the League spread rapidly. For a while some in the country, Motilal among them, stood apart watching the new movement skeptically. They were herded into it, however, by the action of a nervous bureaucracy in jailing Mrs. Besant in 1917. The volume and fierceness of the public protest against her arrest compelled the administration to retreat in confusion and quickly release her.

The founder of the League had long been a friend of the Nehru family. Jawaharlal had been drawn to Annie Besant and the Theosophical Society when he was only thirteen. After her release from jail she came to Allahabad to visit the Nehrus. Her reception in the city was an amazing demonstration of public affection for her and of fervor for the idea she had put forward. Floral arches, garlands, flags, and buntings of course abounded. But the people of Allahabad, apparently feeling that such customary forms of public homage did not express adequately their love for her, went further. The carriage that was to take her to Anand Bhavan was unhorsed, and a group of young men insisted on pulling it through the city as crowds, almost gone crazy with joy, showered rose petals on her. To a shaken but stubborn British bureaucracy, these were unmistakable signs of an impending rebellion or at least a serious confrontation with authority. One of its senior members, Sir Reginald Craddock, wrote at the time: "Sedition in India is like the tides which erode a coastline as the sea encroaches."

It was at this stage of India's troubled history that Mohandas Gandhi arrived from South Africa with his newly designed political weapon of *satyagraha,* or righteous agitation. He was to bring about in India a revolution the extent and nature of which Lord Curzon even at his most apprehensive could not possibly have imagined.

At an early age Gandhi had left his home in Gujarat to take up a rather junior clerical post with an Indian firm in Durban because, though a qualified barrister, his utter diffidence and almost pathological shyness had made it impossible for him to earn a living as a lawyer even in the subordinate court of his home town. In South Africa he suffered his share of the humiliations that were then the lot of Asian settlers. He was thrown out of a first-class compartment in a railway train, ordered to take off his turban in acknowledgment of his racial inferiority, and once severely beaten by an angry white. The experience changed Gandhi: this timorous young man, who had been rendered tongue-tied by the mere presence of a junior magistrate, somehow acquired the courage to take on a well-entrenched and arrogant government in defense of the rights of others like himself. The justness of his cause was underscored by the methods he devised to fight the European rulers of South Africa. In their fight against injustice, he told other Asians in South Africa, they must learn to die, not kill. They must vow never to resort to violence against their oppressor and not even let their minds be sullied by feelings of hatred for him. For eight long years he led the Asians and Africans through an ordeal of repressive measures, including flogging and shooting, until in 1914 the South African Government, wearied by its own violence, agreed to negotiate with Gandhi for the redress of the grievances of the communities he represented.

When Gandhi returned home he was acclaimed a hero. But even though they lionized him, not many in India in 1915 really understood his concept of vanquishing the foe through love and peaceful protest. On Gandhi's part, the great size and complexity of the problem in India seemed to baffle and deflect him for a while. Soon after his arrival in Bombay, he perplexed everyone by publicly declaring his loyalty to the British Empire. Stern as was their hold on power, the British rulers of India impressed Gandhi as being relatively free from the desperation and lack of subtlety that marked the behavior of the whites of South Africa. The next three years did not lessen his ardor for the Empire, even though he frequently protested to those in authority his sorrow over some of their decisions. He was particularly loath to take political advantage of the difficulties the British encountered owing to the war, and he wrote to the Viceroy in 1918:

> I recognize that, in the hour of its danger we must give—as we have decided to give—ungrudging and unequivocal support to the Empire, of which we aspire in the near future to be partners in the same sense as the Dominions overseas. . . . I would make India offer all her able-bodied sons as a sacrifice to the Empire at this critical moment, and I know that India by this very act would become the most favored partner in the Empire and racial distinction would become a thing of the past. . . .

To demonstrate the earnestness of his beliefs, Gandhi even spent several months touring his home province urging people to join the British Indian Army.

After the war, however, India did not become the most favored partner in the Empire. Nor did racial distinctions disappear. Adding fuel to the smoldering disappointment over the inadequate Montagu-Chelmsford reforms, the so-called Rowlatt Acts, passed as the Defense of India Act lapsed with the end of the war, brought a threat of new oppression. This legislation, permitting British provincial governments to try political cases without juries and also granting them the power of internment, so appalled even a moderate politician like M. A. Jinnah (head of the Muslim League and later the creator of Pakistan) that he declared that any government that enacted such laws in peacetime could not claim to be civilized. The Congress, which during the war years had been rendered inert by its own divisions and dissensions, quickly came to life. And Gandhi, who had scrupulously avoided embarrassing the authorities during the war, resolved to mount a nonviolent campaign against what, finally disillusioned, he described as the British Government's determination "to retain its grip of our necks." As he called for *hurtals* (suspensions of work or business) throughout India, the situation acquired an ominous, explosive character.

Confrontation of a history-changing nature occurred in April 1919. The venue was Jallianwala Bagh, a nondescript public park in Amritsar, the second largest city in the Northern province of Punjab. Politics in the Punjab then was dominated by Lajpat Rai, one of the most prominent members of the extremist group in the Congress Party; the administration in Punjab was headed by Sir Michael O'Dwyer who was convinced that in shouldering responsibility Indians were qualified to go no higher than municipal work; the army in the Amritsar area was commanded by Brigadier R. E. H. Dyer who, by his own subsequent admission, saw no difference between the "battlefields of Amritsar or Flanders." The combination of these men and their intransigencies made tragedy inevitable. When it struck, its impact on the Indian mind was so strong as to last for years and end all hope for the peaceful settlement of differences Congress moderates had once visualized.

That spring, hundreds of miles southeast of Amritsar, in Allahabad, the small-boned, big-eyed, black-ringleted Indu was the focus of life at Anand Bhavan. Not even their rising anger over the Rowlatt Acts or their excitement over the spreading enthusiasm for Gandhi's movement deflected her young parents for long from their delight in the child. They and her grandfather Motilal, grandmother Swarup Rani, and all the other relatives, visitors, and swarm of servants in the big house quoted to one another the small girl's amusing efforts to talk, her words coming out sometimes in English, sometimes in Urdu, or even in "kitchen" Hindustani. She was walking, too, in fast short steps, and one adult or another hovered close to keep her from falling on the hard, polished terrazzo floors of the vast rooms or to protect her from the possible cobra or poisonous lizard lurking in the gardens where she chased the blue and yellow butterflies.

Into this child-centered domestic peace, the news from Punjab broke like a bombshell. The politically aware Nehrus had in one sense expected something like it, some lesser trouble, perhaps, that might momentarily shake their world. But when it came, they were as unprepared emotionally for its stark, shocking ugliness and as horrified by it as the people of Amritsar.

The men and women who had assembled several thousand strong in Jallianawala Bagh on April 13, in weather already hot enough to shorten tempers, were undoubtedly angry, but they were doing nothing violent when the British authorities chose to strike them down. It was the day of Baisakhi, a major North Indian festival, and they had taken advantage of the holiday to gather for a peaceful protest meeting. Their action constituted defiance of a ban on public meetings that had been imposed a few days earlier—though by no means all of the people in the crowd were aware of that, as subsequent evidence suggested. The park was situated in the heart of the city and inside a walled enclosure with only a single narrow exit. As the meeting began, troops under the command of General Dyer stood on top of the thick wall surrounding the gathering and began firing into it. They fired until they exhausted their ammunition. Several hundred protestors, including many women and children, were killed like rats in a trap. Many others escaped the soldiers' bullets but were trampled to death by the panic-stricken crowd.

The news of the tragedy—its magnitude as well as the callousness and contempt on the part of the British authorities that it reflected—

shocked the entire country. Many even among the extremists in the
Congress who habitually tended to presume the worst about the foreign rulers could not believe that the British had ordered such a cold-
blooded massacre. But more humiliations were still to come. Sir Michael O'Dwyer, whom Lord Montagu had described in a private diary
even before Jallianwala as "the idol of the reactionary forces," imposed
martial law throughout the province. In the weeks that followed, the
people of Punjab were subjected to repression and indignities comparable only to what Indians had suffered following the failure of the
Mutiny of 1857. Villages were bombed and strafed from the air. Hundreds of men and women were rounded up and punished after summary trials for such offenses as walking two abreast on a road or fraternizing with people of different communities. Students were forced to
march miles in the blazing midday sun and at the end of the trek
ordered to salute the British flag. Many a respectable citizen was made
to crawl on his stomach because some young British soldier thought he
detected a sign of arrogance in the Indian's behavior. All this was a far
cry from the racial equality and place of honor in the Commonwealth
that Gandhi had dreamed of for India at the end of the war. It was not
what Motilal Nehru had expected, either.

That Gandhi was the country's supreme leader and was determined
to fight relentlessly, if nonviolently, was obvious to the custodians of
the Empire. Unnerved by the spectacle of the spontaneous popular up-
surge in his support, they made plans to deport him to Burma, perhaps
in unconscious reflection of the "mutiny complex" that by then pervaded the bureaucracy, perhaps in deliberate repetition of the deporta-
tion of the last Moghul Emperor, Bahadur Shah, who had been exiled
to Burma in 1857. These plans were not put into effect, however. The
government merely arrested Gandhi while he was on his way from
Bombay to Delhi and released him after bringing him back to Bombay.
The news of his arrest caused widespread public rioting and arson in
Bombay and parts of Gujarat, forcing Gandhi to undertake a three-day
fast to atone for his "failure to realize that the people were yet not
ready for a nonviolent struggle."

Gandhi's emergence as national leader and the Jallianwala tragedy
and related events were to have immediate, deep, and lasting impact
on the minds of the various members of the Nehru family.

Motilal turned his back finally and resolutely on hats from Heath's and gloves from Travellette's as well as grand dinners at Government House. He threw himself into the freedom movement so energetically and with such obvious lack of any mental reservations after Jallianwala that he was chosen President of the annual session of the Congress held defiantly in Amritsar in December of the same year.

Even when he lived in the placid atmosphere of Harrow, Jawaharlal had always been a staunch nationalist whose young blood used to boil over British arrogance. As he wrote in his *Autobiography,* he "dreamt of brave deeds," of how "sword in hand I would fight for India and help in freeing her." He was attracted to Gandhi's *satyagraha* movement, but he deferred courting imprisonment in the early years under the Mahatma's personal advice. (Later, of course, he was destined to spend many long, introspective years in British jails.) Gandhi's influence changed him almost overnight from a Western intellectual and a young *sahib* to an Indian.

Jawaharlal had first seen the Mahatma in 1916 during the annual session of the Congress Party at Lucknow and was, in his own words, "simply bowled over" by him. He saw him as "a powerful current . . . like a light that pierced the darkness and removed the scales from our eyes."

Motilal had long since discarded his attitude of reposing confidence in the good faith of the British, but to his lawyer's mind it was inconceivable that any good could come out of a mass violation of law. Jail-going had not yet acquired the political halo that it subsequently conferred, and the prospects of his only son being subjected to the harshness and indignities of a prison appeared to terrify him. When Jawaharlal was torn noticeably between the call of his conscience and his sense of duty to his father, Gandhi was invited to visit Anand Bhavan to adjudicate the matter. (In later years, whenever the family was confronted with a crisis—Vijayalakshmi's romantic involvement with a Muslim, for example—the Nehrus instinctively turned to Gandhi for guidance.) This "small wizened man," as Indira's aunt Krishna described him, wearing a peasant's loincloth and with a small cotton shawl draped around his bare shoulders, arrived on his first visit in 1919 and felt totally at home with the family despite its Western-style sophistication and obvious affluence. During his week's stay he succeeded in averting a possible rift between father and son by sympathizing with and applauding the latter's sentiments but urging him to desist for the time being from active participation in the *satyagraha*. Even if he was not bowled over as his son had been, Motilal was sufficiently captivated by Gandhi during that first meeting to want to see and learn much more of him.

Indira was of course too young to be aware of the changes around her, changes that were to inflict upon her a loneliness excessive and unusual even for an only child and give her a taste for politics that developed as she played with her dolls. She has no memory of Gandhi's first visit to Anand Bhavan shortly before the Jallianwala Bagh tragedy. But she has said that "Bapu was always there." She cannot remember when Gandhi was not a part of her life.

Although the household did not embrace Gandhi's austere ways unreservedly for some time after the first visit, it cut itself away from its Anglicized social past quite quickly and quite firmly. There was no English governess for Indira. Miss Cecilia Hooper, who had been with the family since 1905 and who had taught Motilal's daughters, coincidentally fell in love with an Englishman in 1917 and ended her long association with the family to marry. By the time Indira was old enough to need tutoring, the hiring of another European governess had become unimaginable for the family. That owing to changed circumstances Indira was not exposed to the influence of a European or Anglo-Indian governess was a significant, if negative, factor in shaping her mind and personality. Left to the care of another Miss Hooper— European governesses in colonial India were cast in a uniform mold —Indira might well have grown into a carbon copy of an English *miss-sahib* absorbing European cultural concepts and attitudes of mind to such an extent as to leave little room for anything indigenous. Like her two aunts, she would then have felt at home and comfortable only with foreign-educated Indians or in Western surroundings. She would never have acquired her typically Hindi idiom in language and her ability to think and feel like an Indian that, later, turned out to be her major political assets.

Unlike her aunts, Indira as a child did not encounter in Anand Bhavan British bureaucrats who spoke nostalgically of London and told jokes out of *Punch*. Instead, she found her home crowded by Gandhi's followers and others who were to constitute the national leadership in the decades to come. Among the frequent visitors to Anand Bhavan during her childhood were Vallabhbhai Patel, later India's

first Deputy Prime Minister, Madan Mohan Malaviya, who headed
the orthodox section in the Congress, and Maulana Abul Kalam Azad,
who, much to Motilal's delight, punctuated his political arguments
with couplets from Hafiz, Saadi, and other Persian poets. There were,
of course, many lesser luminaries drawn to Anand Bhavan by Motilal's
open-house hospitality and the warmth of his welcome.

Indira has no childhood memories of her father and grandfather
in Western clothes. Before she was three, they had, in response to
Gandhi's call for *swadeshi* (self-sufficiency, with dependence on Indian goods), put away their expensive Savile Row suits, soft hats, and
silk ties—they were to be burned later in a ceremonious bonfire—and
reverted to the long *achkan* and tight-fitting trousers made of homespun cotton cloth called *khadi*. (In summer, the woolen *achkan* with
its closed collar gave place to a long, loose, collarless *khadi* shirt.) For
headwear both Nehrus had taken to the Gandhi cap, the light, pointed
cap, also of *khadi*, that Gandhi had considered appropriate for a people
the vast majority of whom could afford nothing but the most inexpen-
sive of apparel.

Besides the change in their dress, there were other ways in which
the Nehrus turned their back on their earlier life style. By the beginning of 1921 Motilal had overcome his doubts about the effectiveness
of noncooperation sufficiently to resign his seat in the provincial legislative council and begin winding up his legal practice. The separate
European kitchen in Anand Bhavan was closed down, and replenish-
ments to the vast wine cellar were stopped. The stables were dis-
banded, and the large staff of servants drastically reduced. Exquisite crystal and china and costly drapes and furniture representing several
exciting and extravagant shopping sprees in London and other European
cities were given away or burned, along with their European clothes,
in the bonfire. Many items of the family's movable property were con-
fiscated by the police during a series of raids on the house in the years
that followed. How total the break from the past was was demonstrated
by Motilal's action in even withdrawing Krishna from the local convent school to which she was sent after Miss Hooper's departure. In a
letter he wrote from a mountain resort in the middle of 1921, Motilal
gave Gandhi an account of the extent of change. A brass cooker, he
wrote, had taken the place of the two kitchens and a solitary servant
that of the former retinue. Hunting had given place "to long walks

and guns to books, magazines and newspapers." He ate a single square meal in the middle of the day instead of "breakfast, lunch and dinner à l'Anglaise,' " he informed the Mahatma.

Motilal apparently was trying to dramatize, perhaps even exaggerate, the change, because nothing would be more erroneous than to suggest, as the letter seems to, that in their devotion to Gandhi and political zeal the father and son had imposed on the family a life of excessive austerity bordering on deprivation. Even though he had given up his legal practice, Motilal remained reasonably well off. The family no longer spent lavishly on itself, but all the same it lived comfortably. What was abandoned was ostentation. But when Anand Bhavan ceased to be the abode of a prince, it did not become the lowly hut of the average Indian family either. As a child Indira did not have to roam through a cold, empty, bare-walled house or contend with a servantless existence. The imported drapes were replaced by less expensive, but equally serviceable, Indian materials, and, even after the drastic reduction in their number, there were still numerous cooks, gardeners, sweepers, and other domestic retainers.

Other references in Motilal's papers and the recollections of those who knew the family then suggest the continuance of a certain measure of indulgence in the Nehru household even after Gandhi's impact. Thus, when the family visited Mussoorie, a north-Indian summer resort much favored in those days by rulers of princely states, it lived in the best suites in the Savoy or the Charleville, the two most expensive hotels there. Horses were often sent specially from Allahabad to the holiday resort for the family's use. The Nehrus were able to travel abroad frequently and for extended periods of time. Krishna describes how in 1927 when Motilal visited Europe "he was the same *grand seigneur* in his manner of travelling. Suddenly we were going first class, with chauffeured limousines to meet us and staying at the *grand luxe* hotels." On returning home Motilal presented his younger daughter with a new Citroen motor car, and when she sold it off and asked for another he readily gave her "a beautiful Armstrong-Siddeley." The second Anand Bhavan, the smaller house built several years after the Nehrus had accepted Gandhian austerity as a way of life and given the original mansion to the Congress Party, still somehow grew into a villa with marble floors, graceful stone columns, and elaborately carved fountains. When Jawaharlal could not see the point in giving away the old big house only to build another that was beginning to be almost as luxurious and felt they should live in a modest dwelling, Motilal brusquely told him he could go and live in a hut across the street if he liked but "I am not going to live in one."

Indira's childhood was to be in many ways extraordinary. It was marked by extreme contrasts. Thanks to the resolve of her father and grandfather to follow Gandhi, the child grew up in what was a considerably different if no less vibrant household than it had been prior to her birth. What the second Anand Bhavan, built in 1929, lacked in the way of European fittings and numbers of servants was amply made up in the human warmth and liveliness that normally filled it. Although the constant traffic of political leaders and workers often encroached upon the family's privacy and gave the house a noisy, somewhat chaotic, character, it also effectively rid the new Anand Bhavan of the element of slight stiffness that had pervaded the earlier one despite Motilal's warmheartedness. In the days when Motilal lived the life of an English *sahib*, Indian friends who visited the original mansion usually stayed for short periods and often felt somewhat self-conscious. They were overawed by the family's affluence and daunted by its foreign ways. Members of the Kashmiri Pandit community and even some relatives had come to the first Anand Bhavan almost surreptitiously and departed quietly after meeting Swarup Rani or her widowed sister. For such people the new Anand Bhavan was a different place altogether. Throughout the 1920s they came there in large numbers and brought for the family gifts of shared concern and affection.

Nonetheless, almost half a century later, Indira described her childhood not simply as having been far from "placid or protected" but in fact "insecure." The insecurity, however, was not due to any dearth of love for her.

Motilal, who was still the dominant personality in the household, doted on Indira. Few grandfathers have expressed their love for a child as tenderly as Motilal, who confessed that he was "always thinking of Indira" because he saw her as "a personification of innocence whose very thought is soothing." He showered gifts on her, and by Indira's own admission "he spoilt me terribly." From Dalhousie, where one summer he had taken the family for a brief escape from the heat, Motilal sent a frantic message to Jawaharlal, who had stayed back in

Allahabad, to immediately dispatch a good saddle from there because though the pony he had arranged for young Indira was "quite decent," she found the saddle uncomfortable. Indira responded to her grandfather with matching affection. She loved Motilal and, what is uncommon on the part of a grandchild, "admired" him. She was impressed by his personality and his "tremendous zest for life." She even loved the way he laughed. As she recalled in an interview, Motilal always seemed to fill the room. "Now I realize he wasn't really that tall but at that time I thought he was very tall and broad. He seemed to embrace the whole world," she reminisced.

Indira's relationship with her grandmother was of a different sort but in its own way sustaining. In her dealings with relatives and even some members of the immediate family, Swarup Rani was imperious and haughty. Her indifferent health had impaired her porcelain beauty, and premature age had seemingly imparted to her generally stern attitudes an added element of bitterness. Her widowed sister who lived in Anand Bhavan and in whose company Swarup Rani spent a great deal of her time wore her own sorrow like a badge. Around their *puja* rooms the sisters had built for themselves a small world of their own into which Motilal's boisterousness and Jawaharlal's sense of humanity were not allowed to intrude. Indira's tiny feet, however, were permitted to cross freely and often into that sacrosanct domain and were, in fact, always welcome. Swarup Rani did not fuss over the little child the way her husband did, but she, too, spoiled her. For several years Indira called her grandmother by the unusual appellation of "*dole amma*," for Swarup Rani was constantly feeding her various kinds of sweets and other tidbits that she kept locked especially for her in a *doli*—a kitchen cabinet.

Rajvati, who led the austere life of a Hindu widow, was further impelled by her excessive orthodoxy to run for herself a separate kitchen free from the "uncleanliness" of the general kitchen with its meat-cooking. She could not offer goodies of the type that might win Indira's little heart. She made up for it by telling her fascinating stories from the Hindu epics, the *Ramayana* and *Mahabharata*. Munshi Mubarak Ali, who had narrated stories of British atrocities during the 1857 uprising to Jawaharlal was no longer there to repeat them for his daughter. Indira instead heard accounts of more distant conflicts. Rajvati told her how Lord Rama raised an army to punish Ravana for his evil deeds and how, in the *Mahabharata,* the Pandavas, though representing the weaker party in the war, ultimately triumphed because righteousness was on their side.

The younger Nehrus frowned upon the way the older members of the family indulged Indira. But the love she received from her parents was boundless, even though as time passed and Kamala followed her husband into the front lines of the fight for freedom, both parents were often away in jail and thus unable to demonstrate their affection physically. The enforced absences—of her parents and also her grandparents—was the circumstance that made Indira's childhood insecure.

"Indu" was only four when her grandfather Motilal and father Jawaharlal were jailed for the first time for their allegedly seditious activities against the British Government. When the two Nehru men went to the magistrate's court to stand trial and did not return home, the child's sense of loss was overwhelming. She had sat in Motilal's lap as the court went through the ritual of a trial, and she was inconsolable when both were taken away to prison and she had to return home without them. The frequency of similar occurrences in the years that followed did not entirely blunt Indira's feelings of outrage and shock whenever there was a new imprisonment. That after a while her mother was taken away almost as often as her father strongly accentuated her grief. She was somewhat comforted by written assurances of their love for her. Even before she had learned to read, Jawaharlal appended tender little notes for Indira to his letters to the family from his prison cell. There were gentle inquiries about the state of her health and suggestions about what she might do to improve it. Did she join regularly in offering prayers? he would ask. Often he urged her to be always fearless and brave.

When she herself was not in jail, Kamala welcomed Indira's joining her in her daily prayers, and she supplemented her husband's lessons in fearlessness. She was more than adequately equipped to teach faith and courage. Unlike Jawaharlal, Kamala was a deeply religious person, although without the fanaticism and rigidity that Swarup Rani had acquired through excessive emphasis on ritual. Indira's mother gave her not merely familiarity with the Hindu dogma but also some understanding of the arching spirit behind it. Under Kamala's influence, Indira's Hinduism was not warped by the narrowmindedness that it would certainly have developed had the child been exposed only to

Swarup Rani and her great aunt Rajvati's restricted views of religion. As for fearlessness, Kamala imparted these lessons through her own actions at home and in politics.

Indira's mother inherited the family name of Kaul because her father had been adopted by that family. Originally he had belonged to a Kashmiri Pandit family that had held high ministerial office in the state of Jaipur and acquired the name "Atal"—or unshakable one— because even its autocratic princely employers could not browbeat its members or compel them to act against their wishes. Kamala did not lack the sense of purpose and personal dignity associated with the Atals. In 1921, when Gandhi urged everyone to discard foreign clothes and take to *khadi,* the Nehrus, their respect for the leader notwith-standing, were undecided. Motilal had serious doubts about the value of the gesture, and Jawaharlal procrastinated. Kamala, however, was convinced and by all accounts prodded the family into implementing Gandhi's directive. In Indira's own words, "The whole family was against it but it was my mother's insistence that brought about the change." Kamala's courage was typified by her action some years later in repeating at a mass meeting in Allahabad and under the baleful eye of British authority the very speech for which her husband had been charged with sedition a few days earlier.

Kamala needed all the bravery she had. Swarup Rani and Indira's eldest aunt, Vijayalakshmi, treated Jawaharlal's wife harshly, at times even contemptuously. As was expected of a daughter-in-law in a tradi-tional Hindu family, Kamala suffered this treatment stoically and with-out permitting her anger or sorrow to affect her performance of her own duties. The strain of protracted periods of imprisonment, followed by tuberculosis—then generally incurable—she faced with fortitude. At no time did she lose her poise or sense of dignity. Her mother's inner strength was a characteristic Indira was too young to notice in these years but came to recognize and greatly admire later.

This mother of Indira's as a bride of sixteen had been, in the words of Jawaharlal's younger sister, "dazzlingly beautiful," with a glow of robust health about her. Even while Jawaharlal was still studying in Britain, Motilal had subjected the Kashmiri Pandit community to a constant watch for a suitable wife for his son. He looked for beauty. The choice finally fell on Kamala, whose father was a respected busi-nessman of Delhi. The Kauls were reasonably prosperous, but they were socially conservative and cast in the traditional Indian mold; their lovely Kamala, although intelligent and moderately well educated, lacked the Western gloss that her future sisters-in-law had acquired from their European governesses. Thanks to the special coaching she received immediately after her engagement, Kamala's command of English by the time she arrived in Anand Bhavan was passable but, apparently, not adequate enough to impress Swarup Rani and Vijaya-lakshmi. The structure of the joint Hindu family provides the mother-in-law with enormous scope for treating the daughter-in-law with loving care but also, if she be so inclined, with callousness and tyranny. In her years as a young wife, Swarup Rani had suffered under the domineering ways of the wife of Motilal's eldest brother, Nand Lal. The resentment she felt then Swarup Rani seemed to transfer now to Kamala. Besides settling old scores in this unjust manner, she appeared to believe Kamala was not good enough for Jawaharlal. Her over-whelming love for her only son prompted her to exaggerate Kamala's minor failings and even invest her with some that she did not have.

Vijayalakshmi's treatment of Kamala was, by some accounts, almost cruel. She seemed to take a kind of sadistic pleasure in embarrassing her over her inadequate familiarity with Western social etiquette. She would offer friends and visitors gleeful accounts of how Kamala had employed the wrong piece of cutlery at the dining table or had failed to come up with a proper expression during a conversation. She also carried tales against Kamala to her father and brother. In expressing her contempt and antipathy, Vijayalakshmi did not spare young Indira. She was virtually the only member of the family from whom the child received no affection. Vijayalakshmi regarded Indira as a gangling, awkward girl and made no secret of her disdain for her. (The antipa-thy that the two women developed then has lasted. In the struggle for Congress Party leadership in 1966, Vijayalakshmi—better known to the world as Madame Pandit, India's delegate to the United Nations— was known to be sympathetic to Indira's rival, Morarji Desai. After Desai's defeat, Vijayalakshmi spoke to the press about Indira's "weak constitution" in reference to the immensity of the burdens that the prime ministership must place on her. In this apparent expression of an aunt's tender concern Indira was quick to see a note of waspishness and ill will and issued a rejoinder in the same spirit.)

Jawaharlal himself neglected his wife noticeably. Within a few weeks of their wedding the family went to Kashmir for the summer, and there the bridegroom left his young bride in Srinagar with her new in-laws and took off with a cousin to trek in the mountains for several weeks. In an arranged marriage the bonds of affection between husband and wife develop only after the wedding, and slowly. Jawaharlal made no effort to hasten their development. It is a measure of his insouciant attitude towards the event that in his *Autobiography* of over six hundred pages he dismisses his wedding in just two lines. If he did not give much credence to the tales that Vijayalakshmi carried to him against Kamala, he also did not rebuke her for doing so nor do anything to check his mother's overbearing behavior. At times he was almost callous. A young political associate who later rose to be a Cabinet minister under Nehru recalls how he went to Anand Bhavan one afternoon to accompany Jawaharlal to a political rally in a nearby town. Kamala, whose health had much deteriorated by then, suddenly fainted just before they were to leave the house. Her collapse clouded Jawaharlal's brow with worry but only briefly. He laid her on a couch and called a maid to attend to her. He would not consider canceling his engagement or even delaying his departure.

Eighteen years after their marriage, as Kamala lay on her deathbed, her husband thought sorrowfully about how he had treated her. Referring to the early years of their marriage, Jawaharlal wrote in his *Autobiography* of how despite "all my appearance of worldly wisdom I was very boyish and I hardly realized that this delicate, sensitive girl's mind was slowly unfolding like a flower and required gentle and careful tending." He acknowledged that she gave him strength and then added somewhat guiltily that "she must have suffered and felt a little neglected. An unkindness to her would almost have been better than this semi-forgetful, casual attitude."

Besides being sensitive, Kamala had a strong sense of personal dignity and a quick temper. But she seldom let these traits get the better of her judgment or affect her duties as a good daughter-in-law. She showed due deference to Swarup Rani and as for Vijayalakshmi she considered it inappropriate and beneath her as an adult to engage herself in any wrangle or even exchange of harsh words. She did not permit her frequent spells of unhappiness to affect her enthusiasm for political work. If at times her suffering overwhelmed her, she would quietly retire to her own room to cope with her distress alone and in silence. During such solitary battles with her grief, she would often be joined by Indira, the child sensing her mother's anguish even though she was too young to share the burden with her.

In other ways and on other occasions Indira felt conflict within the family or was exposed to shock and agony alongside affection. Any live and vital family has its share of mutual friction and strife. The Nehrus seemed to have more than usual.

To be sure, Motilal and Jawaharlal loved and respected each other the way few fathers and sons probably have. Jawaharlal's *Autobiography* is full of expressions of his devotion to his father and his admiration for him. Motilal loved his son so deeply that during the latter's student years in Britain he virtually lived, as he confessed in a letter, for the occasional brief visits he paid to Europe to meet him. But they also disagreed violently and often held onto divergent views stubbornly. Both were short tempered, and when they clashed with each other there were no holds barred between them. Their differences often assumed such a noisy, raucous character that Gandhi came to hear about them and was disturbed over the seeming rifts. Motilal, himself fond of the good things of life, would seldom miss an opportunity to ridicule Jawaharlal's Spartan tastes. His self-confidence sometimes manifested itself in abrasive, hurtful forms. To a son who was sensitive about his dependence on his father and who was torn between his desire to devote himself to political activity and his anxiety to make a living, Motilal offered advice not to worry about the latter but then added that he "could earn in a day what Jawaharlal would not be able to spend in a year." On such occasions, a troubled Jawaharlal would spend hours alone pacing in his study or in a secluded corner of the Anand Bhavan garden trying to resolve his inner conflict.

The shocks that the family's involvement in the freedom movement inflicted on Indira's mind were less subtle. Some were almost traumatic. As Prime Minister she described the atmosphere in the house, saying in a BBC interview in 1971:

> As a child, when the freedom struggle was on, the house was being constantly raided by police, our goods and chattels being confiscated, we were being arrested and having to hide contraband literature and I was all part of it. . . . I was part of the processions and the meetings and it was an extremely insecure childhood. One did not know from day to day who would be alive, who would be in the house and what would happen next.

The police would visit Indira's home either to take away some loved member of the family for his or her challenge to British power or to remove some valuable pieces of property. The punishment for participation in the freedom movement usually comprised a term in jail and a sizable fine. Although they would willingly go to prison, members of the Nehru family would, in accordance with the policy prescribed by the Mahatma, refuse to pay the fines. The police would then descend on Anand Bhavan to realize the fine by confiscating furniture, carpets, curtains, crystal, china, personal clothes, in fact, almost anything that could be carted away and would fetch a price in a police auction. The older members of the household accepted the government's high-handedness philosophically and watched such operations in sullen silence, but little Indira could not control her anger. She was barely four when, following the arrest and conviction of Motilal and Jawaharlal, the police paid their first visit to the house to confiscate some movable property. The spectacle of the family possessions being piled up in police vans so infuriated Indira that with tiny fists clenched she charged at the police inspector supervising the operation and screamed, "You can't take them away, they are ours." Some of Indira's subsequent experiences with the police were truly grim. On one occasion police-men mounted on horses and wielding 6-foot *lathis*—wooden clubs—beat up her father, who was leading a protest march. As a follower of Gandhi, Jawaharlal would not turn away from the police blows nor retaliate for their violence, and he returned home bruised and bloodied and with his clothes torn.

In politics, Indira of course had her baptism of fire early. It was clear to her from the very start that what the family was engaged in was not a temporary turmoil but a protracted commitment. She also realized, if somewhat vaguely, that it involved considerable sacrifice on everyone's part. She faced a personal crisis of her own when she was five. The Nehrus had resolved to boycott British goods and destroy those they already had. The dozens of expensive suits that Motilal and Jawaharlal had bought in Europe, costly silks, fancy draperies, and other imported items they possessed were brought out to be consigned ceremoniously to a bonfire on the front lawn of Anand Bhavan. A few weeks after the big bonfire—which was the talk of the town, and, in fact, of the country—Indira firmly refused to accept the gift of a beautiful frock brought by a family friend because it was made of British material. Chagrined by the little girl's stubbornness in the matter, the visitor tauntingly reminded her that the doll she held so affectionately to her bosom was also British-made. For several days Indira pondered the truth in the sarcasm and was pulled in opposite directions by her love for her favorite doll and her sense of duty. She finally ended the torture by arranging a small bonfire of her own on the roof of Anand Bhavan to which she tearfully consigned the doll. Talking about the incident years afterward, she could not recollect what that doll looked like but said "I do remember how I felt. I felt as if I was murdering someone." To this day, she confessed, "I hate striking a match."

Like her father, Indira was an unusually precocious child. At Harrow Jawaharlal had found it difficult to mix with English boys whose tastes and inclinations he found quite different. "Here boys, older than me and in higher forms than me, take great interest in things which appear to me childish," he wrote to Motilal from his school. At seventeen when he wrote that letter, Jawaharlal felt he was too old to "really enjoy the life" in school. Indira acquired a somber attitude to life even earlier.

When the child in her got the better of her grim sense of earnestness and she took out her dolls and toys, she almost always played at politics. Her fantasies seldom related to such usual childhood themes as a marriage between two dolls or acquisition of such riches as a glittering set of glass bangles or a trayful of favorite sweets. Her mind was always involved with the independence movement, and she would make her dolls enact aspects of the fight with the British that she had seen herself or heard her elders describe. Her small doll house would sometimes represent the store that had chosen to ignore the Mahatma's plea and was still selling foreign goods. She would station a number of dolls clad in white *khadi* all around the recalcitrant shop as Congress Party workers supposedly picketing its various entrances and urging shoppers to boycott it the way Indira had seen her mother and aunts do so often. At other times she would play at a more serious kind of game. A set of tiny clay dolls would be British soldiers—so identified by the round, brown pith helmets that they wore. Another set of dolls were given tiny red turbans to identify them as the Indian policemen who acted according to their British employers' bidding. The soldiers would carry guns and the policemen long wooden clubs. Facing the foreign rulers and their native minions would be a row of dolls dressed in white homespun *khadi* and carrying nothing but the Congress Party flag. She would move this row forward in an act of defiance while she herself shouted some of the slogans heard at political meetings and demonstrations. The authorities, too, would move forward menacingly, brandishing the guns and clubs. When the people were undaunted, the soldiers and policemen would act with expected brutality and beat up the demonstrators. The latter would fall on the ground only to rise again, carrying the flag aloft and shouting for freedom even more vigorously. All such games always had a happy, satisfying ending. In the shop-picketing game, all customers would turn away disgustedly, leaving the "bad" shopkeeper no option but to close down. In the confrontation with the police, the doll demonstrators always won, with the pretended British authorities retreating in confusion and leaving behind helmets, turbans, and *lathis* as convincing proof of rout.

Often Indira would organize a live play demonstration of her own. Even at its depleted level, the Anand Bhavan staff included a goodly number of servants, some of whom lived on the premises or in quarters specially built for them in one corner of the bungalow's extensive grounds. Their children, even many among them somewhat older than Indira herself, provided the "manpower" she needed for her games. Dressed in the uniform of a Congress volunteer—a long white shirt over tight-fitting cotton pants and the peaked Gandhi cap—that she had seen her mother wear and insisted on getting for herself, Indira would lead the procession of children, everyone shouting *"Inqilab Zindabad"* ("Long Live Revolution") after her and shaking their clenched fists in a gesture of collective determination. Such demonstrations often ended with Indira's mounting one of the several wooden tables usually left in the garden for the family's occasional outdoor dining and from the improvised platform haranguing the juvenile assembly on how Gandhi's leadership would make the British go home. For one who, in her later years, developed an almost overwhelming stage-shyness that was to make her frequent public addresses always agonizing, Indira, as she herself recalls, would be in her element while delivering these speeches. Not content with a group of children as her audience, she would often herd the gardener, his assistants, the sweeper, and other servants in the house to her "public meeting."

The period of such games and fantasies on Indira's part was remarkably brief. Before she was seven she had tired of the make-believe nature of her involvement in the movement and was eager to do something real. Just playing at being a Congress volunteer did not satisfy her. "I was drawn irresistibly to Gandhiji's teachings about *charkha* and I threw myself enthusiastically into the work of the Charkha Sangh," she said in an interview. By 1924 Gandhi had developed the *charkha,* or spinning wheel, into a powerful weapon of the Indian people's nonviolent fight against the foreign ruler. By enabling people to make their own cloth for their needs, the *charkha* exerted strong economic pressure on Britain. Several textile mills in Manchester already had been rendered idle by the Indian boycott. The spinning wheel, however, did much more. It offered people emotional sustenance in what was a protracted struggle and where concrete results were hard to see. It gave people something positive and constructive to do. Even the lowliest of Indian peasants, whose daily struggle for existence made exacting demands on his time and energy, could, by spinning the wheel for a brief period every day, get a sense of participation in the great national struggle. Like her father, who accepted the *charkha* as an article of faith, she acquired a wheel of her own and religiously spun coarse yarn on it. From Allahabad, various members of her family and others engaged in the movement would visit nearby villages to extend the message of the *charkha* to the areas where the Indian masses mostly lived. Indira was always eager to accompany them on such trips, notwithstanding the physical hardship involved in traveling in areas with only unpaved, rutted rural roads. In the village, while the party volunteers explained the implications of the spinning wheel, she would sit solemnly plying the *charkha* her grandfather had specially got for her.

A childhood political activity of which the Prime Minister remains particularly proud was the organization by her of the Vanar Sena or the Monkey Brigade. She was then almost twelve and the Congress Party was engaged in a truly stern conflict with the British Government. Motilal had completed his second term as Congress President, and young Indira had had the exhilarating experience of seeing her father succeeding her grandfather as the new head of the vast national movement.

Jawaharlal had come to the annual session of the Congress in Lahore (then an Indian city, now in Pakistan) riding a white charger.

Vast multitudes shouted for his long life and victory and showered flowers on him. That he should ride a horse instead of arriving at the session in a bullock-drawn cart reflected a significant change in the Congress's and the nation's mood. Instead of "Dominion status" like Canada and Australia, which was until then the goal, Jawaharlal, in his presidential address, set complete independence as the new national objective. On December 31, 1929, around midnight, as the new year was approaching, the Congress flag fluttered in the bitter cold winds on the banks of the Ravi at Lahore. Jawaharlal and others formally pledged themselves to accept nothing short of total freedom. With the formal adoption of the resolution followed by a boycott of all legislatures, the party and its followers had engaged themselves in what Gandhi described as the "final conflict."

The excitement that swept the country could not possibly have left Indira unaffected. She wanted to join the Congress Party and the movement, but she was firmly told she could not do so until she was eighteen. Saying no to a Nehru is the surest way of egging him or her to tread the forbidden path. If she could not join the party as a member she would, Indira resolved, set up an organization of her own and show those who said she was too young to be useful in the conflict with the British what she could do.

The story of the *Ramayana* provided the name for her organization. When Rama decided to wage war on the evil King Ravana of Lanka and punish him for abducting his wife, he was aided by Hanuman, the king of the monkeys. His army of monkeys—Vanar Sena—built the bridge that enabled Rama to cross the ocean to reach his foe's capital. The Vanar Sena that Indira organized comprised boys and girls who had the agility of Hanuman's monkeys as well as their willingness to help what they believed was a righteous cause. At the inaugural meeting of the Sena in Anand Bhavan over a thousand boys and girls turned up. Indira's voice—always somewhat high-pitched and lacking in volume—could not cope with the task of explaining the purpose of the proposed organization. And, of course, there were no public address systems in India in those days. The problem was resolved through the help of a family friend, Bishamber Nath Pandey, who was blessed with a powerful voice and a sense of humor. Indira stood next to Pandey on the dais and as she uttered a single sentence at a time he in turn would bellow out her commands to the noisy audience.

Not only Pandey but most of her elders and even the local British authority took the formation of the Vanar Sena as something of a joke. Motilal, by then once more in jail, wrote to Indira inquiring about the work of the organization. In mock seriousness he begged her to let him know about its exploits and achievements and added, "I suggest the wearing of a tail by every member of it, the length of which should be in proportion to the rank of the wearer."

If the elders seemed to laugh at the Sena, that did not discourage Indira. She took the work of her Monkey Brigade in dead earnest. Decades later, recalling the work of the group of youngsters, she claimed that the organization was "effective." Those who had looked upon it condescendingly in the beginning were "not so condescending later," she said, "because we really did quite a tough job."

The tasks that members of the Brigade handled under her stern supervision were manifold. They relieved their elders of such routine chores as writing notices, addressing envelopes, making flags, cooking food, and supplying drinking water. They also carried messages and even gathered intelligence about impending police moves. She told Arnold Michaelis, an interviewer for McCall's:

> Sometimes a house might be surrounded by police and you could not send out a message. But nobody bothered about an urchin hopping in and out through the police cordon. Nobody thought that he could be doing anything. The boy would memorize the message (and carry it to its destination) . . . frequently, policemen sitting in front of the police station would talk about what was going on—who was to be arrested, where there would be a raid and so on. Four or five children playing hopscotch outside would attract no one's attention. And they would deliver the news to the people in the movement.

As the supreme monkey, Indira herself coped with some of the more difficult assignments. Munshi Kanahiya Lal, who during Indira's childhood occupied the same position in Anand Bhavan that Munshi Mubarak Ali had earlier, remembers the occasion when the police surrounded the house while the party's top executive was meeting there to plan a new stage of its civil disobedience movement. It was particularly important at that stage of the conflict that party records and documents should not fall into police hands. The secret documents were hurriedly placed in the trunk of a motor car. Indira sat primly on the back seat with her books as the vehicle was driven out. When a suspicious police inspector stopped it at the gate, Indira spoke exasperatedly about being late for school and the punishment that awaited her if she were not allowed to proceed immediately. The car with all its precious documents was quickly permitted to leave.

Despite the hectic nature of her involvement in the movement and the fact that she "was part of the processions and the meetings," Indira still suffered long spells of extreme loneliness in her childhood. Jawaharlal had been a lonely child because he was the only son and all his cousins were too old to be his friends; Indira too was an only child, and, in addition, as she said years afterward, not only "my father and grandfather (but) my mother was in prison, my grandmothers on both sides, all my uncles and aunts on both sides, too, and there were long periods when I was absolutely alone in the house without another grown-up or child for that matter." She had no resident tutor or governess. Curiously, there was not even an Indian *ayah* or nanny specifically assigned to care for her. She did not mind being denied such attention and luxuries, and she grew up with the firm belief that doing without them was the right thing. Referring to those lonesome days, however, Indira the Prime Minister once remarked, "I did resent the fact, perhaps, that my parents were not with me as other children had their parents. But otherwise I was very proud of them and I did not really envisage having another kind of life."

When it was possible, she looked forward to visiting her father and mother in jail. They were, of course, never lodged in the same jail and her father was often imprisoned in Dehra Dun, near the foot of the Himalayas and too far from Allahabad for her to visit him. In any case, the number of visitors that even a political prisoner of Jawaharlal's or Kamala's eminence could receive was strictly limited. Indira had to take her turn in meeting them, for there were others in the family and the movement eager for the privilege. The infrequent opportunities of seeing her parents were supplemented only by increasingly infrequent letters from them as prison regulations became stricter and letters were rationed as were personal visits.

Gentle prodding from her father in his letters from prison drove the young Indira to Anand Bhavan's large library. Motilal's own readings outside law books were limited and rather pedestrian. But Jawaharlal had been a voracious reader, whose tastes ranged from Marx's *Das Kapital* to Jerome K. Jerome's *Three Men in a Boat*, from Nietzsche to Robert Frost. At a very early age, Indira read through Grimm's *Fairy Tales* and the children's editions of Bernard Shaw, Dickens, and Shakespeare that had been specially ordered from abroad for her aunts when they were her age. To these were added numerous books that her father would recommend in his letters and sometimes even order from his jail cell for her from bookshops he had once patronized himself in Britain. Many a book he suggested seemed unusually heavy reading for a child of her age. On her tenth birthday he sent her H. G. Well's *Science of Life* and added to the usual birthday inscription, "Do not get frightened by its size."

Her loneliness, her reading, and her intense imagination made Indira "a serious, solemn child." Her father had dreamed of how "sword in hand I would fight for India and help in freeing her." Indira cherished similar yearnings. Her childhood heroine appropriately was Joan of Arc. The story of St. Joan's life that she first read when she was about seven so fascinated her that in letters to her parents she repeatedly expressed her determination to be another Joan of Arc.

Her aunt Krishna one day found Indira standing in the verandah of Anand Bhavan, one hand resting on a large pillar and the other raised high as if she were addressing an audience. She seemed to be muttering something, and when the amazed Krishna asked her what she was doing, Indira looked at her solemnly, "her dark eyes burning," and said "I am practising being Joan of Arc."

3

Education of a Prime Minister

U NTIL Indira Nehru grew to adulthood, Jawaharlal nursed an obsessive concern—bordering at times on a sense of guilt—about her education. In 1922, when she was not yet five and her father was serving his second term in prison, he wrote frettingly from his cell in Lucknow jail that he wished "some arrangements were made for Indu's lessons." He claimed confidently that he "could have managed her easily" but noted, "I am confined to Barrack No. 4." The same fussy concern was evident in 1936 when Indira was preparing to enter Somerville College, Oxford. Discussing his daughter's plans at that later time, Jawaharlal wrote to a friend that "with all my attraction for Oxford I am not frightfully keen on it; there is just an element of ineffectiveness in it." In the period between the writing of the two letters, he had not only trotted Indira to diverse schools—conventional and unconventional, in India and abroad—and had a much-publicized row with his father over her education but also had used his enforced leisure during various imprisonments to write her scores of letters about world history. These later became a literary classic, but it is clear that they were not written with an eye to publication. They were to educate a loved child.

Nehru had his own concept of what a good educational institution should be. He was not enamored of the schools and colleges that the Raj had spawned in India. In a system of education designed specifically to produce an adequate number of English-speaking "natives" to fill the junior, clerical posts in British bureaucracy, Nehru saw the danger of a numbing effect on the minds of students. He, in fact, thoroughly disliked the "regular official and semi-official universities" because the whole atmosphere that enveloped them he considered "oppressive and authoritarian" and liable to suppress and deaden "the fine instincts of youth." He was, therefore, eager for Indira to escape their "dead hand." He had himself studied at Harrow and Oxford and, while remaining within their general discipline, had been encouraged to indulge his questioning, curious mind by reading about a vast range of subjects. He was anxious that Indira should have similar freedom to pursue what interested her, acquiring an understanding of life generally and a mind not set in a standard stereotype.

Yet another consideration seemed to nag Nehru constantly when he thought about Indira's education. Anxious as he was to give her the finest of schooling, he apparently worried also about the Anglicized character of the prevailing education turning Indira into a stranger in her own country. Before he went to school in Britain, Jawaharlal himself had been taught by Ferdinand T. Brooks, a Theosophist of mixed Irish and French ancestry, working as a resident tutor and companion to the young Nehru in Anand Bhavan. His two sisters had been schooled by their English governess, Miss Hooper. Admirable though these arrangements were for the children of a family striving to associate itself with and emulate its colonial rulers, such education in now changed circumstances struck him as totally unsuitable for a child of a family that had renounced its earlier values and attitudes and established emotional ties with those whom it had previously spurned. The search for a school relevant to the Nehru family's new outlook and yet not devoid of some of the qualities associated with exclusive, Westernized institutions was a difficult one and at one stage caused serious tension between Motilal and Jawaharlal, leading to their row over Indira's education. It is a measure of its intensity that this family quarrel, which occurred in 1924 and even prompted the Mahatma to intervene in it, received extensive notice in newspapers of the day. Many saw it as a serious rift between father and son.

The quarrel grew out of the Congress Party resolution that, as part of Gandhi's noncooperation movement, Indians should boycott not only British courts but state-financed schools as well. In accordance with the party directive, Motilal had already wound up his lucrative law practice and withdrawn his younger daughter, Krishna, from a government-aided school. Thousands of others had responded similarly to the Mahatma's appeal, and private, independent schools were set up hurriedly to provide some education for children who had been pulled out of government institutions. Unavoidably, such schools were makeshift arrangements lodged in cramped, unsuitable buildings with totally inadequate staff and equipment. Often, the paucity of teachers and limitations of accommodation caused students of diverse ages to be herded together in a single large room. Indira was admitted into a "national" institution of this type—the Modern School in Allahabad—in 1923, but within months Motilal's affection for Indira and his life-long aristocratic scale of values got the better of him. His fervor for noncooperation did not extend to what he saw as sacrificing his beloved granddaughter's future to the cause. Abruptly he moved her to St. Cecilia's, a European-style, if privately run, local school. The change became the subject of what turned into a protracted dispute between Jawaharlal and his father. Jawaharlal feared that the three Englishwomen who ran St. Cecilia's would make Indira a little Miss Muffet of the kind exclusive European schools were turning out by the hundreds annually in every British cantonment area. He also vehemently argued that even if St. Cecilia's was not exactly a government school, its exclusively European character brought it within the scope of the Mahatma's boycott.

Jawaharlal's resentment smoldered steadily, occasionally producing enough sparks for many friends of the family and political associates to know about it and wonder why a father and son otherwise so devoted to each other should allow a seemingly small matter to come between them. Jawaharlal did not regard Indira's education as a small matter. He wrote to Gandhi, who had by then been accepted as a friend and mentor of the family, for guidance. The Mahatma, anxious to repair the growing rift between father and son without appearing to interfere unduly in a private family feud, was touched by the extent of the mental agony that the matter seemed to be causing the young man. Pleading Jawaharlal's cause with Motilal in a letter, the Mahatma described him as "one of the loneliest young men of my acquaintance in India." But Motilal, enraged over his son's attempt to justify opposition to Indira's continuance in St. Cecilia's simply on political grounds, fired off an angry telegram from Simla, where he was

Indira's father, Jawaharlal Nehru, as a young boy
with his mother, Swarup Rani

The young Jawaharlal (on ladder) with his father,
Motilal (seated), and friends during a visit to
Kashmir in 1897

Family portrait: Swarup Rani and Motilal Nehru with Jawaharlal

Family portrait, second generation: Kamala and Jawaharlal Nehru with "Indu" on her first birthday

Motilal Nehru in British court dress for the Delhi *durbar*, 1911

. . . and in *khadi* and Gandhi cap less than a decade later, after joining the Indian independence movement

Anand Bhavan, the family mansion in Allahabad

Motilal at the wheel of a family motor car outside Anand Bhavan

The young Nehrus in Geneva, 1926, with Indira and her aunts Krishna and Vijayalakshmi

Indira, aged nine, a Geneva portrait

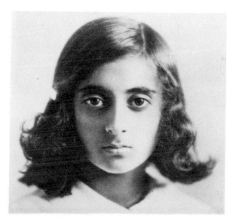

Nehru in the garden in Allahabad, with Indira (on table) and her cousin Chandralekha, daughter of Vijayalakshmi Pandit

The same trio with local Congress Party volunteers

The family, Allahabad, 1927. Front row, left to right: Swarup Rani, Motilal, and Kamala Nehru; back row: Jawaharlal, Vijayalakshmi Pandit, Krishna Nehru (later Hutheesing), Indira, and Ranjit Pandit

Father, daughter, mother, Congress workers all, 1931

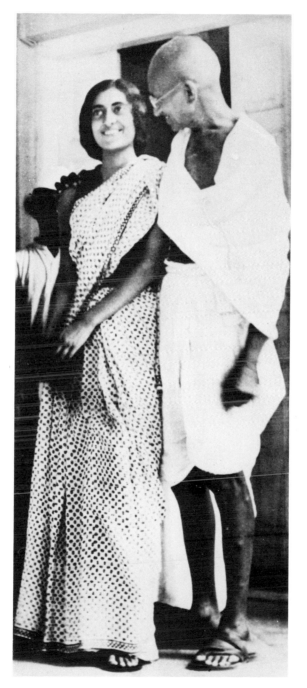

Indira with Mahatma Gandhi, Bombay, 1935

Kamala, Jawaharlal, and Indira on a visit to Ceylon

Kamala Nehru

Leaving Anand Bhavan for prison, Kamala Nehru says good-bye to Indira

Indira with her father in Czechoslovakia, 1938

... and in London that same year (V. K. Krishna Menon is on the right)

The marriage of Indira Nehru and Feroze Gandhi
at Anand Bhavan, Allahabad, March 26, 1942

Bride, bridegroom, and other relatives

The bride and her father

Indira Gandhi with her firstborn son, Rajiv

Family portrait, with grandfather Jawaharlal

Indira Gandhi and her father, Prime Minister Nehru, smeared with the colored powder used by Hindus of all walks of life, "playing *Holi*" in celebration of the spring festival of that name

at the time, telling Gandhi that what had been presented to him was a "tissue of lies from beginning to end." The school, he heatedly pointed out, was totally unconnected with the government, Jawaharlal's aversion to Indira studying there had nothing to do with the principles of noncooperation, and he, Motilal, was prompted solely by his desire "to give Indira companionship of children of her age regardless of instruction." In a further burst of anger he added that anything else reported to Gandhi was absolutely false—"too mean for the proudest father in the world." The furor finally ended in compromise, with Indira withdrawn from St. Cecilia's but not sent back to the Modern School. Instead, arrangements were made for her to be tutored at home.

This episode in which Motilal and Jawaharlal battled over what constituted a suitable education for Indira was not to be a solitary instance of interference with Indira's schooling. As her school years passed, her family's preoccupation with the independence movement and her mother's persistent ill-health and death in 1936 were to be responsible for her moving rapidly from one institution to another, a nomad.

Worried though he always was about Indira's schooling, Jawaharlal was increasingly absorbed in politics. He took to the dusty village roads in a Gandhi-inspired effort to rouse the peasants and other ordinary people of India to become partners of the intellectuals and elite groups in the great undertaking for independence. Motilal had entered active politics after a slow and protracted process of reasoning, but Jawaharlal had been drawn to the movement and Gandhi emotionally, instinctively. His commitment, therefore, was total, leaving little room in his life for anything else. "I lived in offices and committee meetings and crowds," he wrote in his *Autobiography*. " 'Go to the villages' was the slogan and we trudged many a mile across fields and visited distant villages and addressed peasant meetings. I experienced the thrill of mass-feeling, the power of influencing the mass." But as he learned to feel "at home in the dust and discomfort," Jawaharlal had less and less time to spend on the concerns of his own home. "In spite of the strength of my family bonds I almost forgot my family, my wife, my daughter," he confessed.

And Indira was doubly neglected, for Kamala's involvement in the freedom movement, though not as complete as Jawaharlal's, was extensive enough to leave her only limited time and energy for her child. As early as 1921, when Indira was barely four, Kamala had been prompted because of her own preoccupation and the constant din and commotion in Anand Bhavan, now the Congress Party's national headquarters, to send her only child to Delhi to live with her own parents and study in a local kindergarten. Indira has only hazy recollections of her stay with her grandparents, which did not last long. The house in Chandni Chowk, the old city's principal residential and shopping area, was large—almost like a little fortress with high, thick walls designed to shut out much of the summer heat and noise of the surrounding business establishments—and everyone in it showered lavish affection on the child. At the school, which was small and exclusive, her teachers, too, bestowed much personal attention on her. But Indira missed her parents and her grandfather and longed for the more exciting atmosphere of her home in Allahabad. Within months she was back in Anand Bhavan and soon placed in a nondescript private school until her admission into the Modern School and the eruption of the dispute between Motilal and Jawaharlal.

Not only was Indira's mother deeply involved in the politics of the time, but also her health had been increasingly indifferent. In November 1925 her ailment was finally diagnosed as tuberculosis, then a dreaded and usually fatal disease. A year earlier she had given birth to a son who had died when only a few days old. The sad event left perceptible emotional and physical scars. Jawaharlal, though he had recently succeeded his father as General Secretary of the Congress and could ill afford a long absence from the country, on the advice of doctors and with Gandhi's approval, left his new post to take Kamala to Europe for treatment. Indira went with them, swapping instruction at home in Anand Bhavan by her private tutor for a spell in the International School in Geneva.

When the family sailed for Europe in March 1926, it was hoped that they would not have to spend more than a few months away from home. But improvement in Kamala's health was so slow that it was only in December of the following year that it was possible for them to return. Much of the time was spent in Geneva, where Kamala received some initial treatment, and in Montana, a mountain resort, where she was later admitted into a sanatorium. Soon after the Nehrus arrived in Switzerland, they were joined by Jawaharlal's younger sister, Krishna, who, besides attending to various routine household chores, provided Indira some welcome company in the midst of strangers.

Indira has described her stay in the International School in Geneva as one of the happiest years of her life. The school, sponsored by a group of civil servants on the staff of the League of Nations, was situated in a small but attractive Swiss chalet where every classroom offered "a wonderful view of the mountains." Indira, who was then in her tenth year, was one of nearly seventy-five students of different nationalities that the school had on its rolls. On most mornings Jawaharlal walked with her to the school and would return in the late afternoon to escort her home. Even to casual observers of this daily ritual, the bond of affection between the father and daughter appeared unusually strong. Mrs. Ernest Gosnell, then a young University of Chicago graduate who taught Indira French and social studies, remembers Jawaharlal as always smiling when he was with his daughter. "He seemed very proud of her. One would notice that from the way he looked at her," Mrs. Gosnell, in retirement after a long career of teaching at Sidwell Friends School in Washington, D.C., recalled many years later.

The children spent the morning doing their lessons in the chalet. In the afternoon they were taken by bus to Onex in the country for diverse activities ranging from practical gardening and manual training to gymnastics and Maypole dancing. Shy and withdrawn in the beginning, Indira overcame her hesitation quickly, "though she never became one of those students who are always trying to attract attention to themselves," according to Mrs. Gosnell. She took part in everything —even singing European music in accompaniment to a piano—without undue self-consciousness. But her serious demeanor seldom left her. The school motto was "Do your best," and Indira attended to her studies with considerable earnestness. "Her slender long hand was frequently going up in the class. She was a very bright child," Mrs. Gosnell remembers.

When the school closed for the winter holidays, Indira joined her father on the ski slopes where both learned to ski—a process she describes as "a painful experience for a long time" because of the "innumerable falls," but one that became exhilarating and exciting as the two of them acquired proficiency and confidence.

On the family's return to India in December 1927, Indira joined St. Mary's Convent School in Allahabad. At the same time the services of a *pandit* were engaged to teach her Hindi at home. The arrangement lasted for the following three years.

Another change came in the wake of her grandfather's death. Motilal's health had been failing steadily for some years, but when he died in February 1931, his death, though foreseen for some time, came as a tremendous emotional shock to Jawaharlal and others in the family. In a letter he wrote to Indira three months after his father's death, Jawaharlal spoke of his anguish during the last days of Motilal's life as he watched his "suffering and agony" and realized "my own inability to help him whom I loved so much." The new Anand Bhavan that Motilal had fashioned so lovingly and carefully appeared, in Nehru's words, a place "lonely and deserted" whose "spirit seems to have gone." Indira herself was no less stricken by sorrow over Motilal's death. The grandfather who had seen her in her childhood as "a personification of innocence" was, until the very last few days of his life, constantly fussing over the young girl and thinking of new ways to please her. Only a couple of weeks before his death he wrote to Jawaharlal with almost childlike delight of how Indira had converted an old wooden house originally built for a family of deer into a summerhouse where she spent a part of the day reading in tranquility.

It is doubtful if Jawaharlal consciously felt that with Motilal's disappearance from the scene he was at last free to give Indira the type of education he regarded as eminently suitable for her but that his father had frowned upon. Perhaps unconsciously he considered it no longer necessary to make concessions to his father's preference for exclusive, Western-style schooling. Even if there was any such vague feeling at the back of his mind, certain other circumstances made a change in Indira's school seem desirable.

A few weeks after Motilal's death, the Congress held its annual session at Karachi. At the session Indira's parents came across Jehangir Jivaji Vakil, a brilliant young Parsi from Bombay, who, with the help of his wife, Coonverbai, had established an unusual educational institution in Poona. Vakil had been much impressed by Rabindranath Tagore's concept of a real place of learning and had tried to translate the poet's ideas as expressed at the University of Shantineketan into reality on a rather more modest way in his preparatory school. Like

Tagore, Vakil was anxious to incorporate in his own institution the best of the ancient Indian system of teaching as well as of the modern Western theories. He believed that by itself the former did not serve the needs of India of the twentieth century and that the system the British had established in the country would turn Indians into cheap imitations of the West and in the process rob them of their cultural identity. Nehru was quite carried away by Vakil's ideas and the enthusiastic way in which he presented them. He also saw a distinct possibility of him and Kamala's being imprisoned again soon. Indira's continuance in the convent school in Allahabad appeared in the circumstances unreasonable. Before the Karachi session was over, it was arranged that after a brief holiday the family was contemplating Indira should travel to Poona, nearly 1,000 miles from home, to become a boarder in Vakil's school.

Unlike her references to the International School in Geneva and to the universities at Shantineketan and Oxford to which she went subsequently, Indira's recollection of her nearly three years in Poona seldom reflect any nostalgia. The institution was run along the lines Vakil had explained to Jawaharlal at Karachi, and the normal routine was rigorous and exacting. That it was a pioneer institution and that the Vakils were loath to accept any financial assistance from the government accentuated the school's spartan character. For Indira it was quite a change from the comforts of Anand Bhavan and the exaggerated pseudosophistication of a convent school. It required a great effort on her part to adjust herself to it.

The school was housed in an old colonial-style bungalow. Nearly a century earlier, Lord Wellesley, whose success in annexing territory for the East India Company had made the British Empire in India a reality, reputedly lived in the bungalow during a brief visit to Poona. By the time the Vakils acquired it for the school the building had lost much of its former elegance and showed distinct signs of decades of decay and neglect. Vakil and his wife occupied one room, while Indira and about a dozen other boarders lived in a few other rooms, some of which had to be converted quickly into classrooms every morning. The food served them was modest, and Vakil enforced discipline sternly and with the zealousness of one whose faith in what he was doing was unmarred by any self-doubts. Indira, then nearly fourteen, was the oldest among the boarders. She was, in fact, older than her

years and, as such, felt self-conscious and lonesome. The companionship of students of her own age, which was one of the concerns that
precipitated Motilal's dispute with his son years earlier, was conspicuously denied her in the Poona school. A few months after Indira's
arrival at Poona, her aunt Vijayalakshmi was arrested (Nehru himself
was already back in prison) and her three daughters were also hurriedly dispatched to Vakil's school. The oldest of Indira's cousins was
only seven. Their arrival placed on her the enormous psychological
burden of caring for them and helping them to adapt themselves to the
unfamiliar surroundings. Additional responsibility came in the form
of a group of "untouchable" children whom the Vakils had admitted
into the school, most of whom had to be washed and fed daily by their
own daughter, Jai, and Indira. Her beloved grandfather gone, her
father back in jail, her mother seriously ill in a sanatorium in North
India, living a long way from home and with hardly any real friends
and companions, is it any wonder that Indira found life crowded with
stresses and strains? Often, despite the considerable affection she received from the Vakils, she was unable to cope with them and found
relief in lonely tears shed in the privacy of her bed at night or a distant
corner of the large playground.

Not that her stay in Poona was entirely devoid of joyful thrills and
excitement. In September 1932 Gandhi, then undergoing a jail term,
announced his decision to fast unto death to protest against the British Government's Communal Award. The Award prescribed that
henceforth various religious communities of India—Hindus, Muslims,
Sikhs, Christians, etc.—would elect only individuals belonging to
their own faith to represent them in the various legislatures, where the
quota of seats for each community would be fixed. The Mahatma saw
in it a sinister move to perpetuate and enlarge the religious differences
in the country and resolved to fight it by offering his own life as a
sacrifice. His decision caused sorrow and nervousness throughout the
country. On the eve of the beginning of the fast Jawaharlal, who was
himself in jail, wrote to Indira that the news had completely shaken
him. "My little world in which he [Gandhi] has occupied such a big
place, shakes and totters, and there seems to be darkness and emptiness
everywhere. . . . Shall I not see him again?" he asked in unmistakable
personal anguish. Indira was too young to regard the Mahatma as a
mentor and a *guru,* but her bond of personal affection for him was

strong. The possibility that he might starve himself to death disturbed her, but she found that, unlike her father, she did not need to torment herself with the feeling that she might never meet him again. Gandhi was lodged in a prison in Poona itself, barely a few miles from her school, and one day Indira appeared at its gate with her three cousins, demanding to meet the prisoner. In view of the consternation and turmoil that the beginning of Gandhi's self-imposed ordeal had created in the country, the jail authorities felt it would be unwise to turn back Nehru's daughter. Indira, therefore, had what she thought was a delightful meeting with "Bapu" during which she told him how in her school all the children had fasted for a whole day and prayed for him and how she had "adopted" an untouchable child to take special care of because the welfare of the Harijans was so dear to him. Gandhi was distinctly pleased to meet his young visitors and with his puckish sense of humor teased Indira about her matronly responsibilities for her cousins and how she seemed to eat better in the Vakils' house than she had ever done at Anand Bhavan, because, for the first time, her gangly frame showed signs of having some flesh on it. The fast ended on the fifth day, when the government, though not canceling the Award, withdrew its most objectionable feature.

Gandhi's incarceration in Poona was responsible for another wonderful interlude in Indira's life in the school. Jawaharlal was released from jail in September 1933, and he rushed to Poona to meet Indira and Gandhi. He spent several days in Poona, and much of the time he was in the school playing with Indira, his three nieces, and numerous other children, telling them stories from ancient history as they sat around him in the evening, attending some of their classes, and often even trying to improvise toys for them. Even the youngest among the children had heard of Nehru and what a great leader of India he was, and they were proud to have him among them. During that week, Indira was all happiness to have her dear "Papu" with her and delighted by the look of reverence on the faces of her schoolmates as they watched him.

Shantineketan, to which Indira Nehru went after obtaining her school-leaving certificate, was the original on which the school in Poona was modeled, and yet it was a world apart from it. Visva-Bharati was the name of the unconventional university that poet-philosopher

Tagore had established in 1921. He had turned its location, Shantineketan, today generally synonymous with the school, into the real abode of peace that the name meant. Tagore, whose work of philosophic verse, *Gitanjali,* had brought him the Nobel Prize for literature, was revered all over India as a seer and a saint and affectionately called *gurudev,* or "God in the form of teacher." Jawaharlal admired Tagore next perhaps only to Gandhi and his father, and the curriculum at Visva-Bharati appealed to him immensely. He believed that the institution offered a perfect escape from the "dead hand" of the conventional universities. A visit to Shantineketan in early 1934 so impressed both Kamala and Jawaharlal that they resolved to send Indira there as soon as her final school results were available.

At Shantineketan, Indira rose long before daybreak and after a frugal, early breakfast, joined students and staff out in the open at a general assembly at which devotional hymns were sung in chorus. Instruction was imparted in natural surroundings. Unlike conventional universities, which banished them completely, Visva-Bharati gave crafts and classical Indian art forms, including music and dancing as well as painting, a prominent place in the day's program. Twice daily, at sunrise and sunset, everyone at Shantineketan sat silently for a while meditating or in communion with nature.

Her father approved of it because it was different from the official universities, but Indira took to Visva-Bharati because it offered her some of the things she had always yearned for. The idyllic setting and the atmosphere of peace and tranquility that marked the university was for Indira a wonderful change from the turmoil and commotion through which she had lived her life until then. She had always been amidst crowds, noise, conflict, and violence, which, she once confessed to an interviewer, she later came to consider responsible "for the considerable bitterness in me." At Shantineketan she was able to cleanse herself of that bitterness. Instead of slogans of hate shouted by demonstrators and equally angry abuse hurled back at them by the police Indira encountered at Visva-Bharati a pervasive silence broken mostly by the dulcet notes of *Rabindra Sangeet,* Tagore's verses rendered to music, or the singing of the birds that abounded in the thick forest-like foliage of the university garden. Even the chattering of students had a musical quality about it because Bengali, the mother tongue of most of them, is the sweetest of Indian languages. "I seemed suddenly to have landed in another world," she recalled of her arrival at the university.

Even more than the atmosphere of peace she encountered there, Indira appreciated Shantineketan because for the first time in her life she had the companionship of persons of her age. Previously, she had been almost always with adults or, when she was at school, as she ruefully recalled, usually found herself the oldest person there. It was a curiously joyful experience to have around her many individuals with whom she could communicate at her own emotional and intellectual level. Perhaps it was this combination of tranquility and suitable companionship that enabled Indira to overcome much of her shyness. At Shantineketan she continued to read extensively, but books ceased to be the refuge they were earlier, and she took to the Manipur style of Indian classical dancing with much zeal and attained sufficient proficiency in it to be praised even by Tagore.

Like her father, Indira found Rabindranath Tagore fascinating. "In a way, Tagore was the first person whom I consciously regarded as a great man," she remembered. A bond of affection grew between them quickly. The poet was then over seventy-three, and with his tall but fragile frame, flowing white beard, and a robe reaching down to his feet, he seemed a figure out of a Greek classic. As he walked slowly through the various groves or sat reposefully on the terrace of his modest cottage, students would often approach him, touch his feet reverentially, and seek his guidance on personal and scholastic problems. Indira hesitated to "impose upon *Gurudev*" until Tagore himself gently chided her for neglecting him. Of her meetings with the poet, she once wrote, "Many were the evenings when a small group of us sat at his feet and talked of diverse subjects, or silently watched him paint. Often he would recite or read aloud." To her, these were "moments of serene joy, memories to cherish."

The happiness Indira found at Shantineketan was, however, tinged with constant worry about her parents. Nehru had been imprisoned again even before she had joined Visva-Bharati. In fact, he was punished for the three "subversive" speeches he had delivered in Calcutta while on his way to Shantineketan to decide about Indira's enrollment there. Kamala's health had been deteriorating rapidly, and both Jawaharlal and Indira feared that her end might be approaching. Towards July 1934 her condition worsened, and the following month

Jawaharlal was released temporarily to be by her bedside. Indira rushed from Shantineketan to Allahabad to join her parents. A slight improvement in Kamala's condition prompted the government to order Nehru to return to jail after only eleven days' freedom. A few weeks later Kamala, who suffered a setback following her husband's re-arrest, was moved to Bhowali in the mountains, and Jawaharlal himself was transferred to a jail in nearby Almora and allowed to visit her "once or twice a month." What added to the personal anxiety of father and daughter a few months later was the news reaching him in Almora, and Indira back at Shantineketan, that Swarup Rani, Motilal's widow, who had been ailing for some time, had suffered a paralytic stroke.

In May 1935 doctors urgently advised that Kamala again be taken to Europe for treatment. Earlier, messages had been sent by those in authority that Nehru would be released to be with his wife provided he gave an assurance, however informal, not to take part in politics. Anxious though he was to be with his wife, it was unthinkable for Jawaharlal to offer such a pledge. Even Kamala, though in a constant feverish daze by then, begged him to make no such promise to secure his release. When, therefore, it was considered necessary for Kamala to be taken to Switzerland for treatment, inevitably Indira was asked to go with her. She thus left Shantineketan, and her brief encounter with serene living ended abruptly. Tagore wrote to her father:

> It is with a heavy heart we bade farewell to Indira, for she was such an asset in our place. I have watched her very closely and felt admiration for the way you have brought her up. Her teachers, all in one voice, praise her and I know she is extremely popular with the students. I only hope things will turn for the better and she will soon return here and get back to her studies.

Unfortunately, things did not turn for the better. On February 28, 1936, Kamala died in Lausanne. Jawaharlal, who had been released unconditionally some months earlier and had traveled at once to Switzerland, was at her side. After Kamala's death a sorrowful Jawaharlal returned to India where the Congress Party once again had chosen him as its President for the following year, and an equally distraught Indira left for Britain to look into the prospects of studying at one of its prestigious universities.

In 1937 Indira joined Somerville College, Oxford, after passing the usual entrance examination. Apparently, the question of Indira's studying in America instead of Britain was also considered. In a long letter to Agatha Harrison, a friend of Indira and of the Nehru family in Britain, Jawaharlal argued that Indira "must make her own decisions" whether she should go to Oxford or "Smith College in the United States where Dr. S. Ralph Harlow is eager for her to study." Indira opted for Oxford, presumably because for Indians Britain then held a strange fascination. That Feroze Gandhi, whom she later married, was studying in the London School of Economics at the time may also have influenced her decision, though there is also some evidence that he went there because she planned to be in Britain.

At Somerville Indira studied, among other subjects, public and social administration, history, and anthropology. By and large she looks back on her stay at Oxford as a happy one. She found the place itself "lovely," and, as during her brief stay at Visva-Bharati, she was able to read widely on art, archaeology, architecture, and religious thought. She regarded the opportunities to do such reading as opening windows into her mind. She even dabbled in local party politics and was a member of the students' wing of the British Labour Party. Her association with the organization afforded her an experience that, when it occurred, seemed almost traumatic but that she now relates with considerable amusement. V. K. Krishna Menon, who was himself active in the British Labour Party and whom she knew as a friend of her father, asked her to come to a meeting to read a message that Jawaharlal had specially sent for the occasion. At the meeting, however, Indira discovered to her chagrin that she was also expected to make a regular speech. This terrified her. Addressing a gathering of the Monkey Brigade was one thing, speaking at a Labour Party gathering at Oxford quite another. As she narrated the episode years afterward on a BBC program, "I just could not get anything out at all. And there was a drunk in the audience, at least I hope he was drunk, and he remarked, 'She does not speak, she squeaks.' Naturally the audience were in splits of laughter and that was the end of the speech."

Though she enjoyed her stay at the university, Indira does not think she got "as much out of Oxford as I might have." Her heart and mind were in India. "Only a part of me was there. All the time I kept thinking when can I get back and do something in India."

A great deal was happening in India by 1937. The British Government had announced new constitutional reforms, and after much debate and despite serious misgivings about their effectiveness, the Congress Party had decided to give them a trial. The party had contested elections to the provincial assemblies and succeeded in forming governments in many provinces. At the same time it was continuing its struggle for complete independence. It thus found itself in the strange —in fact, fascinating—position of being in authority and yet challenging authority. For one nurtured on the politics of the independence movement, as Indira was, it must indeed have been galling to be thousands of miles away from the country at such a time.

Her health, too, was far from good and caused Jawaharlal a great deal of anxiety. As a child Indira had always had a weak constitution. She was thin and lanky, and her father often wished aloud she would "get strong and plump." During her first year at Oxford the principal of Somerville wrote to Nehru advising him that doctors felt Indira should spend the winter in some place other than Oxford. Her physical strength did not match her spirits, and even a slight exposure or some undue exertion was liable to bring about a debilitating—and for her distant father, worrisome—bout of illness.

In the autumn of 1939 Indira caught a chill that developed into pleurisy. Jawaharlal immediately cabled Dr. P. C. Bhandari, a London doctor who was a close family friend, requesting him to look after her. Later, when she recovered, her father urged her to go to Lysin in Switzerland, arguing that Britain in winter and at war "is no place for an invalid." When she was at last back to normal health after some months in the Alps, Indira returned to Britain via a long and tedious route through Europe, hopping from country to country to evade the advancing Nazi armies. In London Hitler's blitz had begun. She enrolled herself as a Red Cross volunteer and did duty as an ambulance driver. Britain in 1941 was no place for pursuing academic studies. And home was beckoning Indira more strongly than ever. The Empire's prewar experiment in cooperation had failed, and the Congress Party was again flexing its muscles for a major conflict with British power. Accompanied by Feroze Gandhi, who had been feeling equally restless away from India, Indira sailed via the Cape of Good Hope and reached Bombay in March 1941. That she had come away without securing the B.A. degree from Oxford did not worry her much, though it caused some disappointment to her father.

Any account of Indira Gandhi's education that merely mentions the degrees and diplomas she earned or failed to earn and lists the various schools and universities she attended is liable to give an incomplete and inaccurate idea of the real opportunities for learning she had and took advantage of. Notwithstanding the frequent interruptions in her schooling as she was forced to flit from institution to institution, Indira was given an education of a kind few young people are lucky enough to receive. Those critics of her prime ministership who ascribe its mistakes to what they see as her incomplete education seriously miss the mark.

That he was confined to "Barrack No. 4" of the Lucknow jail, as he complained in that letter in 1922, did not deter Nehru from looking ahead and doing something about Indira's learning. From his prison cell he wrote to his then five-year-old daughter the first of a series of what would come to over 200 letters offering what was later described as "a rambling account of history for young people." The letters discussed in a simple, chatty way the various aspects of world history from the functioning of the village republics in ancient India to the impact of the Industrial Revolution on Britain and Europe. When published later in book form, the letters were appropriately entitled *Glimpses of World History*. They were preceded by an earlier, shorter series comprising only twenty-eight letters that Jawaharlal wrote to Indira when she was away from Allahabad on a summer holiday in the mountains. The exercise in letter-writing had a more intimate reason than providing Indira with a general understanding of history. The writing of them enabled Jawaharlal to demolish, at least temporarily, the prison walls that stood between him and his adored child. With these letters, he explained to Indira, "you shall silently come near me and then we shall talk of many things."

The many things he talked about were not all related to events in world history. There were many a lesson in personal courage. In the opening letter of the larger series that he started on Indira's thirteenth birthday as a gift for her, Nehru wrote, "Never do anything in secret or anything that you would wish to hide. For the desire to hide anything means that you are afraid, and fear is a bad thing and unworthy of you." In a subsequent letter he translated an old Sanskrit verse to subtly suggest to its young reader that the individual must be prepared to sacrifice his interests for the larger good of the community and the country.

At the time she received them Indira regarded the paternal epistles as "just letters." She found them interesting, read each of them many times over, and loved them because they came from her dear "Papu." Later, however, she was able to discern the impact they had on her mind and the way they influenced her outlook on things. She told a British journalist that the letters "helped to form my mind in a way that no other education did because they enabled me to see things in perspective and I never saw an Indian problem merely as an Indian problem but as an international one."

Even when he lacked the leisure that imprisonment offered him, Jawaharlal found time to make his contribution to Indira's education. As she recalls those times, he was always telling her of wondrous things about the world, various countries, and life generally. In doing so, he seldom sounded like a teacher trying to impart useful information to a pupil. Instead, he merely seemed to be telling her interesting stories. Whether he was walking her to her school in Geneva or skiing with her later that year or traveling through France, Germany, and Britain or watching the Devil Dancers during a visit to Ceylon, Nehru was constantly pointing out to the girl the fascinating world around them. If they walked through Anand Bhavan's gardens under a cloudless, starry sky, he told her of the mysteries of the universe. If they visited the Louvre in Paris he would talk to her of the world's greatest artists and various countries and ages that had enriched the world's treasury of art. If the daily newspaper reported a new political development in Europe he would explain to her what fascism stood for and the reason why it was so belligerent towards democratic Britain on the one hand and communist Russia on the other. He was not consciously trying to form her mind, but he was so bubbling over with enthusiasm that "it spilt over," she says. Nehru's own vast and diverse reading filtered through an introspective mind to meet Indira's inquisitiveness—she never tired of asking questions—and provide a sound basis for a growing child's education.

Additionally, as Jawaharlal's daughter, Indira at an early age came into contact with some of the world's most important personalities. Besides political leaders the Nehru house drew artists, writers, and scientists. When she accompanied her parents to Europe in 1926, Indira met Romain Rolland many times and occasionally even tried her French on him. Ernst Toller, the German poet, and his wife became greatly attached to her as Edward Thompson, another outstanding literary figure, did later. On her own she met George Bernard Shaw and Einstein and virtually all the leading lights of the Labour Party at the time of her stay in Britain. And Indira was no collector of autographs. She took her meetings with important persons rather seriously. In the presence of celebrities she seldom allowed herself to be overwhelmed by their personalities or her awareness of their importance. In fact, she subjected most of them to a critical, independent appraisal, often disagreeing with what they advocated. Even Gandhi did not impress her overmuch, for all that she loved him. She did not agree with everything he said, and as a young person she felt that "so many of his ideas were so old and out of date." Harold Laski, the noted economist and political thinker who influenced Jawaharlal profoundly, tried on one occasion to influence a decision of Indira's, but she found his reasoning unconvincing and had no hesitation in rejecting his suggestion. When Lord Lothian, a British Cabinet minister noted for the archconservatism of his political views, invited Jawaharlal and Indira to spend a weekend at his ancestral home in the country, Indira promptly turned down the invitation because she said she could not abide her host's "pro fascist" leanings. Nehru went to the Lothian castle at Blicking, but Indira would not.

Finally, Indira's own contribution to her education through her voracious reading, though impossible to assess precisely, has been and even today continues to be considerable. As a child, when absorbed in a book she would forget to eat or play. Her grandmother and often even Kamala would be exasperated by their inability to pull Indira away from her reading. Anand Bhavan had a collection of nearly 6,000 books, most of which Jawaharlal had carefully chosen during his various visits to Britain, and he was constantly adding new books for Indira. Some of these he would urge others to "commandeer" after she had read them. Indira loved her father's interest in reading, and often a few days before visiting him in prison she would write to him requesting him to have a new list of books ready for her.

In 1971, long after Nehru's death and following her own assumption of the time-consuming task of governing India, when unfavorable weather caused a routine stop at London's Heathrow airport to be lengthened by several hours, Indira Gandhi took advantage of the delay to send an aide quickly into the city to buy some recently published titles not yet available in India. The troubles that by then had erupted in blood in Bangladesh were leaving her very little time for books. But old habit is strong. Trained by Jawaharlal in the stretching pleasures of the mind, Indira was still reading when and where and what she could.

4

Marriage
"Conflict and unhappiness are not the worst things that can happen."

U P to the age of eighteen or nineteen, Indira, as she once confessed, was determined "never to get married." Unlike their Western counterparts who tend to regard marriage as the culmination of romance and the establishment of settled personal freedom, for most Indian girls marriage usually means leaving the security of their parents' home and tying themselves for life to someone whom they may have glimpsed only briefly prior to the wedding ceremony. Few can look forward to setting up their own homes, with the joy and excitement that that brings. Rather they become part of a large, already established household—a joint family in whose folds who knows what jealous, hostile in-law might lurk? But Indira's resolve not to get married was not the result of such uncertainties and trepidations.

Jawaharlal had married the girl of his father's choosing. However, by the time Indira approached womanhood, the Nehru family had imbibed Western social thought sufficiently to rule out a totally traditional wedding in her case. Indira was averse to getting married, because a matrimonial involvement, as she explained, would have interfered with her political activities to which "I felt I should devote every minute of my time." Her fantasy about being another Joan of Arc had metamorphosed into an equally demanding, if more realistic, sense of commitment to the national cause.

A few years later, however, when she changed her mind about celibacy, Indira acted in an equally determined manner. "When I decided to get married I just did not think out things any more. I just got married," she remarked to an interviewer. It was 1941, and Jawaharlal was again in prison. When she announced her decision to her father during one of her fortnightly visits to him in Dehra Dun jail, the firmness of her tone surprised him. He could not believe that Indira had made up her mind suddenly and suspected that she had been keeping a secret from him.

If some of her own remarks and the abruptness with which she apparently conveyed her mind to her father suggest that her marriage was the result of an impulsive, impetuous resolve or that she was swept off her feet by someone whom she had met only briefly, the impression would be very erroneous; few women have been wooed as assiduously and over as long a period as Indira was by Feroze Gandhi. Indira was only sixteen when Feroze had first proposed marriage to her. That was the time when Swarup Rani, in the manner of an orthodox, tradition-bound grandmother, had started looking around for a suitable match for Indira. There was also vague talk in Anand Bhavan of a wealthy Kashmiri family being anxious to secure Indira as their daughter-in-law. The fear that his claim to Indira's hand might go by default prompted Feroze to rush with his proposal—a proposal that he reiterated with remarkable perseverence every few months until it was finally accepted almost nine years later.

Feroze Gandhi had the same surname as the Mahatma, but he came from a quite different social and religious background. Unlike Mahatma Gandhi, who was an orthodox Hindu, Feroze was a Parsi, belonging to one of the smallest and most cohesive religious sects in India. The Parsis were so named because they originally lived in Persia from where they had fled over 1,000 years ago to escape persecution by their country's Muslim rulers. As followers of Zoroaster, they worshipped fire, which was anathema to Islam. A few hundred Zoroasterians landed on the west coast of India in the beginning of the eighth century and were assured of safety and freedom of worship by the local Hindu ruler.

Over the centuries the Parsis have lived in harmony not only with the principal religious faith in the country but also with the dominant political force. Their number increased, but they still remain a microscopic minority in India. They are smaller in size than even the Kashmiri Pandit community and more jealous of their cultural identity. Like the Kashmiri Brahmins, the Parsis accepted the language of the region they live in, but in matters of worship they are sternly opposed to dilution of dogma. They also frown at Parsis' marrying outside of the community. There are other striking similarities between the two communities. Both are almost totally free from illiteracy and have produced an unusually large number of outstanding men and women. Dadabhai Naoroji and Ferozeshah Mehta, two of the most influential leaders in the early stages of the freedom movement, were Parsis, as was Sir Jamsetji Tata, who founded what is today the largest business house in the country. India's most eminent nuclear physicist, Dr. Homi Bhabha, who died in an air crash in 1966, was a Parsi. In the brief period since Indian independence the community has provided one army chief and one head of the air force. Yet, the size of their contribution to national leadership notwithstanding, the Parsis, like the Kashmiri Pandits, have remained essentially a middle-class community engaged principally in small-scale commerce and the professions. Before independence, in many district headquarters, the license to sell liquor and guns was granted to what often was the town's only Parsi family.

Most Parsis live in Bombay, although some families have moved into the interior in quest of opportunities for trade and employment, which were scarce in India under the British. Feroze was only two years old when in 1914 his father, a naval engineer, sent the entire family to live in Allahabad. The outbreak of World War I made it necessary for him to be away at sea for long periods, and he felt the family would be better looked after in Allahabad, where his sister was a surgeon in the Lady Dufferin Hospital. Besides his mother, Feroze was accompanied to Allahabad by a sister, Tehmina, and a brother, Faredun, both considerably older than he was.

For nearly three years young Feroze studied in a girls' school, where his high spirits and capacity for mischief made many teachers and female students regard him as a little monster. Later, at seven he was admitted into the city's Anglo-Vernacular School for boys. There many of his classmates shared the same horror of him, but he also made some deep and abiding friendships. At home he drove his brother and sister to distraction through his exuberant, unruly behavior. At twelve Feroze became a Boy Scout and joined the troop of his school's assistant scout-

master, Kesho Deo Malaviya, an association that later grew into enduring comradeship in the field of politics. (Nearly thirty years later,
when Feroze was elected to the Lok Sabha, the lower house of India's
Parliament, Malaviya was a powerful minister in Nehru's Cabinet,
and in party affairs the two worked with unusual unanimity of purpose.)

Feroze's interest in politics was late in developing but, when it did
come, was quick to acquire the characteristics of a hurricane. He was
sixteen when he was drawn into the freedom movement. That was the
period of intense political fervor in India. People's hopes, which had
been roused in the beginning of the 1920s, had by 1928 turned into
frustration and anger, for the British Government showed no inclination of accepting the minimum Congress demand of Dominion status.
The government had announced the setting up of a royal commission
to study the question of constitutional reform in India. The commission, which arrived in India in February 1928, was headed by Sir
John Simon, a distinguished lawyer whom Motilal knew personally.
(Among the commission members was Clement Attlee, during whose
prime ministership nearly two decades later India was granted independence.) The Congress Party, however, was unimpressed. What
was there, its leaders asked, that the British Government needed to
study about India's competence to govern itself. They saw it as an attempt on Britain's part to delay meeting Indian aspirations. Many in
the party and outside regarded it as a national affront. In its decision to
boycott the Simon Commission, the Congress Party was joined by
many other groups, including even some moderate ones on whose support Britain could previously always count. In New Delhi's Western
Court, the palatial hostel for legislators where the commission was
housed, the Indian residents were rude to its members to the extent of
declining to shake hands with them or even acknowledge their saluta-
tions. In the streets massive demonstrations erupted to protest against
the commission. Wherever they traveled, Sir John and his colleagues
were greeted by crowds chanting, "Go back, Simon." So unrelenting
was the public fury against the commission that when it traveled by
railway, mobile police had to be posted all along the track for its security. Its arrival in a city invariably caused a total suspension of business
and a complete students' strike in the local schools and colleges.

It was during one of these demonstrations in Allahabad that sixteen-year-old Feroze received his baptism in politics. He had by then finished school and entered the local Ewing Christian College, an institution run by American missionaries. The college had had its share of student unrest and political turmoil, but, curiously, it had left Feroze unmoved. Enormous though his energy was and restless his spirit, politics somehow had failed to make any claim on them. The change, when it came, was sudden and total. The Allahabad Congress Committee had organized a procession in disregard of the ban on demonstrations to protest against the Simon Commission. Thanks to the frequency and vehemence of such defiance, official nerves had become distinctly frayed. In asserting its authority the police not only beat up the demonstrators but also gave a thrashing to Feroze who, along with numerous others, had stood on the curb leaning nonchalantly on his recently acquired bicycle watching the fun. More physical punishment awaited him at home, where his brother, Faredun, wanted to teach him a lesson for getting involved with "subversive" elements. Faredun's nervousness and anger were understandable. The authorities in those days regarded with strong disapproval any employees who, their own loyalty notwithstanding, failed to keep their wards and dependents away from political agitation. The bungalow they all lived in was given to his aunt by the government, and Faredun and his sister were aspiring to enter the civil service. The presence in the family of an agitator could ruin their prospects. But Feroze, it seemed, could not care less. The unjustness of the beating at the hands of the police had roused the rebel in him. Thereafter it could not be suppressed or overawed by the severity of the beating he received at home after virtually each participation in Congress demonstrations and processions.

Feroze's ardor for political agitation grew rapidly. The Simon Commission returned to London, but neither national anger nor Feroze's enthusiasm subsided. The Congress Party raised its sights to demand complete independence and prepared itself for what it then believed would be its "final conflict" with the Raj. Young men like Feroze were riding the crest of a wave of nationalistic fervor. His family's concern for his future, too, grew as Feroze's involvement became deeper. By 1930 he had had his first taste of British prisons. Soon after his imprisonment his mother, Rattimai, paid a tearful call at Anand Bhavan where Mahatma Gandhi happened to be on a brief visit. She begged the Mahatma to rebuke her son for neglecting his college studies and order him to listen to his family's pleas. The Mahatma who, eleven years earlier had averted a rift between Motilal and Jawaharlal by urging the latter to curb his enthusiasm for the time being, was, somehow, not prepared to act similarly in the crisis in the Gandhi household. Perhaps he realized the futility of offering such advice to Feroze, of whose dedication and commitment to the cause of freedom he had heard some accounts. Gently but firmly he pointed out to Rattimai that her son was engaged in a worthy cause and that she should not pull him back from the performance of a noble duty. As for his future and her distress over his disregard of his college studies, Gandhi told Rattimai that in independent India what would matter would be the number of times one had courted imprisonment and not the degrees one had collected poring over books. As Rattimai later recalled, Gandhi said of her son, "Give me seven young men like Feroze and we shall achieve independence in seven days."

As soon as he was eighteen, Feroze joined the Allahabad City Congress as a regular member and found to his delight his old scout master, Malaviya, holding an important position in the organization. The doors of Anand Bhavan were always open to Congress leaders as well as workers, but Feroze's association with Malaviya, who had by then won Jawaharlal's trust and friendship, gained him entry into the inner family circle of the Nehrus. Soon, he needed no help from Malaviya. His obvious sincerity, his capacity for genuine affection, his selflessness, and his ebullient humor—he could make even a grim occurrence like a police *lathi* charge seem irresistibly funny—made him a dear and welcome friend of the household.

In Anand Bhavan Feroze was particularly devoted to Kamala and Indira. That Kamala was suffering from the dread disease tuberculosis was generally known. She would be compelled to spend long periods on her sickbed either at home or in a sanatorium fighting a battle for her life that she appeared slowly but unmistakably to be losing. Jawaharlal's younger sister Krishna has described Feroze's fondness for Kamala as "romantic, Dante-and-Beatrice" in style. When Kamala was well enough to travel to villages in connection with the Congress Party's program, she was followed by Feroze proudly carrying her tea and sandwiches in a small box. At no time during the political meeting —which could often be long and tedious—would he put aside the precious box or entrust it to someone else's care. Kamala received his attention and affection in even more generous measure in sickness. Owing to the highly contagious nature of her ailment, many near relations tended to avoid visiting Kamala at times when she was bedridden. Those who came would stay briefly and apprehensively. Feroze showed no such hesitation or concern for his own health. During her bouts of illness, he would always be around to run errands for her, keep her amused with his unending supply of anecdotes and current political gossip, and nurse her with tender care. He would not hesitate to do for her such an unpleasant task as cleaning her spittoon, a chore that even the Anand Bhavan sweepers performed reluctantly and with unconcealed distaste. During one of her bad spells, when she was moved to a sanatorium in the mountains, Feroze visited her with unfailing regularity. On yet another occasion when she was in a hospital in Lausanne, Feroze, who by then had joined the London School of Economics, would often leave his studies to visit her in Switzerland.

In his affection for Indira Feroze was relatively less demonstrative. That he was somewhat circumspect and restrained in the matter probably was not due to any inadequacy in his feelings towards her. Though he was young and impulsive and probably deeply in love with Indira, Feroze was intelligent enough to realize the risks involved in any undue display on his part of ardor for the young girl. In a society where the sexes are firmly segregated, as they are in India, young boys and girls must learn to conceal from their watchful elders whatever mutual attraction might develop. Any seeming lack of decorousness in their behavior is liable to deprive them of what little freedom to mix with each other they might grudgingly have been granted. These rules of social propriety were enforced even more rigidly at the time circumstances brought Feroze and Indira together. The Nehrus, though highly Westernized in certain respects, continued to adhere fairly firmly to many traditional social attitudes and values. Blatancy on Feroze's part in expressing his feelings for Indira would almost certainly have caused his immediate exclusion from the inner sanctum of Anand Bhavan. Even his action in proposing marriage to Indira was an act of considerable daring that normally should have earned him a stern reprimand. If it did not, it was probably because for a long while Indira herself did not take it seriously, few others in the family knew about it, and, finally, because Kamala's affection for Feroze shielded him against any ire that he might have invited upon himself.

It was, however, a measure of his attachment to Indira that when she went to Britain for her college education, Feroze constantly traveled to Oxford to be near her. Indira by then was almost twenty and had grown into a young woman of acknowledged beauty. She was slim and delicately built. In her willowy loveliness none could recognize the spindly-legged girl of less than a decade ago whose nose seemed too big for her face and who ran around on the Anand Bhavan grounds dressed in the austere and unattractive uniform of a Congress volunteer, her bobbed hair erupting in ill-set tufts from under a flimsy *khadi* cap. By the time she went abroad, Indira had not only changed greatly physically but acquired the desire to dress well. Her taste in clothes was impeccable, and her instinct about personal appearance faultless. She dressed with care and modishly but not without a touch of sobriety. Those who met Indira in Britain then remember how she could look chic without the least bit of flashiness or loudness about her clothes or hair style. She wore colorful Indian *saris*, North Indian *salwar-kameez* (long shirt over specially cut loose pants), occasionally, even Western dresses. An aunt who visited Britain in 1939 recalls her meeting with Indira who had come to a London railway station to receive her. Young Indira in an elegantly cut skirt and jacket, with a gauzy black veil over her hat, looked as if "she had just stepped out of a high class fashion house in Paris." As they walked down the railway platform towards the exit, the aunt remembers feeling embarrassed and even somewhat irritated by men turning round to stare at Indira.

Feroze, too, stared at her, rapturously. By then Indira had begun taking him a lot more seriously than she had in Allahabad. Shanta Gandhi, another Indian student with whom Indira shared a small flat in London for a while, was once invited to go to a theater with Indira and Feroze, and the evening reportedly left her with the distinct impression that Jawaharlal's daughter was deeply in love with their escort. Strong though their attachment was, Indira and Feroze behaved with the sense of propriety that an old-fashioned Indian family would have expected of them. Mrs. Sheela Kaul, Indira's aunt on her mother's side, met the two of them often in Britain, but her watchful eye noticed no signs of a romance. She remembers how Feroze was always hovering around Indira, helping her in diverse ways and often acting almost possessively towards her, but there was little in their demeanor or their common activities to give her the impression that they were in love. Wherever Indira went, whether it was a meeting of the British Labour Party or of Krishna Menon's India League or a visit to an art exhibition, a theater, or a Soho restaurant, Feroze always seemed to be there. He helped her with any routine problems that might confront her, watched over her health, which then was causing her family some worry, and often traveled with her when she visited other parts of Europe. Indira mentioned Feroze in her letters home. Feroze himself wrote sometimes to Jawaharlal about Indira. From Stanstad in Switzerland, for example, he sent Nehru a number of color slides of Indira and the places they had visited, along with instructions about how to view them. ("They may be viewed by holding them against a light and placing a sheet of paper between them.")

If despite this Jawaharlal was amazed when on her return to India in 1941 Indira disclosed to him her intention to marry Feroze, it must have been because he and others in the Nehru household had got so used to seeing Feroze around Indira that they had ceased to notice him.

Jawaharlal was not only surprised but distressed. He was modern-minded enough to concede Indira's right to make her own decisions. During her stay in Britain, when her education did not appear to be following any clearly planned course, he declined to use his position as her father to decide what she should or should not study. In letters to Agatha Harrison, the close personal friend who looked after Indira in Britain, Nehru repeatedly argued that Indira must make her own decisions about what she wanted to study. He had himself enjoyed similar freedom from Motilal, who had declined to impose his will on his son. That Jawaharlal's first reaction to the proposed marriage should be one of resistance and shock was, apparently, the result of his ever-increasing concern for her welfare. After Kamala's death this had acquired a tender yet tense character. The father, who would urge Motilal not to spoil Indira and who sent her at eight on a long railway journey all by herself to toughen her, had become a doting parent who worried excessively, often needlessly, about her. He had lost his wife ("when I needed her the most") as well as both his parents in a short span of time. All his affection was centered thereafter on his "darling Indu." Any news of her being indisposed even slightly made him send frantic letters and cables to physicians and friends around her. When he himself was confined to Dehra Dun jail where, besides being subjected to considerable physical discomfort, his warders had calculatedly raised the walls of his compound so as to deprive him even of an occasional view of the vegetation and mountains, Nehru would worry whether it was wise for Indira to have traveled from Allahabad to Calcutta—a 12-hour journey—in the heat of summer. From his prison cell he would not only arrange a cottage in the mountains where Indira might escape from the heat of the plains but also urge his sister or others in the family to join her there and keep her company. When, therefore, Indira announced her intention of embarking on something considerably more arduous and prolonged than a train journey to Calcutta, Nehru's mind was seemingly assailed by doubts and worries of proportionate magnitude.

Specifically, he was not sure of Feroze's suitability for Indira. That the person she had chosen to marry belonged to a different religious group scarcely bothered him. Communal bias was decidedly not one of Nehru's failings, and from all accounts it did not affect him even in a matter as personal and important as his only child's marriage. He had spent years challenging religious narrowmindedness and did not hesitate even to chide the Mahatma once for the orthodoxy of his faith. In any event, interreligious marriages were not new to the Nehru family. Two of Indira's cousins married Muslims—one of them is a Pakistani national now—and yet another had insisted on marrying a Jewish Hungarian girl. What really worried Jawaharlal was the fact that Indira and Feroze had come from markedly different backgrounds. This, in his view, was liable to create serious problems of adjustment. Nehru was seemingly guided by his own marital experience in making this assessment. Kamala and he were undoubtedly devoted to each other, but their family backgrounds had been so dissimilar as to cause friction. Surveying his marriage of over eighteen years, Jawaharlal wrote in his *Autobiography*:

> We were attracted to each other and got on well enough but our backgrounds were different, and there was a want of adjustment. These maladjustments would sometimes lead to friction and there were many petty quarrels over trivialities . . . in spite of this our attachment grew, though the want of adjustment lessened only slowly.

The divergence in the family backgrounds of Indira and Feroze was even more pronounced. Feroze had grown up in a family of somewhat limited means. Indira, the family's "renunciation" of high living not-withstanding, had been raised in what by Indian standards was still the lap of luxury. Feroze had no job, nor any visible means by which he might be able to support himself and his wife. As for their tempera-ments, both were, as Nehru probably noted (and later years con-firmed), even more sensitive and proud than he and Kamala had been.

In trying to dissuade Indira, Nehru offered the usual objections. Marriage, he told her, was a serious business, and she must think coolly and at length before making up her mind. The family's involvement in politics and her absence from home for extended periods had denied her an adequate opportunity of meeting young men; now that she was back home she should wait for a while, for she might like someone else even better. He asked her if she was quite sure her heart was not in-fluencing her head unduly in her choice of Feroze. When Indira was unimpressed by his reasoning, he advised her to consult her two aunts. He himself turned, as he often had since his father's death, to Gandhi for guidance.

The advice that Vijayalakshmi offered Indira was brief and against marrying Feroze. Though she herself had at one time wanted to marry a Muslim youth for love, she urged her niece not to disregard family tradition and culture in making her choice. Krishna, who had married Gunottam Hutheesing, a man of her own choice, tried to dissuade her, too, but when Indira insisted she was certain of being in love with Feroze, her younger aunt told her to go ahead. The Mahatma, in the meanwhile, had talked tradition to Feroze and secured from him the promise that he conveyed to Jawaharlal in his jail, that "he would not think of marrying Indu without your consent and blessings."

In the end, once Nehru was convinced that Indira was clear in her mind about her wish to marry Feroze, he had little hesitation in offer-ing her his consent and blessings. He, in fact, helped Feroze's family overcome the doubts and misgivings that it entertained about the pro-posed marriage. To his family, it seemed that Feroze was going to wed a princess. It worried them. The Nehrus had not merely been affluent for years but also the idols of the Indian people. Feroze came from a comparatively humble background and, as members of his family saw him, was a "vagabond," ill-equipped to carry the responsibilities of marriage. Tehmina, who was then the only earning member of the family, bluntly reminded Feroze of the limitation of his financial re-sources. It was left to Jawaharlal to reassure her on this point. As she recalled her meeting with him, Nehru told Tehmina not to worry on that score. He had watched Feroze over a long period, and "whatever he does I am sure he will always land on his feet."

Bigger and more irritating objections to the marriage were yet to come, and they came from unexpected quarters. A month before the marriage was due to take place, the *Pioneer,* a progovernment daily newspaper published from Lucknow, printed on its front page the news of Indira's engagement to Feroze. The news item was small and straightforward, but the storm of public protest that it immediately caused was disproportionately large. All religious communities have their quota of bigots, and the Hindus were not without theirs. In the beginning of 1942, in fact, the fanatics among the Hindus were particularly large in numbers and chauvinistic in mood. Two years earlier a section of the Indian Muslims had formally asked for the country's partition because, as they put it, they were not willing to live under Hindu domination. As the Muslim demand for a separate homeland grew, the Hindus reacted by indulging in much chest-thumping and display of more than usual narrowmindedness and intolerance in their utterances. Normally, a Hindu girl marrying a Parsi would not have upset even the fanatics in the community, but in their sensitive frame of mind they saw Indira's resolve to marry outside the faith as an affront to Hinduism.

Could not a suitable match for her be found from among millions of Hindu young men? they asked. Such "permissiveness" on the part of a national leader like Nehru was considered particularly deplorable, for it would encourage others in the community to emulate his example and thus "endanger" Hindu society. In less than a week of the publication of the news the Hindu bigots' tirade against Gandhi, Nehru, and Indira was in full swing. Many an orthodox Hindu journal criticized the match editorially, speakers condemned it from public meetings (an effective communication medium in India), and thousands of others wrote angry personal letters. Only a very small proportion of the letters they received lauded the couple for ignoring restrictive barriers that had ceased to be relevant in modern India. To young Indira it seemed as "if the whole world was against" the wedding.

The storm blew away as quickly as it had developed. Tolerance, which is among the stronger and more enduring virtues of the Hindu mind, reasserted itself, and the campaign of vilification ended as abruptly as a premonsoon shower. Before it ceased, however, Jawaharlal had to issue a press statement rebuking the critics with gentle dignity. He said,

> A marriage is a personal and domestic matter, affecting chiefly the two parties concerned and partly their families. Yet I recognise that in view of my association with public affairs, I should take my many friends and colleagues and the public generally into my confidence.
>
> I have long held the view that though parents may and should advise in the matter, the choice and ultimate decision must be with the two parties concerned. That decision, if arrived at after mature deliberation, must be given effect to, and it is no business of parents or others to come in the way. When I was assured that Indira and Feroze wanted to marry one another I accepted willingly their decision and told them that it had my blessing.
>
> Mahatma Gandhi, whose opinion I value not only in public affairs but in private matters also, gave his blessings to the proposal.

Gandhi, who had received an even larger number of abusive letters, followed his customary practice of answering them in the form of an article in the *Harijan,* a weekly that he published. He strongly defended Feroze's claim to Indira's hand. Not a single one of his correspondents, he told his readers, had anything against Feroze Gandhi as a man. "His only crime in their estimation is that he happens to be a Parsi," he said. Gandhi reiterated his opposition to anyone changing his or her religion for the sake of marriage for "religion is not a garment to be cast off at will." In the case of Indira and Feroze, there was no question of a change of religion. Having thus disposed of the issue of religion, he said:

> Feroze Gandhi has been for years an intimate of the Nehru family. He nursed Kamala Nehru in her sickness. He was like a son to her. A natural intimacy grew up between them [Indira and Feroze]. The friendship has been perfectly honorable. It has ripened into mutual attraction. But neither party would think of marrying without the consent and blessing of Jawaharlal Nehru. This was given only after he was satisfied that the attraction had a solid basis. . . . It would have been cruelty to refuse consent to this engagement.

He ended the article by inviting his angry correspondents to shed their wrath and bless the forthcoming marriage. "Their letters betray ignorance, intolerance and prejudice—a species of untouchability, dangerous because not easily to be so classified," he told them.

One effect of the irrational public opposition to the marriage was that the ceremony had to be considerably more elaborate than the bride, bridegroom, and their families would have liked it to be. Both Indira and Feroze were sufficiently modern-minded to be anxious to have a simple ceremony attended only by near relations and close friends and totally devoid of the vulgar and noisy displays associated with weddings. In this they were opposed by, of all people, Gandhi. The Mahatma, who dramatized his own abhorrence of high living and needless consumption by wearing a loincloth and living in a peasant's thatched mud hut urged them to have a reasonably elaborate wedding and invite a large number of friends to attend. He reminded them of the hostile public reaction to the news of their engagement. If they were to have a brief, simple ceremony attended by only a small number of close friends an impression might be created that their families had been overawed by the critics and that Indira and Feroze were getting married surreptitiously or that Jawaharlal did not really have his heart in it when he gave them his consent and blessings. The logic of the advice combined with the fact that it came from Gandhi persuaded them to have a moderately large and gay wedding. For Indira this was virtually the only point on which she gave in. The marriage was fixed for March 26, 1942.

In the history of India's freedom movement 1942 was the year that saw the fiercest and the bloodiest conflict between the Congress Party and the British Government. It was the year of Gandhi's Quit-India movement in which, by the authorities' own admission, over 50,000 Indians were jailed. The number of those who were killed by police fire was never officially stated but may well have run into several thousands. The collective impact of the year's happenings on the Indian mind was even more traumatic than the shock it suffered in 1919 over the Jallianwala Bagh massacre. The Congress challenge and the repressive British response was the result of the tension that had been mounting since the beginning of World War II in 1939 when the Viceroy entered India into the war without even a pretense of consulting Indian leaders before committing the country. The Congress Party, which had tried cooperating with Britain and agreed two years earlier to form ministries in a number of provinces even on the basis of limited autonomy was so chagrined by the arrogance implicit in the Viceroy's act that it resigned office. As the war progressed, Indians were frustrated and angered that Britain should claim to be fighting for freedom in Europe while denying them that freedom in India. Britons, in a state of deep apprehension following the spectacular Nazi advance in Europe, found the Indian demand for constitutional change ill-timed and dangerously distracting. Matters did not improve with Winston Churchill's rise and blunt public declaration that he had not assumed the prime ministership "to preside over the liquidation of the British Empire."

Even during the "Battle of Britain" Gandhi was hard put to curb the Indian people's indignation and hostility. Many in India then drew almost sadistic satisfaction from Britain's difficulties, and some seriously believed that India should take advantage of the situation by siding with the Germans. Neither Gandhi nor Nehru shared this view, and in 1940 the former launched the "individual *satyagraha.*" The agitation provided for specially chosen persons to court arrest as a formal gesture of protest. The limited and controlled nature of this *satyagraha* was designed to achieve the twofold purpose of avoiding adding to Britain's difficulties and at the same time providing a safety valve for the mass anger in India. Jawaharlal was the second person chosen for the *satyagraha* and was put in jail by a nervous administration even before he could go through the ritual of violating the law. As 1941 drew to its end, public restiveness in India and Britain's intransigence made it increasingly clear to Gandhi and others that a wider and more purposeful confrontation was unavoidable.

In December 1941, however, only three months before Indira's wedding international developments unexpectedly averted that impending strife in India. Japan had entered the war, and its forces were moving rapidly through Southeast Asia towards Burma. Averse though he undoubtedly was to liquidating the Empire through political negotiations, Churchill feared for its security. As a first gesture of conciliation, Jawaharlal and others were suddenly released from prison. In the beginning of March 1942 the British Government announced its intention to send Sir Stafford Cripps to India to discuss with the leaders there a new constitutional proposal. Sir Stafford had visited India earlier in 1939 and met Gandhi and Nehru, both of whom were impressed by his personal sincerity and progressive political outlook. That a man of his impeccable credentials should be chosen as its emissary was regarded as an indication of a change of heart on Britain's part. Tensions relaxed rapidly and hopes soared. Jawaharlal was cheerful and buoyant in a way he had not been for some years. He was due to meet Sir Stafford in New Delhi over breakfast three days after Indira's wedding.

In the days before the ceremony was due to take place, Anand Bhavan once again sprang to vibrant life. The large portions of the house that had remained barred and shuttered for several years were hurriedly reopened and cleaners and decorators put to work to prepare them for the guests. Death—besides Motilal and Kamala, Swarup Rani and her sister, Rajvati, had died—had reduced the size of the family. But the number of its friends and admirers had grown tremendously, and many were expected from all over the country and some even from abroad. The weather was delightful. The brief North Indian winter with its frosty, blustery winds had departed. The summer heat with its devastating dust storms was still some weeks away. The skies were cloudless and clear, and there was color all around. The banyan and the *peepul* had shed the last of their dead leaves and were covered with shiny new ones. The massive *neem* tree facing Jawaharlal's study was laden with thick bunches of its bright green date-like fruit, inedible but wonderful to look at. At the base of Anand Bhavan's several mango trees lay a thick carpet of fallen blossoms. The oval lawn in front of the main entrance to the house was fringed with rose bushes offering the season's final, luxuriant flush of blooms. Outside the compound itself, as one moved away from the city, fields of mustard with their brilliant yellow flowers dazzled the viewer with their mass and brilliance.

The bride herself looked no less radiant. Eve Curie, daughter of the celebrated French scientist and a journalist by profession, had arrived in Anand Bhavan coincidentally the day before the ceremony and was struck by the atmosphere of joyous excitement that pervaded the household. She noted the glow on Indira's face as she coped with teasing friends and relations and awaited the day of the wedding. One of the chores that she attended to with particular relish was the selection of glass bangles. "To the bride of tomorrow a merchant had brought a basket full of translucent bracelets of glass, in all the colors of the rainbow," Eve Curie wrote. "Indira took pleasure in making her choice at length. She picked carefully the bracelets that would exactly match her saris." This is how Indira looked to her younger aunt, Krishna Hutheesingh:

> She was tall and rather frail, ethereal-looking, with very black hair that fell to her shoulders. She had large dark eyes in an aquiline face, and a complexion the golden color of ripe wheat. In profile Indu looked like the head on a Greek coin.

In dressing for her wedding, Indira adhered to the simple ways the family had adopted since 1921. Although in deference to the Mahatma's advice a large number of friends had been invited—many more residents of Allahabad gate-crashed, and some even climbed the trees in Anand Bhavan to get a good view of the ceremony—Indira would not tolerate any form of personal ostentation traditionally associated with a Hindu marriage. Instead of the customary bridal *sari* of heavy brocade, she wore a simple shell pink *sari* of cotton cloth made from yarn that her father had himself spun during his latest 15-month incarceration. She also wore no jewelry or gold ornaments. No diamond rings sparkled from her fingers, nor could the *tikka,* a bejeweled coin-like ornament, be seen on her forehead. She did not wear even the relatively less expensive ivory bangles that are usually placed on a bride's left forearm the day before the wedding and that she continues to wear for several weeks as a mark of being newly wed, or any of the glass bracelets that she had so excitedly chosen the previous day for their bright colors. Instead of these or the traditional bangles of solid gold, she wore round her wrists strings of the fragrant *motia* blossoms that signal the impending arrival of summer.

The bridegroom was dressed in matching simplicity. He wore the traditional *achkan,* a closed-collar long coat stretching to the knees, but it was not of heavy brocade. Instead, like the collarless shirt and the tight pants that he wore under it, as well as the pointed white Congress cap, it was of handspun white *khadi.* As those who attended the wedding remember it, he looked strikingly handsome. Feroze was always somewhat stockily built person, but he had a way of holding his head that made him look taller than he actually was. Fair—he was fairer even than the bride—and broad-browed, he had perfect features, with a sharp nose and large, bright eyes set in a round, moon-like face. As they got ready for the ceremony, Indira and Feroze appeared a remarkably well-matched couple.

As is customary in India on occasions at which a large number of friends and relations may be expected, a big *shamiana,* a multicolored cloth canopy resting on tall bamboo poles, was erected in the Anand Bhavan garden. The actual rites were performed in a smaller "enclosure" marked by four thick wooden pillars only a few feet high and covered in the traditional style with large banana leaves and branches of mango trees to symbolize man's proximity to nature. The *mandap,* as the smaller structure is called, was set on a marble-floored terrace that Motilal had built as a projection into the garden for use during the monsoon, when heavy rain could turn the rest of the lawn into slush and mud. In the center of the *mandap* was located the sacred fire, the focal point of the Hindu marital rites. The fire was built of a heap of small, dry twigs that were constantly replenished, and it was fed steadily with clarified butter and fistfuls of aromatic mulch. Her father led Indira to her seat of a silk-covered cushion by the sacred fire. Feroze sat by her side and Jawaharlal opposite them. A vacant seat was placed beside him in memory of Kamala.

Following the traditional pattern, the ceremony was in scriptural Sanskrit, which often even the priests do not understand. Indira had insisted that the vows that she and Feroze were called upon to take be clearly explained to them. The Vedic hymns that were chosen for the occasion were, therefore, translated into English. In fact, it was arranged to print the translation in an attractive folder for the benefit of the numerous guests at the ceremony. Perhaps as a protection against the British Government's stern printing laws, the red-colored folder was prominently marked as being "for private circulation only."

The opening hymn paid the young couple's homage to "the law of righteousness." As butter was poured over the flames, Indira and Feroze "resolved to dedicate our lives in the service of that light which leads humanity onwards" and prayed that their "hearts be possessed with love for all." The priest explained to them that in that ceremony clarified butter symbolized thought, the spoon with which it was poured represented thought translated into action, and the fire the "universal spirit in the life of man." The next part of the ceremony was devoted to "man's love of freedom and his determination to preserve it." According to one of the verses chanted during this part of the traditional ceremony, the bride was supposed to say, "If there are any people in the four quarters of the earth who venture to deprive us of our freedom, Lord, here I am, sword in hand, prepared to resist them to the last. I pray for the spreading light of freedom. May it envelop us from all sides."

The ceremony also charged the bride and the bridegroom with the responsibility of preserving inviolate the "sovereignty of the people." This was followed by the most formal and important part of the ceremony, the *kanyadan,* or the giving away of the bride. The bridegroom was enjoined to deal with the bride in matters relating to *dharama* (spiritual and moral life), *aratha* (financial and economic matters), and *kama* (aesthetic pursuits) "with deference and self-control and in harmony with her wishes." The bridegroom was further called upon not to neglect her.

With the chanting of hymns over, Jawaharlal placed Indira's hand in Feroze's. Together, their hands clasped and with a corner of the bride's *sari* tied to the bridegroom's *achkan,* they took seven steps around the fire, binding themselves into the eternal, irrevocable union. Relations and friends then gathered around Indira and showered rose petals on her while chanting hymns urging her to preserve the tradition of dignity and honor established by Indian womanhood.

Shortly after the wedding, Indira and Feroze went to Kashmir for their honeymoon. The weather in Kashmir was heavenly. As they drove to Srinagar, they saw hillsides covered entirely by wild flowers. In the valley itself, the ground was literally carpeted with daisies. Cherry and almond trees were covered with blossoms, and the mountain peaks surrounding the valley still had their dazzling snowcaps. Jawaharlal in a similar situation twenty-six years earlier had departed on an extensive trek with a cousin. Feroze stayed by Indira's side all the time. Their activities included visits to the beautiful gardens built by the Moghuls, walks along the bank of the Jhelum River, rides in a *shikara* (a light, narrow boat) on the serene Dal Lake, short excursions into the mountains, and occasional brief shopping visits to Srinagar's floating emporia.

The honeymoon was blissful but short. The political gloom that had marked Britain's relations with Indian leaders had lifted but only briefly. The proposals that Sir Stafford had brought were disappointing. Once again the government and the Congress Party were on a collision course. Within four months of the wedding Nehru was back in prison. He was soon followed there by the newly married couple, giving Indira her first experience of a British jail.

Before their arrest in September 1942 Feroze had rented a small bungalow in Allahabad not far from where his own family had always lived. There was no dearth of accommodation for them in Anand Bhavan, but Feroze's sense of personal pride ruled out their living there. He did not want anyone to think he had married Indira either for the sake of Nehru's position in the country or of the grandeur and status associated with Anand Bhavan.

Indira was released from jail in May 1943 owing to her indifferent health. Feroze was set free three months later after he had served his 1-year term of imprisonment. Even though they had a separate house of their own, both somehow veered back to Anand Bhavan. Their own house, thanks to their arrest and otherwise unsettled existence, had not grown into a home. Indira's family was dispersed and depleted. Both her aunts had their own homes and families away from Allahabad. Jawaharlal was shut up in an old fort in Ahmednagar, and the government's mood was so stern that Indira was denied even the routine privilege of a fortnightly visit to him. In these circumstances Anand Bhavan, though virtually empty, served as a haven and seemed to offer what emotional stability was possible. Its sizable garden monopolized much of Feroze's spare time and affection. Flowers had always fascinated him, and with loving care he brought the neglected garden back to life. He spent a great deal of time spraying the plants with insecticides and pruning the numerous trees and shrubs, which over the years had become so overgrown as to make the garden look like an untamed forest. Far from resenting his intrusion into their domain, the gardener and his assistants loved him. As the son-in-law he had a highly privileged position in the household, but Feroze was not the person to overlook his modest background. Ram Autar, who was then one of the assistants and is now the head gardener in Anand Bhavan, remembers Feroze as a friendly person who never threw his weight about and treated everyone as an equal. Though born a Parsi in distant Bombay with Gujarati as his mother tongue, Feroze spoke to them in their own local dialect—something that none among the Nehrus, long-time residents of Uttar Pradesh though they were, could ever do. Dahlias, Ram Autar recalls, were Feroze's special love, and the ones he grew were enormous in size and rich in color. Indira, whose physical strength did not match her interest in flowers, joined her husband in the garden occasionally, and when she did she concentrated her attention on roses and narcissi.

In India of those days it was almost impossible to find a job not connected with either the government or the conduct of the war. Feroze, therefore, had to content himself with selling insurance and occasionally writing free-lance articles built around the large collection of photographs he had taken during his travels in Europe. The income from both sources, needless to say, was meager.

Besides being worried by a certain degree of financial stringency, Indira and Feroze fretted about the indefinite nature of Jawaharlal's imprisonment and the noticeable deepening of his sense of loneliness. Temperamentally an introvert, the loss of Kamala had left Nehru almost desolate. He recorded his helplessness and anguish in his *Autobiography*, "Our joint life was only now properly beginning. We relied so much on each other; we had so much to do together." The fact that he was not allowed to meet anyone from the family had added to his gloom. Even the number of letters he could write or receive was exceedingly small and subjected to rigid censorship, and many were lost on the way or delayed by weeks in delivery. The state of Jawaharlal's mind was reflected in one letter he wrote to Krishna, wondering if on his release, meeting as they would be after a long interval, they would "recognize each other in the old way." He added:

> The private worlds each one of us lives in, worlds of fancy and feeling and imagination, have so long laid apart that they are apt to become strangers to each other, separate circles overlapping less than they used to. Partly that happens as we grow older, but the process is accelerated by the abnormal conditions we have been living in.

Jawaharlal was still in jail pining to meet his darling Indu ("the thought of you haunts me," he wrote to her from prison on her birthday once), when he received news of the birth of his first grandson in August 1944. Happy, though not excited, as he claimed, Nehru promptly urged Indira to get a proper horoscope of the newborn cast immediately. With his characteristic fastidiousness he reminded her that owing to the war the Indian standard time was set one hour ahead and that the permanent record he was suggesting should be based on the proper solar time.

The Allied victory in World War II happily brought an end to the

Gandhis' concern about Jawaharlal. Elections in Britain had placed the Labour Party in power. In its anxiety to end the constitutional impasse in India the Attlee government ordered the release of the Mahatma, Nehru, and other Congress Party leaders and initiated the process that ended two years later in the country's partition and independence. In September 1946, almost a year ahead of independence, Nehru became the head of the Interim Government and the leader of the Constituent Assembly, abandoning for good the role of the political agitator. He had also seen the last of prison, where he had spent altogether nearly ten years of his life. About the same time a position was found for Feroze that appealed to the young husband. Shortly after Nehru left for Delhi to join the Interim Government, he appointed Feroze as managing director of the *National Herald* in Lucknow.

Nehru had founded the *Herald* in 1938 as the exponent of the nationalistic viewpoint and as a rival to the *Pioneer,* which supported the government stand unabashedly. Following Gandhi's Quit-India movement, the *National Herald* had suspended publication, because it would not submit itself to censorship and official scrutiny. Feroze joined it when it reappeared in November 1946. Indira and Feroze moved to Lucknow to set up a new home. A second son arrived a few weeks later.

The following three years posed for Indira two of the most difficult and significant questions of her life. Now that freedom was won, the first question went, should her involvement in politics continue or should she become a good housewife? The second, not unrelated, was: Should she stay in Lucknow where her husband had a job or move to Delhi where her father had become the Prime Minister and needed not only an official hostess but also someone to care for him in his old age and relieve some of the loneliness that preyed upon him constantly?

Probably these questions were never posed in clear, precise terms. They were raised only vaguely over a period of time by a combination of circumstances. Similarly, in finding the answers, Indira was pushed, usually without her being aware of it, in slow steps to a decision determined as much by a constantly developing situation as by her own wishes.

Perhaps it was impossible for Indira to turn her back resolutely on politics and become a housewife. Many of those who have known her intimately assert that left to herself she would have enjoyed nothing more than looking after her home, husband, and children, attending to their needs, and filling the traditional woman's role in a family. But, apparently, she had little choice in the matter. Interests and associations developed over nearly three decades could not be turned off like an electric light. Such abrupt abandonment of politics was rendered all the more difficult by the basic philosophy of the freedom movement that, first, considered women as equal partners in the struggle and, second, insisted that independence was the beginning, not the end, of the real task before everyone. Her father and husband were still deeply involved in politics. Her house in Lucknow as well as her father's imposing official residence in New Delhi were constantly thronged by people who spoke of the new phase in the nation's life and its challenges with an enthusiasm that must have been infectious. In any event, Indira never pondered the issue calculatedly with the intention of carefully weighing the pros and cons and then making a firm resolve. Things, she once said, were happening so fast that she did not have time to think. She merely reacted. When author Betty Friedan asked her to locate the particular moment in her life at which she was drawn into politics decisively and unreturnably, Indira recalled the time she agreed to campaign for a woman candidate in an election because her father was unable to keep his promise to speak in her constituency. "That is when it all began," because at the meeting she discovered she had the capacity "to make people listen" to her. Why did she go? Her answer reflected a touch of fatalism typical of the Indian mind. "The good Indian would say it was just not in my stars to be that little housewife."

Even with the realization of her powers of political persuasion, Indira would have stayed out of active politics if her husband had disapproved of it. But Feroze did not oppose it. Being in politics himself, Feroze could not have asked a woman of Indira's background not to participate. Indira herself offers another interesting reason why Feroze did not object to her increasing preoccupation with politics. She told an interviewer, "I am so intense in whatever I do, he [Feroze] must have been frightened to have it all concentrated on him. He wanted me occupied." Later, when Indira became Congress President and made a success of the job, Feroze was not particularly happy and probably regretted not having stopped her from entering politics. In Indira's own words, "he liked it, and he did not like it." But, obviously, it was too late to reverse the process.

In the matter of whether she should stay in Lucknow or join her father in Delhi, Indira made the decision relatively more consciously and in greater awareness of its impact on her own marital relations. However, in this, too, she was impelled, at least partly, by Feroze's desire to keep her occupied and his lack of opposition at an early enough stage.

An occasional clash of personalities notwithstanding, their first two years or so in Lucknow brought Indira and Feroze a great deal of joy and a sense of fulfillment. In size and elegance their house was no match for Anand Bhavan or Nehru's new official residence in Delhi, but it had the warmth and excitement that only a young family can generate in its process of growing up and coping with the world around it. Their children were attractive and intelligent, and both parents doted on them. Should Indira need to go out to attend to some family or political chores she usually arranged her activities in such a way that she would be home when the boys returned from school. She frowned upon the common practice in affluent Indian families of entrusting the burdensome task of bringing up the children to hired nannies. She spent time and thought on the boys at home, and one of their teachers contrasted Indira's visits to the school to check on their progress with those of other mothers "who never seemed to pay any real attention to their children." Mrs. Gandhi talked to them, discussed things with them in such an interested way that "they never felt rejected when she had to leave," the teacher recalled. Feroze was seemingly even more devoted to the boys. He seldom missed an opportunity of playing with them, making toys for them—he had a special flair for making and repairing mechanical toys—and taking them out to the zoo and the local museums. Their home itself drew a considerable share of their attention and energy. Feroze personally designed the furniture and had it manufactured by skilled artisans under his own supervision. In the garden attached to the house his green fingers were as evident as they had been in Anand Bhavan during their stay there. His work on the *National Herald* brought him much satisfaction because his efforts to give it a stable financial base met with quick and measurable success.

This seemingly idyllic state did not last long. Her father and his house were making steadily growing demands on Indira's time and attention. The house that Nehru had chosen to live in as head of the Interim Government was found to be too cramped and unsuited for the official residence of the chief executive of independent India. Lord Louis Mountbatten, who had stayed on in India as its Governor General, persuaded Nehru to move to the palatial residence that in the days of the Raj had been occupied by the British commander-in-chief of the armed forces. Besides having to cope with the onerous task of running a huge establishment, Nehru was constantly being called upon to entertain world leaders who came to New Delhi in large numbers. Vijayalakshmi could not help him, as she was drawn abroad by U.N. work and ambassadorial assignments. Krishna, who lived with her husband in Bombay, would sometimes fly to Delhi to act as the hostess at formal receptions and banquets, but she was deterred by the distance and the fact that air travel in India then was slow and tedious. Indira was only a comfortable night's train journey away from Delhi, and Nehru turned to her with increasing frequency. For a while she led what one of her household staff described as the life of a "traveling salesman," continually commuting between Lucknow and Delhi. But by the end of 1948 she had virtually shifted her headquarters to Delhi, for she felt it was her duty to be near her father. The boys moved with her. As she saw it, the duty that goaded her into leaving Lucknow was not so much to her father as to the country, which at that chaotic time needed a leader of his charisma and cohesive force. Whatever her reasoning, it cannot be doubted that in her decision Indira was influenced by the fact that her husband was young, confident, a happy extrovert full of himself and his professional concerns, while her father was tired and lonely and showing distinct signs of nervous and physical strain caused by the magnitude of his responsibilities.

From Delhi Indira traveled regularly to Lucknow to meet Feroze. The boys always went with her because they were fond of their father and Indira did not like leaving them behind even for brief periods. They thus lived in two houses until Feroze insisted it would be more convenient and sensible for him to travel to Delhi than for the three of them to visit him in Lucknow. His traveling too ceased, when the family was once again reunited under one roof in the beginning of 1952. Now that the *Herald* was on its feet again, Feroze's love of active politics reasserted itself. With independence and the installation of a national government, the focus of political power shifted to Delhi. Feroze had been feeling restive in Lucknow, and when the first general election held under India's new republican Constitution offered him an opportunity to maintain his long-standing association with Uttar Pradesh politics and yet be in Delhi where his family and the real political action was, he ran for election to the Lok Sabha from Rae Bareli in Uttar Pradesh and won convincingly. Five years later he was re-elected to Parliament from the same area.

As a member of Parliament, Feroze was an acknowledged success. By 1960, when he died suddenly following a heart attack, Feroze had won for himself a nationwide reputation for fearlessness in challenging authority and a deep compassion for the downtrodden. During his second term in the Lok Sabha, he was among the best-known MPs—better known than even many members of the Cabinet, whose names were being constantly aired by the state-controlled All-India Radio. Even if he had lived longer, however, he would probably never have been a minister. He was too much of an iconoclast for any Prime Minister's comfort, not the sort of MP chosen in a parliamentary system to serve in the Cabinet.

His constituents probably would always have returned him to Parliament, nevertheless. Rae Bareli had a population of over a million, much of it poor, living in underdeveloped rural areas. When Parliament was not in session—and sometimes even when it was—Feroze would leave Delhi to travel extensively in his district. As a rule, he never permitted more than three months to elapse between visits. In maintaining his contact with his constituents he was held back neither by the hardship of travel by open jeep on unpaved village roads, dusty or muddy according to the season, nor by any family and personal commitments. He often spoke derisively of legislators who would not leave the air-conditioned comfort of Parliament House to meet those who had placed them there. During visits to Rae Bareli he would talk to hundreds of people, listen to their gripes, advise them on their problems, rebuke them when necessary, and eat and live with them. He spoke to them in their own peasants' dialect and not the chaste Hindustani he customarily used in Allahabad and Delhi.

What, however, brought Feroze national acclaim was a different set of qualities. It was not often that he rose to speak in the Lok Sabha, but when he did he made sure that he understood the subject of his speech thoroughly. His mind was sharp enough to separate the essentials from the extraneous. In addition, he worked hard and had all relevant details of the issue at his command. Unlike many others in the house who had received their training as speakers at mass meetings and, therefore, tended to talk in vague generalities, Feroze dealt with his brief with the competence of an experienced lawyer. Temperamentally, he was averse to pulling punches on any issue or to being overawed by a person's position and power. At meetings of the Congress Parliamentary Party, the closed-door caucuses at which the ruling party discussed its policy on important, controversial issues, Feroze would not hesitate even to criticize Nehru. He acquired a David-like image when his attacks on some big and politically entrenched business houses and convincing exposés of the corrupt methods they adopted to amass wealth and power prodded the government into moving against them. One of his disclosures in Parliament led to a judicial probe and caused the resignation of India's Finance Minister, T. T. Krishnamachari. Krishnamachari was one of the most influential members of the government and much liked by Nehru who made no secret of his personal distress over his exit. If he was loved by the powerless of Rae Bareli, Feroze had come to be feared by the moghuls of politics and commerce. A small enclave in the Parliament lobby where he usually sat discussing politics over coffee with friends and colleagues had come to be known as the "Feroze corner," and ministers were often anxious to know what was being discussed there. In the last year or two of his life, the Establishment came to regard him as a deadly enemy. A fellow MP, who is also a poet, once summed up Feroze's career as a Lok Sabha member by describing him as "the gentle breeze that quickly developed into a storm."

As Feroze grew in stature as an MP, he also seemed to grow apart from the Prime Minister's house and from Indira. When he moved to Delhi from Lucknow in 1952, Feroze lived in Nehru's official residence. Indira and he had a large suite of rooms that together they decorated with some care. After a while, however, Feroze took the small bungalow to which he was entitled as an MP and used that as his office. Later, he began using it as his regular residence, though he would visit Nehru's house frequently—almost daily, in fact—and took many meals with Indira. In India, where family ties usually have the strength and holding quality of shackles, Feroze's action caused many eyebrows to be raised and gave rise to much gossip and speculation about marital estrangement. Much of this was in the form of word-of-mouth innuendo—India's press is remarkably loath to discuss the private lives of even public figures—and undoubtedly was exaggerated. But an observer as close as Indira's aunt, Krishna Hutheesing, has acknowledged in her book *We Nehrus* that Indira's living with her father "was not a good arrangement from a family point of view and they [Indira and Feroze] finally drifted apart." As Feroze's friends recall, he felt "shut out" by his wife and resented his "inferior" status in the Nehru household.

The ostensible reason for Feroze's moving into a separate house was that as an MP he was required to receive many constituents and political associates, not all of whom might be suitable visitors for the Prime Minister's official residence. It was obvious and understandable that he yearned for greater personal freedom than he could exercise in a household not his own and unavoidably somewhat starchy in atmosphere. That his family background was different from that of Indira—a fact that had worried Jawaharlal when the marriage was first suggested— undoubtedly strengthened Feroze's desire to live apart. He abhorred the official banquets that he sometimes had to attend as a member of Nehru's family. He felt uncomfortable in formal attire, and the conventional polite conversation at such occasions bored him to tears. Apart from finding them tedious, he found the ease with which Indira and Nehru conducted themselves at these functions an irritating proof of their growing distance from the Indian masses. He regarded life in Nehru's house as unreal in the context of Indian poverty, and he wanted to be as little a part of its elegance as possible. Even when there were no visiting dignitaries present on the occasion, the meal with Indira and Jawaharlal was usually overlaid with the atmosphere of stiff propriety of an upper-class English home. Nehru ate carefully and selectively, and, though genial and affectionate with members of the family around him, his wit would be dry and subdued. Feroze liked to eat almost gluttonously and was boisterous in his jokes and remarks. When Feroze and Nehru were together socially, the young man felt constricted and confined, the father-in-law irritated and exasperated.

These seemingly superficial temperamental differences were accentuated by certain strong factors in Feroze's psychological make-up. Feroze had what seemed like an overwhelming sense of personal pride and self-importance. He was not prepared to play second fiddle and resented being outshone by anyone around him. In the corner of the Parliament lobby where he customarily "held court" every morning, he was in his element surrounded by the young or the back-benchers among MPs or by those who echoed his own resentment of Jawaharlal. Senior, responsible legislators or those who made no secret of their admiration for Nehru were seldom welcome in the corner.

His attitude towards his father-in-law appeared to suffer from a touch of schizophrenia. Although he was always willing to accept his help, he was resentful of his greatness. But for Nehru's support, he could not have been appointed as the managing director of the *National Herald;* at the time his qualifications for the post were negligible. His association with the Nehru family undoubtedly helped him win his election to Parliament in 1952. When he moved to Delhi, in addition to his duties in Parliament, he took on a well-paid job on a leading newspaper, the *Indian Express.* The employer apparently believed—and Feroze must have been aware of this—that by placing him on his payroll the firm was getting a useful contact in the Prime Minister's house. Many of those who brought him the confidential information on which he based his famous exposés did so because he was Nehru's kin. Yet in many ways nothing seemed to irritate him more than this kinship. He would decline to go to functions where he suspected he had been invited as a member of the Prime Minister's family and not in his personal capacity as an MP. His own sense of humor was more than rambunctious, often coming perilously close to heartlessness, but he himself would be deeply offended if someone jested about his Nehru family position. One joke he relished in the beginning but later could not stand was to be described, as he often was, as "the nation's son-in-law."

After Indira was named to her first important party post in 1959, he was asked how it felt to be married to the Congress President. Such unthinking jocular remarks as this would upset him so much that it would take her "weeks to win him over." As she remembers such occasions, Indira thinks that to hurt the male ego is "the biggest sin in marriage." When Feroze was hurt, he would talk of Indira in deprecating terms. For if he was kind-hearted, generous, self-sacrificing, and bubbling with fun, he also had another side to his character and when provoked could be coarse and vicious. Many legislators and newspaper columnists habitually gave the "Feroze corner" a wide berth out of fear that something in their speeches or writings might unintentionally have offended the thorny MP and that they would not be equipped to answer the crude insults he might fling at them. Neither Indira or others in the Nehru family had even that choice. When he made wounding remarks about them, the victims were not there to answer him back had they wished to. But usually there was someone who heard the taunt and would carry an exaggerated report of it to Indira or Jawaharlal. Then they, for their part, were hurt and angry.

Feroze died just about the time his temperamental angularities were beginning to lose their sharpness. As an MP he was getting tired of his role as a muckraker and turning his attention to less sensational but more significant problems of the country. Maturity and a growing realization of the usefulness of his own role as an MP was mitigating his resentment at being overshadowed by Indira and Jawaharlal. Although Indira had made a convincing success of her term as Congress President, she had firmly declined a second term. One of the principal considerations that weighed with her in that decision was the fact that Feroze had suffered his first heart attack in 1959, and she was anxious to devote more time to caring for his health. Feroze was touched by her resolve and was spending increasingly more time in the Prime Minister's official residence. In Indira's own words, "Towards the end we were somehow getting very close." The summer before his death they had what she regarded as "a nearly perfect holiday." Feroze died in September 1960. He felt the symptoms of a second heart attack while sitting in Parliament. Instead of sending for his doctor to come there, he got into his small Fiat and drove to the doctor's clinic. Indira was away on a tour of South India. On hearing of his illness she immediately flew back to Delhi, but he died before her return. In his last hours Feroze repeatedly inquired when Indira might be expected.

Indira today takes a philosophic view of her marriage. She does not accept that it was not a success. "I did not have less love. I think my husband gave very deeply to me and I to him. I think giving is what makes for happiness," she told a woman journalist. "I do not think he would have been the person he was if he had been married to the sweet little woman in an Indian movie. He would have been just an ordinary husband. I think this conflict helped him to grow also. Conflict and unhappiness are not the worst things that can happen. It is all the experience one has that makes one what one is—the wider the experience, the stronger one's personality."

PART II

Freedom and Politics

5

Prison
"Unless you have been through it"

INDIRA believes that at least in one respect going to jail is like being in a war. Just as one has to have fought in a battle oneself to realize the horrors of war, one can understand what life in prison means only from personal experience. "Unless you yourself have been through it, you cannot really get the correct picture," she once remarked.

Even as a child Indira was no stranger to British prisons. She paid her first visit to a jail when she was not yet five. The games she played with her dolls sometimes represented her fantasy of a freedom-fighting mob attacking a jail and freeing the Congress prisoners lodged there. The characters for such a game—armed guards, tyrannical superintendents, and heartless warders—were usually drawn from life as she witnessed it during her frequent visits to Naini Central Jail, across the river from Allahabad, to meet Jawaharlal or to Mallaccas jail on the other side of the city, where sometimes her mother was imprisoned. During the brief periods they were in Anand Bhavan, her parents, grandparents, and uncles and aunts would often describe their life in what they had come to regard as their "other home." Indira would hear them with rapt attention, almost sensing the distinctive atmosphere and character of each jail; yet, as she discovered when she herself was imprisoned, she had not until then really understood what it meant to be "shut in and being so completely cut off, not only from events and day-to-day happenings but cut off from things one could regard as quite normal."

She was twenty-five when she experienced her first and only imprisonment. Her arrest came almost at the heels of her honeymoon and, curiously, both Indira and Feroze were jailed the same day and during the latter portion of their term lodged in the same prison, though in different wings and separated from each other by a massive wall and stern regulations.

By the time the young Gandhis had returned to Allahabad from their honeymoon in Kashmir and started setting up their small home, the political tension in the country had begun to mount more rapidly than even the temperature in an Indian summer. The hopes roused on the eve of her wedding of a rapprochment with the British Government and an early and effective transfer of power had receded quickly. Jawaharlal, who had left Allahabad for New Delhi even before the *shamiana* erected in Anand Bhavan for Indira's marriage had been dismantled, was deeply dismayed by what Sir Stafford Cripps had to offer India. The constitutional reforms that Britain proposed were to be effective only after the war was won. For the time being Indians were required to give British authority their wholehearted cooperation in the conduct of war and in return for it receive a few ineffective posts in the Viceroy's Executive Council—something that Congress leaders had rejected two years earlier. After the war India was to be accorded Dominion status, but its various provinces were to be guaranteed the right to secede from the union.

The party and the country were shocked by the sheer niggardliness of the proposal. Indian leaders' estimates of British nervousness over Japan's entry into the war had obviously been exaggerated. They had read more than was perhaps justified into the few signs of conciliation from Britain and the fact that Sir Stafford was chosen as the emissary. As they saw it then, the attitude of the British Government, even when challenged by a powerful foe, was marked by a stubborn unwillingness to share with Indians the substance of power. They also saw in the offer to provinces of the right of secession a Churchillian design to ensure India's balkanization. The Congress Party rejected the Cripps offer categorically. Gandhi, who seldom used hurtful language even in reference to his opponents, was seemingly so exasperated by the proposal that he described it as "a post-dated cheque on a failing bank."

Indira and Feroze, who had just started setting up their home (the bulk of their furniture had still not been delivered), were suddenly drawn back into the politics of fist-shaking and flag-waving. Gandhi and Nehru—particularly the latter, whose personal abhorrence for fascism was pronounced—were reluctant to embarrass Britain at that stage. But they were prodded into action by the dark mood in the country and restiveness among their followers. The situation, they realized, had gone far beyond the stage at which something like the earlier individual *satyagraha* could be usefully revived. They saw no way by which they could express India's indignation without distracting the British Government in its fight against Japan. The leaders, however, were not merely pandering to the mood of their followers. They were themselves angry and frustrated. Writing in the *Harijan* Gandhi told the British: "You have sat too long here for any good you have been doing. Depart and let us have done with you. In the name of God, go." The Quit-India movement that the Congress launched in August 1942 reflected a sense of national desperation and led promptly to the arrest of the entire party leadership.

On her return from Bombay, where Nehru and other leaders had assembled to discuss the Quit-India resolution, Indira found herself the only adult besides the servants in Anand Bhavan. Besides Jawaharlal, her aunt Vijayalakshmi had been arrested. Feroze had decided to evade arrest as long as he could and organize an underground movement for the overthrow of British power. Anand Bhavan, under constant police surveillance, was obviously no place for him. Indira would have liked to join him in such work, for it greatly fired her youthful imagination, but certain family obligations stood in the way. Living in Anand Bhavan, besides her, were the three teenage daughters of Vijayalakshmi, and Indira felt that it was her duty to look after them. Perhaps the loneliness and insecurity she herself had suffered in similar situations as a child influenced her resolve.

For Indira, those were agonizing days. The girl who at twelve would not be thwarted from participation in the freedom movement was being held back when she was twenty-five and when the national confrontation with the foreign rulers was at a crucial stage. Adding to her concern and chagrin were widespread rumors that her father and some other top leaders had been removed from the country and taken to the Andamans, a group of inhospitable islands in the Indian Ocean that had long served the British as a dreaded maximum-security penal colony. Apart from causing her personal distress, the rumors, floated presumably with the authorities' approval, had the effect of demoralizing the party workers and mitigating much of what Feroze and others were trying to accomplish. Vast parts of the country were in a state of deep turmoil. Following Gandhi's arrest in Bombay the movement was frequently meandering into violence. Official buildings were being burned down, railway tracks removed, bridges damaged. Such sabotage provided the government with justification for its ruthlessness in suppressing the movement. Official sternness, in turn, led to more vigorous demonstrations and larger processions in what seemed a heady defiance of the government ban. While all this went on, Indira wondered fretfully if she would have the opportunity to be more than a mere observer.

The conflict in Indira's mind was resolved within a month of the start of the movement. Chandralekha, the eldest of her three cousins, was arrested for joining a political demonstration by university students. The care of the two younger girls was placed in the hands of a Chinese governess whom Vijayalakshmi's husband had engaged and found to be trustworthy. Indira's worry about her father's whereabouts, too, was eased somewhat. The police had removed Jawaharlal to some secret destination away from Bombay, and a month after his arrest Indira had still not received any letter from him. Official secrecy notwithstanding, it soon became fairly widely known that he had not been taken to the Andamans and, as was later confirmed, that he was probably housed in the old fort at Ahmednagar in the southern plateau of the Deccan. Indira could thus join the agitation undistracted by domestic commitments and filial concern. She made up her mind to go to prison, because without that her political experience, she felt, "would have been incomplete."

It was not for some future political rewards that Indira went in search of imprisonment. When Mahatma Gandhi tried to soothe her mother-in-law Rattimai Gandhi's fears about Feroze's involvement in politics, he had said that in the India of the future no one would worry about university degrees. All that would matter would be the number of times her son had courted imprisonment. But imprisonment as a caste mark to wear for future benefits was not what Feroze or his young wife had in mind in mid-1942. In that wartime year, national freedom and the personal benefits that it might bring to some seemed remote and hazy. Like tens of thousands of others in India at the time, Indira contemplated going to jail simply because it was an honor to be imprisoned in the cause of independence.

Indira exposed herself to arrest at a flag-hoisting ceremony in Allahabad's Ewing Christian College. All political activities were banned, and the boundary walls of an academic institution offered no protection against the police. The students had planned to raise the national flag, sing "Bande-mataram," a patriotic song, and perhaps shout some slogans. In the past such a function would receive little official notice, but in the agitated state of mind of British authority after the Quit-India movement the college program appeared highly subversive. At the appointed time not only the local police but also troops appeared on the scene and surrounded the student gathering. Indira was not supposed to address the crowd or participate in the proceedings in any other way. But the presence of Jawaharlal's daughter amidst them added to the students' fervor immeasurably. A police inspector's order to them to disperse was greeted with derisive remarks, taunts, and a vigorous shouting of slogans. The inevitable police attack with *lathis* followed, with the attackers converging rapidly and systematically on the young man who was holding the Congress flag. As he was struck and fell, he handed the flag to Indira, who had been standing next to him, urging her to keep it aloft.

The advice was unnecessary. Though unprepared for the responsibility, Indira held on to the flag firmly, not letting it fall even when she herself fell to the ground under the policemen's blows. Letting the police snatch the flag would have been tantamount to British success, and permitting it to fall to the ground and be trampled in the melee would have been sacrilege. Indira, as she recalls it, would allow neither. She talks of the incident with considerable pride. "I tried to hold it [the flag] up. I was quite badly beaten but I did not let it fall." Even today she remembers the "heavy boots" of the policemen and the troops that came perilously close to her face when she fell on the ground. That night, Feroze, much perturbed over reports of the incident, emerged from "underground" briefly to visit Anand Bhavan. Indira was quite casual about the beating she had received. Even though she carried many visible bruises, she would hardly talk of the physical punishment she had suffered that day. But she was full of the fact that she had not let the flag drop. She remembered how fairly early in his involvement in the freedom movement Jawaharlal had been similarly attacked by the police but had stubbornly retained his hold on the flag he carried and the handbills he was distributing. She felt in that morning's encounter with the authorities she had lived up to the standards set by her father.

Indira's only regret about the Ewing College incident was that she was not arrested. However, she did not have to wait long. A few days after the flag-hoisting, she arranged a meeting of party workers. Since the Congress Party had been outlawed and the press was subject to stern censorship, there was no way of announcing the meeting except through word of mouth, which reached the police as quickly as it did the party sympathizers. At the appointed time there were more police-men and soldiers than party workers. Police vehicles set up a ring around the venue. Troops, some armed with the usual long, heavy, steel-studded clubs and some carrying guns, stood near the dais de-termined to prevent the meeting from proceeding. When Indira had addressed the gathering for no more than a few minutes, a British soldier ordered her to stop speaking. When that did not produce the desired response from her, he raised his gun and moved menacingly towards her. In a move that in retrospect seems melodramatic, almost comical, Feroze, who was in the audience unknown to his wife, sprang forward and planted himself between the angry soldier and Indira. The gun was not fired—though, considering the mood in which the government then was, its firing could be regarded as a distinct possi-bility—but Feroze was promptly arrested and hustled into a waiting prison van. When police pounced on Indira, a section of the assembled crowd intervened angrily to prevent her arrest. That caused a tug of war—brief but, for Indira, painful and embarrassing—in which party workers and policemen tried to pull her in opposite directions. Her *sari* was torn in the process. While this was going on, Feroze somehow managed to get out of the police van, scrambled to its roof, and was, much to the discomfiture of the law official in charge, haranguing a section of the assembly. In time, however, Feroze was pulled off his perch and pushed back into captivity, while Indira was dragged away from her zealous defenders and taken to Anand Bhavan to pack her bag quickly for a term in jail.

Her earlier familiarity with prisons notwithstanding, Indira was sur-prised by the drabness of prison life as she now saw it from the other side of the massive oak gate of the Naini Central Jail. She had not imagined anything like what she saw. She had believed—somewhat naïvely—that inside the jail "life went on as usual except that you could not see people from outside." She soon realized that there was much more to it than being deprived of contact with others. One was denied, she discovered, so many things that one took for granted in life such as being able to receive a newspaper or pick up a book to read or write letters or get food of one's own choosing. Things were made somewhat worse for her than they might normally have been by an act of magisterial absent-mindedness or perverseness. Political prisoners in those days were allotted to an A, B, or C class according to their political and social status. As Jawaharlal's daughter, Indira should normally have been accorded A-class treatment, but while sentencing her the judge somehow marked her card with an X. Since there was no such category, the jail officials interpreted it to mean that she was to be treated as an ordinary convict and given none of the privileges customarily enjoyed by political detainees. It was several months before the mistake was corrected, and until then Indira could neither write nor receive letters nor supplement her food with gifts from outside nor even talk to a visitor.

Indira's response to the situation was practical even though made instinctively rather than after any prolonged intellectual exercise. As she explained it many years later, she virtually sealed her mind "so that while I was in prison I did not consciously feel that I was missing anything." Some of the other prisoners would talk yearningly about food and other things they did not get in jail, but Indira "did not miss a thing." She seemed to live at what she described as "only at a surface level"—an existence in which emotions were temporarily frozen. The walls she quickly erected between her mind and her day-to-day life were apparently so massive that after she left the prison it took her some effort to demolish them. "It was some time before my feelings thawed out and I could look at a color without feeling the shock of it or hear a noise or even feel a texture," she recalled.

As the Central Jail, the Naini prison to which Indira was taken was bigger than the district jail. It could hold more than two thousand inmates, but the fact that it was larger than the ordinary jails did not mean it offered better amenities. The women's wing of the Naini prison comprised two large courtyards separated by a high wall. In one wing were housed criminals, while the other, comprising two sheds or barracks, was earmarked for political prisoners. One of the barracks was empty when Vijayalakshmi arrived there about a month ahead of Indira, and, as an experienced inmate of British prisons, she hastened to occupy the best part of the structure, which was the farthest from the barracks' only lavatory. The other consideration recommending that corner to Indira's aunt was the fact that from there she could get a brief glimpse of the outside world should the warder be slow in closing the gate when entering the main courtyard.

By the time Indira arrived in the prison, the barracks had begun to fill up. Chandralekha had come ahead of her and set up her small string cot, which the prison issued to every inmate, next to her mother's. Even though denied the customary privileges of a political prisoner owing to the ambiguous category classification on her conviction order, Indira was placed among the political prisoners and not in the wing reserved for criminals. She found a nook near her two relatives, creating what they jokingly called the Naini Anand Bhavan.

This august description for their part of the shed did not mitigate the harshness of their existence. The two barracks accommodated nearly twenty other woman prisoners, some of whom chattered incessantly. The barracks itself was comprised of four crumbling walls and a roof that leaked like a sieve every time it rained—which was often during the first few weeks of Indira's jail term. When it did not rain, the ceiling shed large chunks of plaster on the unwary residents. The barracks walls had been broken up at several points and masonry replaced by steel bars to enable jail authorities to keep a watchful eye on the prisoners. Besides depriving the women of any little privacy that might otherwise have been possible, these openings admitted flies during the day, ugly bats at dusk, and hordes of mosquitoes at night. After every shower came large frogs—creatures that most Indians regard with particular distaste. One night a large poisonous snake of the kind in which the Naini area abounded was found lying along the wall just opposite Vijayalakshmi's bed. All the efforts the prisoners made to get the sentry to come and kill it were of no avail, and ultimately the snake slid away on its own.

Winter brought them some relief from flies, frogs, and mosquitoes, but rats, cockroaches, and bats continued to pester them. The jail had electricity and a solitary light, dim and unshaded, hung from the center of the barracks ceiling, but, for security reasons, it was turned off as dusk fell. If Indira wished to read after the normal lights-off time, she had to borrow the kerosene lantern issued to her aunt in consideration of her A-class status. The three women had a rickety iron table among them, but their request for a chair was brusquely turned down as being contrary to jail regulations. Some of Indira's irritations were unrelated to the hardships prescribed in the jail manual. Two convicts from the adjoining courtyard who were permitted into the political prisoners' section to help a wardress quarreled with each other frequently, and when they did the entire jail rang with their hysterical shrieks and the filthy abuse they exchanged. When they were not brawling with each other, the peace of the yard would be broken by the shrill, raucous chanting of the hymns from the scriptures by an old political prisoner from Maharashtra.

For food, Indira was allowed daily rations worth nine annas, which, on the basis of the prevailing exchange rate, was less than a shilling. (The allowance was raised to twelve annas a few weeks before her release, following her elevation to A class.) The amount had to suffice not only for rice, *dal* (lentils), milk, sugar, tea, and vegetables but also for the cooking fat and the wood to cook the meal on. The rice and *dal* were always full of stones, the sugar of dust, and the milk of the water from the hand pump outside the yard wall. In a corner of the yard Vijayalakshmi had improvised an oven by arranging a few bricks in such a way as to hold a small cooking pot over a handful of twigs. That became the "Anand Bhavan kitchen" that Indira shared with her aunt and cousin. Vijayalakshmi prepared the morning tea and breakfast, while the two younger women jointly produced the supper. Cooking the meal was not much of a chore, especially on the days the wood was reasonably dry, but cleaning the rice and *dal* of their stones was tedious and took a long time. The jail authorities had assigned a young convict named Durgi to help Vijayalakshmi with the cooking chores, but though a cheerful person—she was serving a life term for the murder of her husband—she was an atrocious cook. Indira was unwilling to risk their meager supplies of groceries in the hope that in time Durgi would improve her culinary skills and, therefore, insisted on doing much of the cooking herself.

By 1942 restrictions on supplementing the jail rations with food from outside had become pretty rigid. As an A-class prisoner, Vijaya-lakshmi was entitled to receive food parcels from friends and relations,

but the jail superintendent permitted exercise of this privilege grudgingly and, as time passed, infrequently. He, in fact, seemed to possess
a sadistic streak of mind in these matters. Indira recalls with particular
chagrin the episode of the mangoes that her father, himself in prison
over a thousand miles away, had specially arranged to be sent to her.
Indira was partial to mangoes, and Jawaharlal thought she would like
nothing more than a basket of them to add some variety and taste
to her coarse, unvarying jail food. At his request his younger sister
Krishna, who lived in Bombay and had somehow escaped being imprisoned, sent Indira a basket of choice Alphonsos, one of the best
variety of mangoes in India. Instead of permitting Indira to receive
them, the superintendent consumed the entire consignment himself.
In addition, he had the gall and audacity to come to Indira and thank
her for the wonderful mangoes. The incident has stuck in her mind
over the years, because that was virtually the only time during her
8-month stay in prison that Indira lost her self-control and became
really distressed and angry.

As a rule Indira succeeded in her resolve to stay calm and not let
anything cause her irritation and aggravation. She took the incon-
veniences and deprivations of jail life in her stride. Unlike Vijayalakshmi, who, by her own account, often fretted and fumed, Indira
tended to laugh at things and greet official provocations with cheerful
nonchalance. In this, the presence of Chandralekha in the barracks
helped her greatly. Both saw much around them to cause them amusement. There was, for example, Zainab, the very fat wardress whose
walk was like "the satisfied waddle of an old duck." Zainab was perpetually worried about the advancing Japanese, because someone had
told her that the Japanese soldiers had cannibalistic tendencies and she
feared that her bulk would make her an obvious subject of their atten-
tions. Even the Maharashtrian woman, the clamorousness of whose
religious devotion exasperated Vijayalakshmi, afforded Indira occasional opportunity for laughter. Almost everything in the barracks had
been given a special name by the two young women. Their corner of
the large room was called the "Blue Drawing Room," deriving its
name from a small and rather old blue rug that Vijayalakshmi had
foresightedly brought with her as part of her bedding roll when she
was arrested. The lantern they used after lights were switched off was
"Lucifer," while a bottle of hair oil that had lost its cap was named

"Rupert—the headless Earl." Indira called her corner of the barracks "Chimborazo" after the mountain in the Andes that seemed to her to symbolize "all that was beautiful but far away." The part occupied by Chandralekha was "Bien Venue." Vijayalakshmi, whose exposure to Europe was not as recent as theirs, was content to have her corner called rather staidly "Wall View." The jail cat was named "Mehitabel," and despite the fact that it often consumed all the milk they had been allotted for the day and thus deprived them of their tea and coffee, it received from Indira much tender attention when it had kittens.

Besides vowing not to permit jail officials and regulations to upset her, Indira had come to Naini determined not to get bored. She quickly found much to occupy herself usefully and ordered her day to be able to attend to it in a systematic way. Sharing the courtyard, as she was, with over twenty other political prisoners, she saw the danger of being drawn into a pointless pastime of gossip and idle women's talk. She, therefore, made a firm rule that until 5 P.M. every day none of the other jail inmates might speak to her except when absolutely necessary. In the observance of this rule she did not relent even when some of the prisoners seemed to resent it or regarded it as a manifestation of arrogance on her part.

Indira read voraciously. She had brought with her from Anand Bhavan "a suit-case full of books—serious, less serious, and frivolous." Additionally, she was able to borrow the books that her aunt and cousin had with them. Occasionally, Vijayalakshmi received books from outside that she shared with her niece. The catholicity of Indira's reading in jail is evident from the fact that books she read included Upton Sinclair's *Dragon's Teeth,* Plato's *Republic,* George Bernard Shaw's plays, an anthology of world letters, Lin Yutang's latest novel *A Leaf in the Storm,* and a book ironically entitled *Escape from Freedom.* Nehru, who had always anxiously watched over Indira's reading, sent her some of the books that he had read and liked in his Ahmednagar jail. The parcel that, unlike the parcel of mangoes, was duly delivered to her included a collection of Greek plays, Gilbert Murray's translation of *Alcestis,* and a number of books about the United States that Pearl Buck had specially chosen for Jawaharlal. There were, of course, no newspapers to read, except when some were smuggled into the yard. Vijayalakshmi's second daughter, Nayantara, left in Anand Bhavan in the care of the Chinese governess, tried ingeniously, though not very effectively, to fill the need by wrapping newspaper clippings of important stories around toothpaste tubes she sent her mother.

While Chandralekha was in jail—she was released a few weeks before the other two—Indira helped her with her French. With the jailer's permission they had converted a part of the extensive yard into a garden. Tending the flowers and vegetables was engrossing and rewarding. Nasturtium and pansies did particularly well, but their larkspur, Indira recalls, was something of a disappointment. The vegetable patch provided some of the herbs so extensively used in Indian cooking and helped mitigate the blandness of their daily diet. After lock-up time, with "Lucifer" providing the necessary light, Indira and Chandralekha would occasionally spend the evening play-reading, while Vijayalakshmi acted as the audience.

What, however, engaged Indira's attention even more than reading and gardening was the responsibility she undertook to educate one of the young convicts. Almost twenty years earlier, when Jawaharlal had come to Naini jail to serve his first term in prison, he had found much solace and satisfaction in teaching some of his fellow inmates to read and write. Indira, too, collected a group of pupils from amongst the detainees and convicts. For some curious reason she was particularly drawn to a young woman prisoner who had brought a few-weeks-old baby with her to the jail. As part of her own marriage earlier in the year, Indira had acquired extensive, if bookish, knowledge about child care. She taught the mother to read and write and tried her academic expertise on the baby. In the process she became so fond of the child that after her release she wanted to legally adopt him and was dissuaded from doing so with some difficulty.

In the beginning of May 1943 Indira and her aunt were told they would be released provided they gave an understanding not to indulge in political activity. Such a conditional release was unacceptable to them, and the offer was promptly turned down. A few days later, however, after Indira had completed eight months in jail, they were set free.

Jawaharlal spent almost ten years in prison. He lightly dismissed his long, often solitary, confinement to a prison cell as "enforced leisure," but in fact it gave him an opportunity for serious, introspective thinking and enabled him to hone some of the political concepts he put into practice as Prime Minister. Indira's stay in jail was too brief to have made any durable impact on her mind. Her claim about what she gained from Naini prison is quite modest. It enabled her to understand her father better when, later, she stayed with him in the Prime Minister's house, and, she says, "perhaps it strengthened my character—strengthened me as a person."

6

The Extraordinary
Apprenticeship

For one who arrayed her dolls in elaborately staged political battles, whose childhood fantasies drew sustenance from the life of Joan of Arc, and who sometimes indulged in political demonstrations with courage bordering on recklessness, Indira Gandhi accepted the role of a leader with curious hesitation and lack of enthusiasm. A friend of the Nehru family who had watched her from her childhood once remarked that as a politician Indira belonged to "the late-flowering variety."

By the time she reached her early twenties, her childhood reveries about leading the country into heroic battle against the British had given place to more practical and modest ambitions about herself. When an interviewer asked her what she would have liked to be if the choice had been completely hers, Indira, who had then just been named Prime Minister, suggested a handful of fields in which she would have been happier than in politics. She would have liked to be a writer, she said, or a research scholar in some branch of history—preferably in anthropology. Or an interior decorator. She might even have become a professional dancer, she mused, and reminisced how, when she was studying at Shantineketan, she had attained such a degree of proficiency in the Manipuri style that Tagore had suggested her joining a troupe that he proposed taking around the country.

But Indira did not take up any of these professions, and she even adopted politics as a personal career somewhat belatedly, partly because of circumstances and partly because her ties of affection with the immediate members of her family were particularly strong. With the atmosphere in the country what it had been since her childhood, and especially with the Nehru family's involvement in politics, no child of Jawaharlal's could have insulated herself from her surroundings to such an extent as to become a dancer or an interior decorator or a conventional historian. At the same time, however, her sense of commitment to her family—as a daughter, a wife, a mother—prevented Indira from throwing herself into politics with anything resembling the near total abandon that her father had displayed when he joined the independence movement in his youth.

Govindvallabh Pant, Chief Minister of Uttar Pradesh, urged Indira to run for election to the state legislature in 1946 when she was only twenty-nine and expecting her second child. Freedom then was just around the corner, and the legislatures were where its principal rewards were to be found. In Indira's case election to the state assembly would almost certainly have meant a Cabinet post. But she was not tempted. Her children needed her more than the Uttar Pradesh assembly, she told Pant.

When freedom came at last to India, it came with the swiftness of a monsoon storm. Churchill and his Tory Party had been defeated in Britain. The head of the new Labour Party government, Clement Attlee, lacking his predecessor's imperialistic predilections, saw the pointlessness of a war-enfeebled Britain trying to retain its Empire. In sharp contrast to its earlier obstinate hold on authority, Britain was suddenly anxious to relinquish power, and it did so with a speed that left even Nehru and others around him almost flabbergasted.

Until the middle of 1945 Jawaharlal was a prisoner charged with treason. In September of the following year he was heading the Interim Government. On August 15, 1947, he took office as independent India's first Prime Minister. The previous night, as dark clouds hung low over the capital and the air was thick with the heavy fragrance of jasmine and queen of the night, Earl Mountbatten, Britain's last Viceroy, had formally handed over power to India's Constituent Assembly. A message from His Majesty King George VI, which Mountbatten delivered to the assembled Indian leaders at the solemn ceremony, said, "It is inspiring to think that all this has been achieved by means of peaceful change."

In a voice choked with emotion, Nehru responded that "at the stroke of the midnight hour India will awake to life and freedom." That, he said, was the moment "when we step out from the old to the new, when an age ends and when the soul of a nation, long suppressed, finds utterance." Indira watched the transfer-of-power ceremony in the big-domed Central Hall of what later become India's Parliament House, and she was rendered "numb," she said years later, by the immensity of the event. After "all those years of thinking, dreaming and working for independence," Indira found it, when it finally came, "so big a thing that it just could not register. . . ."

It was almost four years after independence that another attempt was made to lure Indira into active politics. The Constituent Assembly had by then completed its work, and India had become a republic with a Parliament in New Delhi and assemblies in the states, all elected on the basis of adult franchise. In the first general election Indira was offered the party nomination for a seat in Parliament. Her children had by then entered a good private school in New Delhi, and she had acquired the services of a European governess to look after them, but Indira again declined political honors. She felt that her father, past sixty and as Prime Minister lonely and bowed under the weight of running a country of India's size and problems, was entitled to her time and attention to the exclusion of all ambition on her part.

The family had well-established traditions of filial devotion. Jawaharlal had tended to his ailing father when both were in jail and served him with such love and gentle care beginning with "early morning tea to the time I retire for the night" that Motilal said he wished "there were many fathers to boast of such sons." Indira was determined not to let political prospects or the fact that she was a daughter, not a son, stop her from bestowing similar affection on her father when, in her judgment, he needed her. She once told Lord Chalfont, who was interviewing her on behalf of the BBC, that she "hated the thought of housekeeping" and "hated most" to be hostess at a party "as I always disliked parties and having to smile when one does not want to." But she did both, though the tasks, despite a surface glamour, were particularly demanding. The house she kept was large and formal. The social calendar was crowded with events for a stream of dignitaries, as it had to be for a leader whom events had suddenly placed at the center of international politics. Indira told herself that "if one has to do a thing one might as well do it well"—and "so I grew into it." After some initial hesitation and confusion she was able to cope with her duties as her father's official hostess and companion with aplomb and even, in time, with noticeable gusto. The problems she tackled in her self-assigned role were varied. They ranged from deciding what to do with the imposing but huge and ugly gilt-framed portraits of the former British generals and viceroys that covered the walls of what was now the Prime Minister's residence, to nursing a tiger cub whose paws had been needlessly cauterized, to making her father control his temper, to combating the jealousies that her proximity to Jawaharlal inevitably brought from other family members (including her aunts) and senior political leaders.

In her capacity as Jawaharlal's household manager, unpaid secretary cum-nurse, constant companion, and conscience-keeper, Indira encountered irritations and frustrations almost daily. Unlike Motilal, who had been ailing for years before his death, Jawaharlal was in excellent health. But he was under considerable mental strain. The partition of India and Pakistan had created several million refugees, whose rehabilitation seemed beyond the country's limited resources. Pakistani leaders were constantly shaking their fists at India and periodically driving more refugees across the border. Gandhi's assassination in 1948 and the death of Nehru's deputy in his first Cabinet, Vallabhbhai Patel, in 1950 removed from the scene two men on whom Nehru had always leaned heavily, despite his occasional sharp differences with them. The Congress was going through a protracted period of ideological confusion caused by having to adjust to its new role as a ruling party. Much of its top leadership was wearied by long years of the freedom fight. In international politics there was distinct hostility towards India's aspirations and Nehru's concept of nonalignment. Jawaharlal's nerves were badly jangled a good deal of the time, rendering the task of looking after him essential and exacting. Indira was herself under a strain, torn between the desire to stay with her husband in Lucknow and the desire to respond to what she felt was a call of duty as a daughter. Some of the close relatives, especially her older aunt, Vijaya-lakshmi, frequently indulged themselves in nit-picking and often hurtful criticism of the way she ran the Prime Minister's residence. Many others, resentful of Indira's presence because it interfered with their access to Nehru and reduced their influence on him, let her feel their pique. Even some members of the Prime Minister's personal staff, notably his private secretary, M. O. Mathai, appeared to regard Indira as a curb on their power. (Mathai, a highly intelligent and ambitious person from Kerala succeeded in winning Nehru's confidence to a remarkable extent but had to quit in 1959 following a scandal involving the acceptance of gifts from a business house.)

Yet all the stresses notwithstanding, Indira's years in the Prime Minister's house were among the happier periods of her life. Jawaharlal's need of her was obvious, and fulfilling it brought her deep satisfaction. The very presence in the house of Indira and her beautiful, lively sons plainly had a soothing effect on Nehru. Quick-tempered and highly strung as he was, without them around him Nehru would probably have found the task of controlling an amorphous political organization and administering an almost chaotic country intolerable. Although she was completely in the background and overshadowed by her father's personality, Indira knew the importance of what she was doing. What moved her was "not just duty to her father but her sense of what her father meant to the country." On his part, Nehru was not only grateful to her but repaid her devotion with unbounded affection for her and her children. After a visit to India in 1966 and an interview with Indira, writer Betty Friedan wrote on the authority of what an unidentified "elder statesman" told her that "in the early years Nehru used to bully Indira in an absolutely shocking way," that "he would shatter her self-confidence," and that "she was a mass of nerves," although she stoically "took the tongue-lashings." Those in India who had access to the Prime Minister's residence during Nehru's tenure find this depiction of Indira's position in that household totally unfounded. Jawaharlal was notoriously short-tempered, but he was never ill-tempered. His anger was always like a brief gust of wind, which people around him accepted in good part. They knew he bore no grudge towards anyone and that, in fact, he was a man with a strong sense of consideration for others. Indira was confident not only of his love but also of his respect. Far from having to accept "tongue-lashings" meekly, she could sternly tell Nehru to "cool down" and chide him, sometimes in the presence of others, for needlessly losing control over himself.

Like Anand Bhavan during Jawaharlal's youth, the Prime Minister's house, called Teen Murti or "the house with three statues" on account of the bronze figures in front of its gate representing India's three armed services, had its moments of tension. But it had many more moments of laughter and warmth. Once the portraits of former British generals had been banished to Defense Ministry "godowns," or warehouses, the house had an air of colonial elegance without the forbidding look that had previously characterized it, and it offered Indira an excellent opportunity, quickly seized, to show her skill as amateur interior decorator. The Teen Murti house was considerably bigger than either of the two large Nehru residences in Allahabad and Jawaharlal's household was comparatively small, yet the airy rooms always seemed full and crowded. Besides friends and relations, the house drew a large number of distinguished guests, from visiting heads of government or state to renowned scientists and men of letters. Foreign dignitaries invited to visit the country were usually put up in Rashtrapati Bhavan (the splendid former palace of the Viceroy, now occupied by India's ceremonial President) for the first two or three days to satisfy protocol and then moved to Nehru's own house for the rest of their stay. The doors of the house and its lovely gardens were also open to the lowliest of citizens, hundreds of whom came every morning for *darshan*, or an "edifying glimpse" of the nation's leader, or to speak to him of their problems as he strolled about after breakfast. And besides people there were the animals. Thanks largely to the enthusiasm of Indira's children, Teen Murti early acquired what amounted to a miniature zoo. There was a pair of pandas from Sikkim, three tiger cubs—President Tito later asked for one of them and took it to Belgrade—and numerous birds of diverse kinds, as well as the great dane that Nehru loved dearly. Looking after the animals and birds was as much a part of Indira's daily chores as taking care of the members of the family.

Although Indira in these years was of necessity, and choice, so engrossed in seemingly interminable housekeeping tasks that she had little time for politics, Teen Murti nevertheless gave her, largely without her being conscious of it, the finest political training that a future Prime Minister could have acquired. Her presence near Nehru was so constant that many of those who saw her scarcely took notice of her. She was always around when world leaders discussed wide-ranging in-

ternational issues with her father and when Indian politicians brought
to him their problems and disputes—seeing and hearing everything
from her anonymous perch near the seat of power. She could not help
but collect a rich store of political experience and understanding of
men and matters.

The education of Nehru's daughter in world affairs was particularly
useful. In this arena few young women have ever had opportunities
anything like those that came her way. Not only did the great of many
nations come to sit in the flower-decked rooms of the house she ran,
but as Nehru's companion, in the exciting early years after India's independence, Indira visited the United States, China, the Soviet Union,
and France, attended the coronation of Queen Elizabeth and the first
conference of Afro-Asian leaders in Bandung, Indonesia, and met on
their home ground such world figures as Truman, Churchill, Khrushchev, Tito, Nasser, Sukarno, and Chou En-lai. (Some of them she had
already, or would, play hostess to at Teen Murti.)

The Britain to which Indira Gandhi paid her first foreign visit after
independence in her father's company in 1948, and to which she returned almost every year in connection with his annual participation in
the Commonwealth Prime Ministers' Conference, held few surprises
for her but offered her welcome opportunities of meeting old teachers
and friends.

During these visits she also saw Britain win its post-World War II
battle for economic recovery but lose the one to remain a world power.
Even though she could not attend the actual meetings of the Commonwealth premiers, her presence in London at the time gave her a sharp
sense of history. With Nehru and his Pakistani counterpart, Liaqat Ali
Khan, joining its deliberations, the Prime Ministers' Conference ceased
to be the exclusive white man's club that it had previously been. There
were other changes. Nehru's first attendance at one of these meetings
had been as the chief executive of a Dominion owing allegiance to
the British Crown in the same way Canada and Australia did. By the
time of the 1949 Prime Ministers' Conference India had resolved to
shed the subservient garb of a Dominion and become a sovereign republic with an elected constitutional head of its own. As it existed
then, there was no room in the Commonwealth for a member nation
that did not formally accept the British monarch as its own head. As

the leader of a totally independent country, Nehru was free to lead India out of the Commonwealth. If he had, the extremists and many other sections of the populace at home would have lauded the move. Besides nursing resentful memories of British colonial rule, many in India were embittered by the massacres and travails of the partition for which they held Britain responsible. Socialists, conservatives, even much of the Congress Party membership regarded snapping all ties with the Commonwealth as the only appropriate course. Nehru, however, was not swayed by such sentiments and painstakingly negotiated with Clement Attlee, then Britain's Prime Minister, a formula that enabled India to stay in the Commonwealth even after becoming a republic and ceasing to owe allegiance to the Crown. The rather vague constitutional compromise that the two evolved enabled, in the following decade, other Asian and African former colonies to remain within the Commonwealth and profoundly affected the institution's character.

It came as a surprise to Britons on the whole that a people who had fought for independence as tenaciously and uncompromisingly as the Indians had done over many years should wish to preserve a relationship with their erstwhile oppressors. Churchill apparently was among the incredulous. Indira describes an encounter she had with him during her visit to London with her father to attend the Queen's coronation in 1953—an encounter that, besides reflecting British puzzlement, explained Nehru's basic approach to the relationship with Britain. At one occasion during the coronation festivities Indira found herself sitting next to and chatting amiably with the leader who had so bitterly opposed and obstructed Indian independence and said terribly harsh things about her father and the Mahatma. Suddenly, Churchill remarked, "Is it not strange that we should be talking as friends when we hated each other such a short while ago?" Indira replied promptly, "Sir Winston, we did not hate you." To which Churchill, who was then back in office, responded by confessing, "But I did, I did."

Indira's first visit to the United States in 1949 offered her a stack of new impressions, some of which disturbed and presumably had a lasting impact on her. She had never been to the United States before, and like most Western-educated Indians of her generation had in her mind a picture of the country that was exaggerated and overdrawn in some parts and fuzzy in some others. Having lived in England and studied its literature and history, she understood Britons well, but she regarded Americans more or less as their distant cousins, rather naïve and uncouth despite the riches they had struck. During her travels as the guest of the U.S. Government Indira saw a great deal of the country but, as she put it, "through colored glasses," referring, apparently, to the conducted nature of her tour. She was overwhelmed by the "abundance and luxury which must be seen to be believed." Food was so plentiful and hospitality so lavish that she worried constantly about putting on weight. Like many foreign visitors she found New York's skyscrapers unattractive. She remembers that she was intrigued by the fact that in the Waldorf Astoria, where the Prime Minister's party stayed, the hotel envelopes in the rooms had peppermint-flavored gummed flaps.

What, however, truly distressed her, as it did Nehru, was not so much the impersonal nature of high-rise living or the wasteful consumption she saw in the United States but the blatancy with which Americans—in government and in commerce—tried to influence Nehru. His American hosts fussed over Nehru, who was then the most important and articulate leader in Asia. They made it clear, not surprisingly, that they hoped he would place his prestige and influence on the side of the United States in its cold-war confrontation with communism. But they also assumed that as the Prime Minister of a poor country he would be overwhelmed by a display of material wealth and that the way to his heart must be paved with promises of economic aid; it seemed more or less taken for granted that he could not resist such tempting offers. All the courtesy extended to Nehru and his daughter was marred by this assumption and by the unfortunately patronizing attitude many Americans adopted most of the time. The Indian Prime Minister was told more than once, usually with an all too noticeable lack of subtlety, that his country could achieve prosperity only through passionate commitment to the path of capitalism. At a luncheon held in his honor in New York Nehru's host for the occasion proudly told the visitors that sitting around the table were individuals who among themselves controlled nearly $20 billion in capital. Clearly, he expected the Indian Prime Minister to be impressed and flattered; Nehru was, in fact, shocked by the crudeness of the observation. The Indian party was also distressed by the naïveté of Americans in not realizing the significance of Mao's success in China and in permitting ideological prejudices to compel their government to adopt unrealistic foreign policy postures. Nehru sounded as patronizing to Americans as they did to him, and some of the newspapers said so.

If Indira's visits to the Soviet Union on her own in 1953 and China in 1954 with Nehru did not cause her the same kind of irritation and exasperation as her first contact with the United States, it was due in no small measure to the fact that she went there in a friendlier and more relaxed frame of mind. Instead of being wary and expecting to be subjected to blandishments and pressures, as she was in the United States, Indira was responsive and receptive when traveling in the two Communist countries. The reason was not ideological. Her travels occurred at the right time.

When she decided, on her way back from London, after the Queen's coronation, to stop over in Moscow, Stalin had just died, and the country appeared to be experiencing the first, hesitant signs of spring after a bitter, harsh, and what had seemed endless winter. Besides the buoyancy in the atmosphere, which she could sense, Indira noted a new warmth towards India. During Stalin's days the Soviet Union had regarded India's supposedly bourgeois leadership with scorn and dismissed India's attainment of freedom in 1947 as a sham that had merely transferred power from foreign imperialists to a group of Indians who were themselves eager to rule the country on behalf of their British masters. But even in the last few months of Stalin's rule the Soviet Union appeared to have begun to realize the fallacy of its earlier assumptions and started the process of thawing towards India. Stalin himself had signaled the change in April 1952, when he received India's Ambassador Dr. Sarvepalli Radhakrishnan (later President of India), even though he had not granted an interview to any foreign diplomat for the previous two years. By the time Indira reached Moscow, Soviet good will towards India had acquired a positive character, and K. P. S. Menon, who had succeeded Dr. Radhakrishnan as the Indian Ambassador and whose guest she was, enthusiastically testified to it.

Indira accompanied the Menons on a tour of certain parts of the Soviet Union that by all accounts was a happy and rewarding experience. In Georgia she was fascinated by the expanse of its capital, Tbilisi, particularly at night, and stayed awake until early hours of the morning watching the scene from her hotel room. The view, as she told the Ambassador the following morning, "intoxicated" her. With the Ambassador and his wife she visited Sochi, the well-known health resort on the Black Sea, and Matsesta. She was much impressed by the health and recreation arrangements at Sochi and the realization that a coal miner from Siberia could enjoy the privilege of basking in the southern sunshine for a few weeks every year. In Matsesta, famed for its sulphur springs since the time of the Roman Empire, she took a dip in the sulphur baths against suspected dandruff. From there she went on to Tashkent, a city that gave her an idea of how much a distant, backward region of a large country could do for its economic development. Wherever she went, her _sari_-clad figure and her good looks attracted attention. Many Uzbeks could not believe she was from India. In Menon's words:

> Where, the Uzbeks wondered, had Indira come from? For despite her sari, she was so fair, had short hair and chiselled features. She might come from any part of the world yet could belong to none.

Russians, apparently, were fascinated even by her name. A Soviet Ambassador to India later reported to her that a large number of little girls born that year in the parts of the Soviet Union she had visited had been named "Indira" after her.

Like the cordiality with the Soviet Union, in 1954 India's relations with Peking had not yet developed the hostility of later years. Since the communist victory in China in 1948, Jawaharlal had studiously tried to create circumstances in which Asia's two largest nations could co-exist. According to his calculations the new leaders of China would need a decade, perhaps longer, to consolidate their power, and during this period they would let others alone. The Chinese leadership did nothing to give him the contrary impression. Earlier that year Peking had extended its administrative and military control over Tibet, and India had endorsed the move, arguing that historically the Tibetan region had been a part of China and it was only the notorious weakness and divisiveness of the central Chinese Government that had enabled Tibet to exercise autonomy in the past. In return for India's readiness to appreciate the Chinese position, Chou En-lai had signed with Nehru the _panchsheel_ declaration, enunciating the five principles of co-existence and mutual respect. When, therefore, Indira accompanied her father on a state visit to China in October, she, like Jawaharlal, believed she was watching a country that was trying frantically to pull itself up by its bootstraps and at least for the time being had no territorial ambitions. Their Chinese hosts were warm and gracious as perhaps only the Chinese can be when they are so inclined. A great deal of what they were shown impressed them by the purposefulness of its planning and resoluteness of its execution. In India people had been shouting, under undoubted official orchestration, that the Indians and the Chinese were brothers (*"Hindi-Chini bhai-bhai"*), and when the Prime Minister's party returned from the China tour there was nothing in its experience to suggest any need to check the public exuberance.

At Bandung in Indonesia, to which she accompanied Jawaharlal for the first Afro-Asian conference in 1955, Indira received another lesson in diplomatic wariness, besides those she had learned on her American trip in 1949, as far as the United States was concerned. Nehru later became disenchanted with such assemblies, but Bandung he approached with enthusiasm, hoping that there he might mold the newly independent Asian and African nations into an element of considerable strength and influence in world politics. For almost eight years he had stubbornly kept India out of either power bloc and had hoped that others, acting similarly, would strengthen their own independence and lessen the chances of a big-power conflict. At the conference he introduced Chou En-lai, who acted with sweet reasonableness calculated to allay the fears of those countries that regarded the rise of communist power in China with trepidation. Nehru urged the assembled leaders of twenty-nine nations to endorse the five principles of peaceful co-existence that India and China had accepted the previous year. Their formal support for *panchsheel* would, in his view, promote mutual trust and unity and also demonstrate that independent Afro-Asian governments were disinclined to get involved in the cold war over ideological issues. His talks with the assembled leaders had given him the impression that his proposal would be accepted without challenge. He was, therefore, taken aback when the resolution was not only opposed but was countered with another that sought specifically to condemn "the neo-imperialism of the communist bloc." The alternative five principles were presented by Ceylon's Prime Minister, Sir John Kotlewala, were supported by Pakistan's Prime Minister, Mohammed Ali Bogra. Both these men were known to have established strong personal and political links with the United States. Nehru, whose philosophy of nonalignment had by then been condemned by John Foster

Dulles as "immoral," had no reason to expect enthusiastic support from U.S. allies and friends, but somehow he had not anticipated such a frontal attack on his attempt to forge some kind of precarious unity among the underdeveloped countries. He saw the rival resolution as a blatant attempt on the part of the United States to inject cold-war divisiveness into a group of nations who could ill afford the luxury of such disputes. Livid with anger, Nehru very nearly stamped out of the conference hall. Indira sternly rebuked her father for losing control of himself. But she also noted, as she told an interviewer subsequently, how big powers tended to "use" the countries to which they offered their supposedly disinterested aid.

With her election to the Congress Working Committee in 1955, shortly before her visit to Bandung, Indira took what may be regarded as the first step on the road that ultimately led her to national leadership. The step was small. The organizational wing of the party had lost much of its former prestige, and a large measure of its real power had shifted to the parliamentary wing. Her move was, however, significant in that she took it after serious deliberation.

It represented a real change in her own view of her role. Of the committee's twenty-one members, fourteen were customarily nominated by the party President, while the rest were elected by the organization's large national council. The competition for the seven seats was always hectic. The Congress President, U. N. Dhebar, would gladly have nominated Indira to the party's executive group, but she preferred to enter it through election. Her election, in fact, was never in doubt, and she polled the largest number of votes. But by spurning the convenience of a nomination Indira indicated that she was ready to accept the rough-and-tumble of elective politics. She had placed her foot on the bottom rung of the ladder of political authority.

Even after her election to the executive, Indira displayed a certain degree of diffidence and self-consciousness. She worked hard as a member of the Working Committee but most of the time in unspectacular fields. Much of her energy was devoted to the women's department of the Congress Party, which, though important, did not bring her any attention from the press and public. She continued to be shy and somewhat withdrawn. At the closed-door meetings of the executive she reportedly spoke little. Whenever the party's larger council, the All-India

Congress Committee, was convened to debate general issues, other members of the executive, especially the relatively junior ones, would jostle with others for a seat on the dais and endeavor to be seen in earnest confabulation with top leaders. But Indira preferred to sit in the pit with ordinary delegates. If she did occupy a place on the main stage she would sit quietly in a corner somewhere behind her father. Most people in the press and the party still regarded her as Nehru's daughter and gave almost no heed to her new role as a political leader in her own right.

Those politicians who were closer to the top and the better-informed among newspapermen, however, knew that Indira's influence had been growing steadily during those years. By the mid-1950s Jawaharlal's authority had increased tremendously. So had his dependence on Indira. Death had removed most of the comrades who had played parts comparable to his in the freedom movement and who had a claim on public affection. None could now challenge Nehru. Among the new crop of leaders many had risen with his help and needed his support to retain their perch. He dominated the party and the government, and leaders at the center as well as in the states exercised authority in proportion to the measure of confidence Nehru reposed in them. Almost nothing of any consequence was decided without his approval. At meetings of the central government Cabinet and the party executive, even senior members with supposedly secure political bases of their own tended to watch his mood before expressing themselves. Anything in direct conflict with Nehru's view was almost never voiced. Even Govindvallabh Pant, the powerful Chief Minister of Uttar Pradesh who had moved to Delhi as India's Home Minister at Nehru's own request, carefully avoided open expression of disagreement with the Prime Minister and would convey his opposition through indirect, veiled means. A few individuals could speak to him freely in private but only in the specific area of their expertise. Nehru, for example, listened to Krishna Menon in matters relating to foreign policy and defense, but Menon did not dare to venture an opinion on any aspect of domestic policy. Until his death in 1956 Rafi Ahmed Kidwai, who had been a personal friend and a dynamic member of Nehru's Cabinet, could influence Jawaharlal on matters relating to Kashmir and the position of the Muslim minority in India—but seldom on anything else. Later, Kesho Deo Malaviya, who as Minister for Oil succeeded in ending the dominance of the foreign oil companies, had Nehru's ear about the factional politics of Nehru's home state to which he, too, belonged. Such friends of the Prime Minister, however, had to guard against exceeding the bounds of their influence or placing undue strain on Nehru's trust in them. Indira alone had the unique privilege of being able to speak to her father freely on issues as diverse as his conception of a park being planned in New Delhi to his reaction to some major international development. She did not have to mind her p's and q's as others did, and she sometimes spoke to him with a bluntness that Jawaharlal had not encountered from anyone else since the death of Gandhi and Patel. She also, sometimes, ventured to correct his behavior in public places.

An American diplomat's wife remembers sitting one night late in January in a drafty New Delhi theater behind Indira and her father and Lady Mountbatten, who had become a friend of such devotion in the hectic months before independence when she was Vicereine that she returned every winter to visit the Nehrus for Republic Day and, usually, much of the month following. The three were watching a dance recital by Martha Graham and her company. The modern techniques of the great American dancer obviously were not to Nehru's taste. As he fussed and fidgeted in his front-row seat, Indira scolded, gently, raising her dark eyebrows expressively over her father's slumped head at Lady Mountbatten, who joined Indira in her attempts to make Jawaharlal behave. When the performance ended, the two together very nearly propelled the Prime Minister from his seat to accept from the lady who had organized the recital a sheaf of roses that he was to carry to the stage to present to Miss Graham. He did as he was told, reluctantly, but with a little show of gallantry in the end, while Indira and Lady Mountbatten giggled unobtrusively together from their place in the audience.

Unavoidably, over these years Indira became not merely the principal sentinel at the seat of power but also the most effective line of communication with it. Men and women in government and politics realized that through her they could convey to Nehru what they hesitated to express directly. A junior minister who felt his merit or loyalty was not being rewarded adequately would take his grievance to her and hope that she would put in a word for him. A former chief minister who coveted the sinecure of a gubernatorial post (state governors in India are appointed by the central government) would similarly seek Indira's help to plant the idea in Nehru's mind.

Not a small part of Indira's role during this period was to protect her father from some of his own friends. By no means was all of the advice he received from those he trusted always disinterested, and often it was left to Indira to point that out to her father. Without her constant presence near him, for example, Krishna Menon would almost certainly have exercised much greater influence over Nehru than he actually did. In most matters, particularly those concerning factional tussles within the party, there was always the other side; Nehru often saw it only with Indira's help. The streak of stubbornness in Nehru's character sometimes prompted him to act unreasonably. Indira, possibly without being altogether conscious of it, more and more tried to check it through unobtrusive intervention.

Typical of Indira's role and its importance at the time was the case of Dwarka Prasad Mishra. A strong and assertive politician from Central India, Mishra had been driven into the political wilderness shortly before independence by his rashness in aligning himself with Nehru's opponents and coming into direct conflict with him. Nearly a decade later Mishra, chastened and more mature, was eager to seek Nehru's forgiveness and get back in line behind him. Through Malaviya, he sent Nehru his regrets for the past and a pledge of loyalty for the future. Nehru was still disinclined to forget the past and accept Mishra in any responsible position in Madhya Pradesh. Some of the harsh things Mishra had said about him personally at the time of the quarrel still rankled, and several of his colleagues in the government and party were suspicious of Mishra's motives. However, he advised Malaviya to discuss the matter with Indira. Indira reacted favorably. Mishra, she felt, had done his penance. She reminded her father that the death in 1956 of Ravi Shankar Shukla, Madhya Pradesh's powerful Chief Minister, had created a void in party leadership in the state that might well be filled with Mishra's return. Soon afterward, Mishra was readmitted into the party and quickly rose to be the state's Chief Minister.

Indira's ability to sway Nehru was probably the main reason why in 1959 she was urged to accept the post of President of the Congress Party. Although the position was elective, the party traditionally accepted as its official head anyone whom the top leadership appeared to favor. The vacancy had occurred because U. N. Dhebar had given up the party presidentship a year before his term was due to end. Govindvallabh Pant, originally reluctant to support the suggestion of Indira's

election, was persuaded to endorse it when, as a close associate later recalled, he saw it as a means of influencing Nehru and occasionally
placing some restraints on his authority. When endowed with an independent political identity of her own, Indira, Pant and others argued,
might become something more than a line of communication with
Jawaharlal. She might be induced to stand up to him openly.

Indira accepted the offer with but token hesitation, and during the
eleven months she was Congress President she proceeded to display
an independence and assertiveness that surprised even Pant. Since the
country's independence the office of Congress President had lost much
of its former authority and prestige. Even those who cynically believed
she had been given the post because of accident of birth, later acknowledged that she proved to be a dynamic leader of the aging organization.
Under her the party took several difficult and controversial steps and
at times appeared to lead the government rather than to act, as it had
tended to do previously, as its handmaiden. The contrast with her predecessor, who had held the office for three years, was sharp and refreshing.

Perhaps the most controversial initiative that Indira took was the one
that culminated in the dismissal of the Communist government in the
Southern state of Kerala. The Communist Party's success there was
unique inasmuch as it was the only instance in the world up to then of
Communists coming to power through a peaceful parliamentary election. Nehru was deeply conscious of the significance of the phenomenon and its possible impact on the psychology of the Communists not
only in India but in the world. Perhaps, as he told a journalist shortly
after the Communist victory in Kerala, the Communists would realize
that they could attain power through the ballot box and become more
tolerant of democratic political processes. Additionally, he was reluctant to do anything to invite the charge that the central government
under him was hostile to a state government where his own party had
been defeated. Communists in Kerala, who were themselves astounded
by their success, were eager to consolidate their power by announcing
reforms in land ownership, injecting supporters into the state bureau-
cracies, and trying to make some structural changes in the prevailing
system of education. Some of the steps the Communist ministry took
were improper, perhaps even somewhat unconstitutional, but Nehru
hesitated to punish the state government for them.

Indira did not share her father's qualms in the matter, nor was she impressed by the philosophic implications of the Communist rise to power through peaceful means. She was the head of a political party that had been ousted from office by a rival, and she apparently felt it was her duty to fight back by the means available to her. The principal means offered was the agitation that two sectarian groups, the Catholics and the Nayyars, had started against the Communist ministry. Though separated normally by strong religious prejudices—the Nayyars are Hindus—the two communities were united in their fight against the Communist government by a common set of grievances. Both administered their own parochial schools and, taking advantage of the state's extraordinarily high rate of unemployment among the educated, they exploited the teachers quite blatantly. The state government introduced measures designed to wrest control of the schools from the hands of the Catholics and the Nayyars and check some of the malpractices they had perpetrated in the past, thus diminishing the patronage enjoyed by the leaders of the two communities. The land reforms that the Communists sponsored, too, affected the influential among the Catholics and Nayyars.

The Congress Party, always proud of its secularism and averse to associating itself with sectarian elements, let its principles be subordinated to its political interests and joined the Catholics and the Nayyars in denouncing the Communist administration. In the furor that the joint agitation created, the state government was accused of sins it had not committed, its motives were distorted, its political selfishness was exaggerated, and the good it had sought to do was completely over looked. The country's predominantly anti-Communist press joined in the campaign to bring about the Kerala ministry's downfall. The state government's attempts to curb the agitation were denounced as Communist highhandedness. Indira not only blessed her party's participation in the movement for the ministry's overthrow but also exerted relentless personal pressure on Jawaharlal and Pant to use the central government's special powers to dismiss the ministry on the grounds of its alleged failure to preserve law and order. At the midyear meeting of the party's national council in New Delhi in 1959, over which she presided, Indira made a strong plea for immediate central intervention. The Communist ministry was duly dismissed, because, as the central Home Ministry claimed, a situation of lawlessness had arisen in Kerala.

In the fresh elections that followed six months later the Communists were defeated, but to return to power the Congress Party had to make an electoral alliance with the Socialists on the one hand and the Muslim League on the other. Although the Socialists had much in common with the Congress, the Muslim League, as the party whose rabid religious-based politics had been a principal factor in bringing about the country's partition, had previously been treated by the Congress as little better than a pariah. That Indira, as Congress President, should authorize an alliance with the League was regarded as the ultimate in compromised principles. It shocked many, even among those who were apprehensive of another Communist victory in Kerala.

In the other major development during her stewardship of the Congress Party Indira displayed markedly greater highmindedness and sagacity. The year saw the partition of the bilingual state of Bombay into separate Gujarati- and Marathi-speaking states of Gujarat and Maharashtra. Indira's contribution to the making of that decision and the resulting end of a protracted period of bloody strife was no less significant than the dismissal of the Communists in Kerala and was accomplished to much less criticism.

When the boundaries of Indian states were reorganized in 1956 to provide a separate home for each of the fourteen languages recognized in the Constitution as official Indian languages, three exceptions were made: The claim of Punjabi speakers to a state of their own was overruled for strategic considerations, and the Gujarati and Marathi language states were denied because the protagonists could not agree to which of them the metropolis of Bombay should belong. The majority of the city's over 4 million residents were Marathi-speaking, but the bulk of its industry and commerce was controlled by Gujaratis. Although Maharashtrian anger over being denied a linguistic state erupted frequently into arson and bloody rioting, Nehru, with uncharacteristic obstinacy, stuck to the concept of a bilingual Bombay. As Congress President Indira realized that the party's opponents were exploiting the issue to alienate the public and that the next general election might cause its defeat. She also saw the pointlessness of preserving an arrangement that neither of the two constituents liked. The bilingual state's Chief Minister at the time, Y. B. Chavan, too, saw the wisdom of undoing the enforced unity. Between them Indira and Chavan persuaded a reluctant Jawaharlal to reverse what until then he had re-

Feroze Gandhi with one of his sons on his shoulder

The PM and Indira at breakfast early in Nehru's prime ministership

...and with Rajiv, Sanjay, and a favorite dog some years later at Chakrata, a hill station in North India

Prime Minister Nehru and Indira Gandhi with Madame Pandit on the *Maid of the Mist* at Niagara Falls during U.S. visit, 1949

... with Chou En-lai in China, 1954

... with Indonesia's Sukarno and Balinese relatives of his at the time of the Bandung Conference

...at a state dinner in New Delhi for Yugoslavia's President Tito and Madame Broz

...and with Vice-President Radhakrishnan (right) and Soviet leaders Khrushchev and Bulganin during the Russians' visit to India in late 1955

Indira Gandhi and Prime Minister Nehru with Jacqueline Kennedy during the U.S. President's wife's semi-official holiday in India, 1962

Indira Gandhi advising her ailing father during a Congress Party
meeting at Bhubaneshwar, 1964

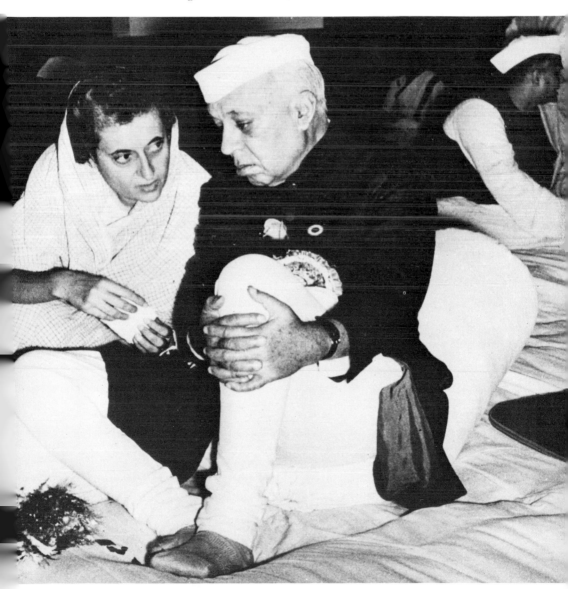

Indira Gandhi at the cremation of Prime Minister Nehru, May 1964. Beside her is Prime Minister Sirimavo Bandaranaike of Ceylon (now Sri Lanka).

garded as an irrevocable decision. Since their separation Gujarat and Maharashtra have been singularly free from linguistic tension, and the continuance of Gujarati investments in Bombay, which is located in Maharashtra, has created little conflict.

Her success as Congress President notwithstanding, Indira firmly turned down the offer by top party leadership of another term. The ostensible reason for her resolve to bow herself out of office was her double concern over the health of her husband, who had recently suffered a heart attack, and her father, who at seventy was beginning to show signs of advancing age. She had discovered during the eleven months of her Congress presidency that she needed to be away from home much more than she had realized she would. Undoubtedly, she felt she should spend as much time with Feroze and Jawaharlal as possible and be always within their call. But other considerations also undoubtedly influenced—perhaps unconsciously—her decision. As head of the organizational wing of the ruling party, she had found herself standing not behind Jawaharlal, as she had always done, but at times out in front of—and even confronting—him. On those occasions when she felt forced to prod him into action, her responsibilities as the party head seemed to him to deprive her action of the gentleness that Nehru expected of his daughter. Friends close to the household recall how her party position occasionally injected a new element of tension into Indira's relationship with her father. There was another problem: she herself seemed to suffer from a certain vague sense of inadequacy in the post. Not yet senior enough in the organization to run it the way she would have liked to, she recognized that much of the strength she enjoyed as Congress President derived from her proximity to Jawaharlal. And though Nehru's authority was unchallenged, under the canopy of his power there had grown several regional or provincial satraps with considerable scope to manage—or mismanage—politics in their own areas. With them Indira found herself unable to cope except when she could persuade her father to use his authority on her behalf. For a proud, self-willed person like Indira that must have been galling.

When Indira Gandhi was Congress President and even earlier, Jawaharlal Nehru undoubtedly tried to help his daughter gather experience and confidence and acquire a place in public life. What political father of a politically minded daughter would not? But did he connive at Indira's ultimate rise to the prime ministership? Did he, as some Indian politicians and writers have suggested, deliberately blur the line of succession and remove persons with stronger claims to succession in order to clear the path for Indira?

The charge that Nehru had a secret plan to install Indira in the direct line of succession appears in retrospect to have drawn its sustenance from a remark he reportedly made in 1961. In referring to a party wrangle over the election of a deputy leader, Nehru discouraged the belief that the post was a stepping stone to the prime ministership. The future leader, he said, "may well not emerge from within the parliamentary party and may be someone from outside." The background to this remark apparently was his often-expressed belief that in a democratic government a person could seldom be chosen as the future leader and appropriately groomed for the responsibility. Anthony Eden's failure as the British Prime Minister, despite his years of training under Churchill, was a case in point Nehru sometimes mentioned when he was ruminating on this subject. A leader was produced by a combination of diverse political and personal factors, many of which could not be foreseen, he would argue. His statement that a future leader might well be from outside the legislature was taken when he said it as indicative of his general philosophy of democratic government. Much later it came to be described as an inadvertent glimpse into his thinking regarding his "plans" for his daughter's future.

From time to time Nehru did deliberately muddy the waters somewhat on the issue of future leadership. But his objective appeared to be the solving of some immediate problems and aimed far more directly at setting back Morarji Desai's prospects than ensuring Indira's succession.

A man of acknowledged seniority in politics and the Congress Party, Desai had left the chief ministership of the important state of Bombay to come to Delhi as a senior member of Nehru's Cabinet, but he had never won the Prime Minister's trust and good will. The conservatism of his ideological beliefs, his supposed close links with big business, his self-righteousness and rigidity, and his personal quirks—he is not only a strong prohibitionist but also declines to be vaccinated or inoculated— kept Desai's relations with Nehru always cool. After Pant's death in 1961, Desai was the seniormost member of the government and the party and should normally have been entitled to the second position in the Cabinet, to Pant's portfolio of Home Affairs, and to deputy leadership of the Congress Parliamentary Party. He was given the second-ranking Cabinet position, but the Home portfolio, which traditionally carried enormous political prestige, went to Lal Bahadur Shastri. As for the deputy leadership of the party, when time came for the formal election, a serious challenge to Desai's claim developed unexpectedly and presumably with Nehru's blessing. In resolving the dispute, Nehru downgraded the post to such an extent that it was not worth Desai's while to fight for it. With the party choosing, at Nehru's bidding, not one but two rather nondescript members as its deputy leaders, Desai's claim to succeeding Nehru was weakened. Whether this move was designed to improve Indira's prospects in any way is doubtful.

Desai was deprived even of his place in the Cabinet two years later in 1963 through the implementation of the controversial Kamaraj Plan. The plan, named after Kumaraswami Kamaraj, who was later an assertive President of the Congress Party, was and is regarded by some of Nehru's critics as a Machiavellian device by which the Prime Minister eliminated from the government all those who could have had any claim to succeeding him and thus secured the post for his daughter. Nehru, of course, vehemently denied these insinuations and described them as the "most fantastic kind of motive hunting" on the part of his opponents. He did not need the camouflage of the Kamaraj Plan, he argued, for his mass support gave him the strength to discard any minister, however senior, from the government should he have wished to do so.

The origin of the plan was much more modest in intent than what evolved from it. Kamaraj, who had been Chief Minister of Madras for over a decade, had begun to notice disturbing signs of public disenchantment with the Congress. As a dedicated party member he wished to step down from ministerial office to devote himself exclusively to strengthening the organization and its links with the people. At the same period Biju Patnaik, the young Chief Minister of Orissa, whose brashness and unconventional approach to administration had just begun creating difficulties for him, also was anxious to quit office before his troubles became too serious. He clutched at Kamaraj's idea—of resignation in order to work at party problems—as an excellent solution of his own troubles. He traveled to Kashmir, where Nehru was holidaying that summer, to persuade him to extend its application to other state chief ministers and senior ministers in the central government. Nehru was receptive to the idea. He was himself eager to find some way to rid both his government and the Congress Party of the self-doubts and depression that had followed on India's swift and unexpected military humiliation in November 1962, when the Chinese had crossed the northern borders of Kashmir and Assam. Only timely American and British support and the sudden deliberate withdrawal of the Chinese had saved India from possible disaster. It had left many in the country, and especially in the Congress, demoralized.

From the discussion with Patnaik in Kashmir and a subsequent round of private talks with other party members later that summer in Hyderabad in Southern India, there emerged the full-blown Kamaraj Plan. Under it, ministers would be expected to resign to form a high-level cadre to devote themselves exclusively to the task of revitalizing their aging party.

The novel idea of voluntary renunciation of power fascinated the Indian public, and the announcement of the plan caused such enthusiasm that even Desai, who saw in it a sinister plot against him, and others like Desai had no option but to submit their resignations. Inevitably, Nehru was requested to make the final choice from among those who expressed a willingness to serve as saviors of the party. And out of what was a near avalanche of resignations he picked those of six central ministers and six state chief ministers—Desai among them.

The Kamaraj Plan was unusual and unconventional. But to suggest that it was conceived to promote Indira's chances of becoming Prime Minister is far-fetched. Reluctant as he always was to wield the knife, Nehru did undoubtedly use the Kamaraj Plan as a means of removing, without seeming harshness, what he regarded as the deadwood that his Cabinet had accumulated over the years, including certain individuals who had forfeited his confidence or whose reputations were tarnished. Furthermore, almost all the state chief ministers whose offer to renounce office was accepted were those against whom there were charges of corruption, nepotism, or highhandedness. And the plan harmed Desari's prospects only slightly. If in June of 1964, following Nehru's death on May 27, the party chose Lal Bahadur Shastri and not Desai as the new leader, it was because Shastri had all along enjoyed greater personal popularity and not because Desai had had to be without ministerial office a few months.

The fact that now seems most telling is that, at the time the Kamaraj Plan was implemented, Shastri was generally acknowledged most likely to succeed Nehru. Far from placing obstacles in his way, Nehru promoted Shastri's claim. Shastri had insisted on being allowed to quit the government along with other officials, but four months later Nehru persuaded him to return to the Cabinet. Nehru had suffered a mild paralytic attack at the beginning of the year. He needed someone to relieve him of some of his burdens. Significantly he did not accept, or even seriously consider, a suggestion by a dozen state chief ministers following his illness that Indira be appointed to the Cabinet as Foreign Minister. Instead, having recalled Shastri to the Cabinet, Nehru nominated him as his special adviser and assigned him tasks that kept him in the public eye and further burnished his image—surely a curious thing for him to do if, as was subsequently alleged, he had not long before incubated the Kamaraj Plan to ensure Indira's election as party leader and Prime Minister.

Another obvious indication of the fact that he was not conniving at Indira's succession can be seen in the attitude of indifference—almost of disdain—that Jawaharlal displayed towards most members of the "Syndicate," that close mutual association among five powerful regional leaders derisively nicknamed by the press. It was no secret that the Syndicate had existed for almost a year before Nehru's death and that it hoped to influence the choice of his successor. Yet Jawaharlal made no efforts—not even after his warning paralytic stroke—to mend fences with Syndicate members and secure their good will for Indira.

Kamaraj was the obvious leader of the Syndicate. Others in the group were Atulya Ghosh and S. K. Patil, acknowledged party bosses in West Bengal and Bombay city, respectively, and Sanjiva Reddy and S. Nijalingappa, who were the chief ministers of Andhra and Mysore. Similarity in temperament and political views had drawn them together. They were all strong and assertive regional satraps who maintained a tight grip on their own party machines and political power; all belonged to non-Hindi-speaking parts of the country and were conscious of the fact that none of them stood any chance of becoming Prime Minister himself. They had been in touch with each other for some time earlier and formed themselves into a deliberate if informal group in October 1963 when four of them met at Tirupathi in Andhra to contemplate the period after Nehru and devise their strategy as far as the choice of a successor. Their announced objective was to preserve party unity when the task of choosing a new leader had to be performed and ensure a smooth transition of authority from Nehru to someone who might not have the long-time leader's qualities and strength. It was a time when many were asking, with real worry, "After Nehru, what?" However, as the press was quick to note, the real reason they banded together was to bring into office someone pliant and beholden to them for election. They would then be the power behind the Prime Minister. Since each of them could influence the party MPs from his own state or area, their pooled influence, it was admitted, could be a decisive factor in the choice of Nehru's successor. Shastri realized that and went out of his way to cultivate the Syndicate and extend to its members much personal courtesy. He made no secret commitments to them, but if they believed that on being chosen Prime Minister he would be "their man" he did nothing to dispel that impression.

Nehru certainly was aware of the Syndicate's plans and motives. Consummate politician that he was, he could foresee the role that its members would play in the selection of the party leader after his death. If he had been anxious to strengthen Indira's chances of becoming Prime Minister, he should have tried to win them over, even though at least three of the five members of the Syndicate—Ghosh, Reddy, and Patil—were anathema to him. He made no such attempt. At his death, her extraordinary apprenticeship ended, Indira Gandhi stood alone.

PART III

Years of Power

7

Death and Succession

CHESTER Bowles, then U.S. Ambassador in India for the second time, called on Indira Gandhi two days after Jawaharlal Nehru's cremation. He found her noticeably averse to the idea of political office. What she would most like to do, she told the American who was an old, close friend, was "to drop everything and go to London for a few months to live with her sons." To an aunt, she even mentioned what she wanted to do on her return from London. She wanted to find a cottage in Dehra Dun or some other place in the foothills of the Himalayas and live quietly, she said.

As subsequent events showed, Indira's reluctance to take up the inevitable invitation to join the central government was short-lived. It was the result of her devastating grief over losing her father. Nehru's death, though far from sudden, had left her dazed. He had recovered from the stroke he had suffered in the beginning of the year, but it was obvious to everyone, including Indira, that his life was drawing to an end. He was old, bent, his face swollen, his eyes—always dark-circled—sunken. Yet, when it actually came, her father's death seemed to overwhelm and bewilder Indira, as if fate had struck a wholly unexpected blow.

The two had always been close. They had drawn even closer in the three years following Feroze's final heart attack. Immediately after Nehru's death, Indira, to the surprise of all, the satisfaction of many, and the consternation of some Indians, took it upon herself to arrange for a traditional Hindu funeral against Jawaharlal's express wish as stated in his will. He wanted only a nonreligious cremation. Whether at the last he had changed his mind or whether Indira decided that his choice was not the correct one, no one except herself knows or will say. The body was carried to the burning ghats on the sacred Jumuna, where priests intoned the ritual prayers as Jawaharlal's younger grandson, Sanjay, lit the funeral pyre. Indira, white-faced and perspiring in the hot, dust-laden May wind, stood with other family members in the forefront of an unending crowd of sophisticated and simple Indians that stretched out of sight from the ghats down the banks of the muddy river and away in the other direction to the heart of the city. That burst of duty, as she so unexpectedly saw it, done, Indira went into a period of silent withdrawal, tending to burst into tears every time a friend or relative tried offering condolences.

Before the monsoon rains had come to freshen the Indian capital, however, she had pulled herself together. As her grief abated, her earlier inclination to renounce politics and leave New Delhi also waned. Some of her relatives and family friends had been quietly urging her not to contemplate giving up politics. The work that her father had begun, to make India not just free but strong, needed her to help continue it, they argued. She must do her part. Only her wish to get away physically from India persisted for a time after she had reached a decision not to abjure politics. She really had wished to go live for a while with Sanjay and Rajiv, both of whom were then studying in Britain. To ponder her future plans away from Delhi's distracting atmosphere seemed wise as well as tempting. Also, as she reportedly mentioned to some friends, she felt that entering politics after a period of absence from India might discourage the public impression that she was there merely as her father's daughter.

Lal Bahadur Shastri, quickly chosen Prime Minister in Nehru's place, prevailed, however, persuading Indira to join his government as a senior minister though acquiescing in her insistence that she would actually assume office only after a month-long period of mourning for her father.

In dealing with Mrs. Gandhi at the time, the new Prime Minister was gentle and understanding. He did not, as was widely reported in the press, invite her to assume leadership of the party and become the country's Prime Minister instead of himself. If Indira had been in the running at the start, and with a reasonable chance of being elected leader, he probably would have supported her. But, in fact, her name had hardly figured in the party's initial inner councils. She lacked the strength to defeat Morarji Desai in an open contest. After Shastri had been duly chosen party leader and invited by the President to form the new government, he did call on Indira and remarked that he wished she had been chosen to succeed her father. But this was merely a courteous expression of Shastri's personal regard for her and not a plea for her to take over the party leadership.

Shastri did not suggest any specific portfolio for Indira in his government. He left the choice to her—although implicit in the offer was the understanding that she would not ask for Home, Defense, or Finance, already held by three senior members of the party whom Shastri would be loath to dislodge. She could have requested that she be appointed Foreign Minister. Nehru had held the portfolio in addition to being Prime Minister, and it could have been allocated to her without causing any powerful party member to take umbrage. Had she wanted it, it is unlikely that Shastri would have denied her wish. Instead, she asked for the Ministry of Information and Broadcasting because, as it was explained to the press, she was conscious of her administrative inexperience and preferred a relatively light charge for the time being. Shastri obliged her readily, ranked her fourth in the ministerial hierarchy (a ranking of honor for a new entrant to the government), and, as further demonstration of his consideration for her, included her in the prestigious and powerful Emergency Committee of the Cabinet.

Indira Gandhi's stay in Shastri's government was singularly unimpressive. Her lack of familiarity with administrative procedures turned out to be even greater and more of a handicap than she had imagined. In charge of a ministry that not only controlled the government's propaganda machinery but also held a complete monopoly on broadcasting in India, she had a powerful weapon in her hands. But somehow she had neither the skill nor, apparently, the motivation to use it effectively. Her contributions to the deliberations of the Cabinet, which met almost every week, were from all accounts small and inconsequential. At the meetings of the Emergency Committee, which were held much more frequently and at which most major decisions were taken, Indira often sat silently or merely asked some routine questions.

Her limited role in the government notwithstanding, Mrs. Gandhi was frequently in the news during this period. When Shastri floundered, as he appeared to almost continuously in the first year of his prime ministership, public attention at home and abroad inevitably turned to those who might be regarded as possible alternatives to his leadership. Indira Gandhi was by no means the most prominent among those who could claim the right to replace Shastri, but as the daughter of Jawaharlal she continued to receive public acclaim and notice out of all proportion to her lackluster political performance.

On two occasions during this period her performance, however, was worthy of note. Both gave a hint of the courage and decisiveness that she was to manifest later.

In January 1965, seven months after Shastri had assumed the prime ministership, the southern state of Madras witnessed large-scale lawlessness over the sensitive issue of replacement of English by Hindi as India's national official language. Under the Constitution the deadline for the complete change-over was set for January 26. The southern states had accepted the constitutional provision with marked reluctance. They regarded Hindi as the language of the north and feared that the planned exit of English, in which they had acquired considerable proficiency under the British, would further strengthen the northern states' hold over the central government and reduce other parts of the country to a relatively subservient position. As the day for the formal change in the status of English approached, agitation in the South increased rapidly. A few days before January 26 the Tamil-speaking state of Madras erupted in a frenzy of violence in which government buildings were burned down by the mob, railway tracks uprooted, all business came to a standstill, and demonstrators clashed extensively with police and troops. So strong were the public sentiments against what was regarded as the imposition of Hindi that two central ministers from the South, though personally close to Shastri, thought it politically expedient to offer their resignations from the government as a protest against the official language policy. Shastri was badly shaken by the vehemence and volume of the southern anger and the disunity within his own government. His capacity for conciliatory action was limited by the fact that as the country's chief executive—particularly as one who was previously criticized for weakness and vacillation—he could not afford to appear to be overawed by street violence. Also, since he himself hailed from Uttar Pradesh, the sanctum of Hindi fanaticism, his promises carried little conviction in the disturbed areas.

Unexpectedly, Indira took it upon herself to help resolve the crisis, even though the issue of official language as well as of law and order concerned the Ministry of Home Affairs and not Information and Broadcasting. She flew to Madras, arriving there at a time when it was unsafe for anyone from the North to walk the city's streets. The presence of a central minister was an invitation to the mob to renew its orgy of violence. Yet Indira seemed to have the opposite effect. Tempers began to cool. She talked to authorities as well as to leaders of the language agitation and was heard by both groups with attention. In her efforts to mollify the South, Indira remained within the periphery of what Shastri had publicly promised. But her words carried credibility, which the Prime Minister's own lacked. Like Shastri, she, too, belonged to Uttar Pradesh. The public, however, apparently did not associate her with any particular state or region. It must have been the first time that Indira felt the all-India mantle of her father brush her slender shoulders.

Within months she found herself involved in an even bigger crisis. In the previous few years her general health had improved markedly, but she was still bothered occasionally by a slipped disc, which necessitated her wearing a wide neck collar. The collar was particularly irksome in summer when Delhi's heat, first too dry, then too humid in the rainy season, caused perpetual chafing and irritation. In the beginning of August 1965, suffering from a bout of her old affliction, Indira decided to seek temporary relief by spending a few days in Kashmir. Her arrival in Srinagar, the state's capital in the famed beautiful valley of her ancestors, coincided with the beginning of the Pakistani attack on Kashmir—a development that culminated four weeks later in a full-scale war between the two countries.

Several thousand Pakistani armed military personnel had infiltrated into Kashmir from across the cease-fire line in the guise of tribal raiders. As was subsequently revealed, the Pakistani Government had hoped to catch India's security forces in Kashmir unawares and capture the coveted territory with the help of local supporters and sympathizers. At the time Indira's plane landed at Srinagar, the raiders were only a few miles from the capital and were moving purposefully towards the airport, the capture of which would have caused a serious military setback for India. Indira was advised to fly back to Delhi immediately as the Pakistanis were within shelling distance of the airport. She declined and instead drove to the city and went directly to the military control room then just established.

Kashmiri leaders and officials recall the resoluteness with which Indira faced the situation. They also remember that in the earlier stages of the situation her instinctive assessment of the magnitude of the Pakistani threat was noticeably more accurate than that of the central government, the military authorities, or even of the Central Intelligence Bureau. The latter believed, at least in the initial stages, that only a handful of Pakistani guerrillas had entered the state and that they might achieve nothing more than some disruption in communications and cause some public nervousness. Indira insisted that the assault was much more serious. Pakistan, she argued, would not organize something small and "liable to explode in its face." The number of raiders would be large and, if necessary, their infiltration would, she felt sure, be backed by less covert Pakistani involvement in the plan. One of the topmost state officials, who was himself deeply concerned with the situation, later confessed that Indira's instinct proved infallible. Besides attending all emergency deliberations of the Kashmir cabinet, she was in constant touch with Shastri in Delhi and was able to communicate to him the gravity of the situation and warn him about its possible escalation into a regular war.

Pakistan's assessment of the inadequacy and unpreparedness of Indian security in Kashmir was correct. But the Muslim nation exaggerated the readiness with which the Kashmiri people would rise in its support. A considerable number of Kashmiris, particularly those living in Srinagar, were emotionally drawn to Pakistan. Such elements would possibly have come to the help of the raiders and even challenged India's control of the valley if they had known about the real extent of the Pakistani attack or if rumormongers had succeeded in creating the impression that Pakistani victory was more or less assured. As Minister of Information and Broadcasting, Indira saw the importance of keeping up morale and influencing the public mind appropriately. She was anxious to see for herself how Kashmiris, especially in areas known to be hostile to India, were reacting to the development. When Kashmir's Chief Minister, G. M. Sadiq, frowned upon her plans to visit areas of Pakistani sympathy in the city for reasons of her personal security, Indira tried to persuade the director of Radio Kashmir, an official of her own ministry, to drive her in his own car through such parts of Srinagar. She also drew heavily from her own experience as the nonofficial chairman of the Citizens' Committee during the Chinese attack in 1962, when public morale in India was particularly low, prodding the state's noticeably reluctant leadership to organize citizens' committees in all parts of the city and in areas exposed to Pakistani attack or propaganda. Besides discouraging exaggerated and unnerving accounts of what the raiders had done, these bodies gave Kashmiris a sense of involvement in the conflict and had the effect of isolating the pro-Pakistan elements. By the end of her "holiday," when Indira returned to Delhi, the Pakistani plan to annex Kashmir through infiltration by guerrillas had failed. Its frustration prompted Pakistan's rulers to deploy more conventional military means, a development for which India had had prior warning. Shastri made no secret of his appreciation for the role Indira had played in the situation.

Shastri's praise for Indira following the Madras and Kashmir crises and the mutual cooperation and cordiality that the two occasions represented were the exception, not the rule, in the relationship that developed between the two during his prime ministership.

As he once told an Indian journalist, Shastri invited Indira to join his Cabinet because he regarded her presence there as "a tribute to Nehru's memory." Indira confessed to the same reporter that she accepted the invitation because she believed her association with the government would give it stability. These two views of the matter are not identical, but they do not necessarily presage mutual conflict or tension. When Nehru suffered his stroke some months before his death and it was suggested that Shastri should end his "renunciation of power" and return to the Cabinet to assist Nehru, Indira favored the move. Genuine warmth and respect for Shastri were reciprocated by him. Shastri's presence in the government at the time of Nehru's death gave him a decided advantage over his rivals in the succession battle. Indira could have easily obstructed his return but did not. As for Shastri's sentiments towards Indira, he was so moved by her sorrow over her father's death that in his acceptance speech to the party following his election a reference to her brought him to tears.

Undercurrents of tension and distrust, however, had begun to affect their relationship within weeks of Indira's entry into the government. Perhaps both of them entered into the association with mental reservations. Besides her anxiety to lend stability to Shastri's government, Indira's decision to give up her intention to visit Britain and join the Cabinet may have been influenced by the realization that after some months there might be no place for her in the government or even in Parliament. She must have noted how the political prospects of several powerful politicians had shriveled up when they were obliged under the Kamaraj Plan to give up ministerial office. Her own father, whose mass popularity had been a modern-day phenomenon, frequently expressed his intention to leave the government but never actually risked doing so. Shastri probably had his own reasons, too, for wanting to have Indira in his Cabinet from the outset. As a member of the government, her actions would be circumscribed by customary parliamentary discipline and her own sense of propriety; outside the Cabinet, she could provide a rallying point for elements opposed to Shastri. Desai had been frustrated but not routed, and in time he and his supporters, Shastri probably feared, might join forces with Indira for Shastri's overthrow.

Unlike Desai, who tended to wear his heart on his sleeve, Shastri was remarkably taciturn and seldom gave expression to his true sentiments about a person or a situation. Nevertheless, some of his actions combined with chance remarks to a few trusted friends and confidants indicated that fairly soon after assuming the prime ministership he came to regard Indira as a potential rival—perhaps his most serious rival. Shastri understood that Desai belonged to an era that had very nearly ended. His prospects of becoming Prime Minister declined with every passing day. Others in the party, such as the members of the Syndicate, though somewhat younger in years than Desai, lacked the image of personal rectitude and integrity that the Indian people demanded of their top leader. Indira, however, belonged to the new generation of leaders, for whom the future held much promise.

Shastri was also anxious to step out of the shadow of the Nehrus. He had thrived under the umbrella of Jawaharlal's trust and good will, but as Prime Minister, he felt, he must acquire a standing of his own. If close association with the Nehru family helped his rise in politics, doubtless it must also have left Shastri with feelings that surfaced as a noticeable inferiority complex. Certain actions on the part of Indira, and of her aunts, did little to assuage Shastri's feelings that they looked down upon him and resented the fact that he had stepped into Jawaharlal's shoes. Besides being of a lower caste, Shastri came from a poor family. He suspected that Indira's family, Brahmins and aristocrats that they were, remained unwilling at heart to accept him as Prime Minister and party leader.

When, following his election as Nehru's successor, the question arose of his moving into the stately official residence of the Prime Minister that Nehru had chosen for the purpose and occupied for seventeen years, Shastri himself was disinclined to occupy the house. Other considerations apart, his life style was still so humble that he believed he would feel uncomfortable and awkward in a big house built in the regal style of the Raj. Some newspapers suggested that the house be converted into a memorial for Nehru (it now houses the Nehru Museum and Library), and Shastri seemed to favor the idea. However, before he could make up his mind in the matter, he received a blunt—almost rude—letter from Jawaharlal's younger sister, Krishna Hutheesing, suggesting that his living in the same house in which the great departed leader had lived would be unpardonable presumption on his part. Indira's other aunt, Vijayalakshmi Pandit, lashed out against Shastri in Parliament and derisively described him as being "a prisoner of indecision." Indira herself assailed Shastri vehemently three months after he took over and at a party forum accused him of abandoning her late father's policies and program.

Shastri, whose feelings of personal inadequacy had been compounded by a mild heart attack that he suffered within a month of his election, saw these attacks on him as the Nehru family's rejection of him and part of what he began to suspect was its endeavor to put Indira in his place. From almost the very start of his term, therefore, he appeared anxious to isolate Indira politically and to ensure that she would not grow into a formidable rival. Following his heart attack, when he was unable to travel to London to attend the annual Commonwealth Prime Ministers' Conference, he asked Indira to represent India at the prestigious gathering—but not alone. With her he sent T. T. Krishnamachari, his strong assertive Finance Minister, in whose presence it was impossible for a ministerial novice like Indira to shine. And although he was truly appreciative of Indira's help in resolving the crisis over language, her action in rushing to Madras at the same time strengthened his suspicion that she regarded her mandate as larger than that of a minister and was trying to build a national following. He seldom consulted her in important official or party matters. As this fact became generally known, politicians drifted away from her, and as he consolidated his hold on the government, Indira's sense of neglect and bitterness in turn increased.

The unbending stand that Shastri took in the face of Pakistan's challenge over Kashmir and India's success in the war that followed greatly increased the Prime Minister's stature. It dwarfed others around him, including Indira. Only a few weeks before Shastri's sudden death in Tashkent from heart failure at the beginning of 1966, it was rumored in Delhi that Indira was proposing to leave her Cabinet post and accept the relatively lower position of India's High Commissioner in London. This Commonwealth post would have taken her, with the status of ambassador, back to the city of which she was so fond. The report was totally without foundation, but the fact that it gained wide currency and seemed credible reflected the decline in Indira's position.

Seldom have a politician's fortunes risen as dramatically as Indira's did in the first few days of January 1966. On December 31, 1965, three days before proceeding to Tashkent to negotiate a peace treaty with Pakistan's President Ayub, Shastri made a major change in the Cabinet. He virtually dismissed the Finance Minister, T. T. Krishnamachari, and quickly nominated a successor. Krishnamachari was a senior and assertive member of the government. He was also influential, inasmuch as he enjoyed the personal support of the party President, Kumaraswami Kamaraj. His exit was liable to have repercussions within the Congress Parliamentary Party, for he had many admirers as well as detractors. Before making the change Shastri consulted the Home Minister, G. L. Nanda, but not Indira. Indira, in fact, learned of Shastri's decision only when it was announced to the press. She regarded that as the ultimate humiliation. To a party associate who called on her that evening, Indira spoke bitterly of how Shastri had steadily isolated her and how little she counted for in the Cabinet and the party. Little did she know that night that in less than three weeks she herself would be the country's Prime Minister.

Her uncanny shrewdness in judging the mood in the party and devising strategy to harmonize with it undoubtedly facilitated her unexpected elevation. But she was also remarkably lucky. A number of circumstances combined to make her success possible.

The suddenness of Shastri's death in Tashkent a few hours after he had signed the controversial but important agreement with Pakistan was the most important factor in the situation. Before he left for Tashkent, his popularity at home was at its peak. The firmness with which he had faced the challenge from Pakistan and the measure of military success that India had achieved in the war had won Shastri national acclaim. Instead of inviting derisive laughter, as it had previously, the appearance in a newsreel of his puny figure caused cinema audiences to burst into prolonged cheers. A few weeks before he died, nearly a million residents of Bombay had turned up to hear him at a political rally—an indication of personal popularity that even Jawaharlal had ceased to enjoy in the latter years of his life. If he had lived, he could not easily have been dislodged. Indira would have sunk deeper in frustration and isolation—or, more probably, removed herself, as a part of her had wished after her father's death, from the Indian scene.

But by itself Shastri's passing away would not have assured Indira's election as his successor. As in 1964 Desai was there to stake his claim to the prime ministership on the basis of seniority. A plot hatched by what he contemptuously called "a caucus" had denied him his right after Nehru's death. Now that Shastri was no more, he felt confident of being chosen party leader. Conscious of his seniority in national politics, he had declined to serve under Shastri, but, remarkably, though he had been out of office for nearly thirty months, he continued to enjoy the loyal support of a sizable section of the parliamentary party. His claim to seniority as well as his position in the party was thus fairly strong. Normally, he should have been chosen the new leader with no more than some routine opposition. But neither his failure in his earlier attempt nor the fact that he had been out of power for a fairly long spell had mellowed Desai noticeably. He had not forgiven Kamaraj and others whom he considered responsible for depriving him of his due in 1964. Far from building any bridges with the Syndicate during Shastri's term in office, Desai continued to speak of its members with unconcealed contempt and hostility. He also retained his reputation for obstinacy in thinking and unwillingness to share power with anyone else. Thus, from almost the moment that the news of Shastri's death reached Delhi, the Syndicate launched its efforts to keep Desai out of office once again. A seemingly meek and gentle person like Shastri had dexterously curtailed the Syndicate's influence; someone like Desai, with his reputation for personal abrasiveness and selfishness in the exercise of power, would reduce them, Kamaraj and his associates feared, to a state of utter political impotence.

The question before the party leadership, therefore, was not who would make the *best* Prime Minister but who was most likely to gather a sufficient number of party backers to defeat Desai. A quick look that the Syndicate took at itself was discouraging. Though adept in behind-the-scenes maneuvering, none of its members enjoyed anything but regional support. Even Kamaraj, well-known as he was, could not command national attention because he spoke neither Hindi nor English. Some others had unsavory public reputations. As for candidates outside the Syndicate, Y. B. Chavan, who had left the chief minister-ship of Maharashtra to become Defense Minister when Krishna Menon was dismissed, still had a strong base in his home state, but support for him from other parts of the country was negligible. G. L. Nanda, who on Shastri's death became acting Prime Minister for the second time, advanced his claim with considerable vigor, but he lacked even re-gional support, and to most in the party his exertions to win support for his candidacy seemed almost comical. It was a simple process of elimination, rather than any positive preference for her, that led the Syndicate to Indira. She was Jawaharlal's daughter. She was nationally known and invited no special antagonism from any region or party fac-tion. All those who were apprehensive of Desai in power for reasons either of his imperiousness, acerbity, or ideological conservatism could be persuaded to unite behind Mrs. Gandhi. What additionally en-deared her to the Syndicate at that stage was her limited experience in running the government and the fact that as Minister for Information and Broadcasting she had been unassertive, almost ineffective. There can be little question but that Kamaraj and other members of the Syn-dicate felt confident that, if chosen leader, Indira, of all possible candi-dates, would be the one least likely to try to break free from their halter.

The news of Shastri's death had reached the Indian capital at about 3 A.M. Within an hour a small group of friends and confidants had assembled at Indira's modest government house on Safdarjang Road to consider the development. About half a dozen who gathered there were those who for various reasons—personal or political—had stayed near her when her future had seemed unpromising. Indira had not summoned them at that early hour of the morning; they had arrived on their own, just as other politicians and friends were assembling at that very time at the residences of other factional leaders. At the informal meeting, as the early Indian dawn began to break and the crows to chatter loudly in the *neem* trees, the possibility and desirability of Indira's seeking the prime ministership began to be clearly visualized. And that morning Indira offered her friends and followers the first glimpse of her unerring instinct for devising political strategy.

It was an instinct, a gift of inheritance, perhaps, that greatly helped her subsequent rise to supreme power. Willing though she was to make the bid for succession, she cautioned her friends against any display of excessive or premature eagerness. She reminded them of the damage Desai had caused his prospects in 1964 by staking his claim before the appropriate time and aggressively, publicly announcing his candidacy and behaving at Nehru's funeral as if he were all but chosen—to the outrage of many in the party. Desai, she was sure, would once again proclaim his right to be the leader. So would Nanda. She should not enter the ring as long as the two of them were involved in what would be an unseemly brawl. She, in fact, should, as far as possible, not appear to be seeking the office. The office should come seeking her.

This is exactly how the situation developed in the following few days. Desai let it be known almost immediately that he was a candidate. He rejected with unconcealed anger a suggestion by the party's top executive body that as in 1964 the new leader be chosen on the basis of a consensus. He saw in the proposal another devious attempt to deny him his rightful place at the top. On the earlier occasion Kamaraj had individually consulted members and then declared that the majority favored Shastri. Kamaraj was authorized to follow this peculiar procedure because it was felt an open contest between Shastri and Desai might divide the party when it needed unity badly. While bowing to the verdict, Desai did not accept that it had been reached fairly and honestly. He was not prepared to be victimized again and so ended the consensus move by declaring his firm resolve to contest the decision, come what may. Nanda, who had been sworn in as acting Prime Minister, asserted that he should be confirmed in the post.

He had ranked as No. 2 in the Cabinet under Nehru and Shastri, he had acted as Prime Minister twice, his association with the Congress Party was of long standing, and his ideology was impeccable. Why should he not be chosen leader? he asked. For a while the Syndicate —or at least some of its members—toyed with the idea of supporting Nanda but gave that up quickly. Few felt sure of his being able to defeat Desai. Some in the party proposed that Kamaraj, though not a member of Parliament, be drafted as leader, but Kamaraj, conscious of his limitations, shrank from the thought. Several other names were considered and quickly discarded. Both Desai and Nanda meanwhile kept announcing loudly and repeatedly their determination to fight it out.

While this acrimonious debate and noisy search for a suitable candidate was going on, Indira stood decorously in the wings. Her low-profile strategy was so effective that most political reporters in Delhi did not even mention her name as a possible aspirant for several days. Those who did so tended to place her name fairly near the bottom in a long list of candidates.

Not until the fifth day of the hectic party confabulations did Kamaraj turn decisively to Indira with the suggestion that she be the new leader. Office, as she had hoped, had come seeking her. Her house, which had previously often worn a somewhat deserted look, suddenly became the principal—and a very crowded—center of political activity. Kamaraj was right in his assessment of her ability to unite behind her the majority of the party members. Desai's opponents, who could not persuade themselves to back Nanda or Kamaraj or Chavan, seemed to endorse her candidacy readily. They were joined by many whose devotion to Nehru had not abated during the twenty months since his funeral. Prodded by Kamaraj, the chief ministers of ten states where the Congress Party was in office publicly supported her nomination. Their joint statement was a virtual directive to MPs elected from those states to vote for Indira. Her success, should a contest be held, was assured.

Even after accepting Kamaraj's plea and announcing her candidacy, Indira continued to act in a reserved, diffident manner. She had joined the battle, but she studiously avoided raising needless dust. She made no tall claims about her strength in an attempt to influence the undecided elements, as Desai and his associates had done. Nor would she bandy words with her challengers or speak harshly or disdainfully about them even in private conversation. Her attitude was that the Congress President had urged her to offer herself for leadership and she had agreed because she felt it was her duty to do so.

When the ten chief ministers supported Indira, Nanda saw the writing on the wall and quit the race. His ambition unfortunately deprived his action of grace, for he quietly tried to pitch Chavan against Indira by insinuating to him that Indira's election would ruin Chavan's prospects of becoming Prime Minister for all time to come. Indira was irritated by Nanda's clumsy maneuver (it amounted to little), but she did not show it. Then, a day before the party was due to meet to elect its leader, Nanda, despite his earlier action, went to Indira to inquire if she would withdraw her candidacy and support him in the interest of party unity. Although she had good reason to be angered by the demand and appalled by the man's overwhelming personal ambition, Indira merely told him politely that she would be with him if others in the party would back him.

A posture of calm dignity over Desai's verbal attacks was relatively more difficult, but Indira succeeded in maintaining it. Desai regarded the chief ministers' endorsement of Indira's candidacy as an attempt to coerce MPs into voting for her, and he said so in a press statement. "I hope Members of Parliament are mature enough to exercise their vote in the national interest," he remarked. He sent a long letter to each member urging him not to succumb to pressure and followed it up with personal telephone calls to most of them. He turned down Kamaraj's appeal to him on the eve of the party meeting to desist from contesting Indira's nomination and sarcastically told press reporters that while he was "the MPs' candidate," Indira was the "Congress President's candidate." Indira issued no rejoinders.

It took the 526 members of the Congress Party in the two houses of Parliament nearly four hours to cast their ballots and have them counted under the close supervision of the representatives of both candidates. As expected, Indira won convincingly, securing 355 votes against Desai's 169. (Two ballots were declared invalid.) Thousands of Indians had gathered outside the circular, red-stone Parliament House with its massive Roman pillars to associate themselves with an event that, although it was no surprise, had a distinct touch of history about it. India had chosen its first woman Prime Minister and demonstrated the catholicity of its political institutions.

8

Victory and Survival

·

W ESTERN politicians and reporters, men and women alike,
representing what are supposed to be economically advanced
and socially emancipated societies, can seldom conceal their
puzzlement over the fact that a conservative, tradition-bound people
like the Indians should have chosen a woman to rule their country.
When foreign visitors inquire—and few seem to resist doing so—of
Prime Minister Gandhi if her being a woman handicaps her in the
exercise of her authority, she assures them, sometimes with a faint
touch of irritation, that "I have not yet come across a problem or a
situation where sex would have made a difference."

In India few objected to her election as leader on grounds of her sex;
Indians were accustomed to seeing women occupy positions of prestige
and authority. During the years of the extensive freedom movement
thousands of them had gone to jail, and at early periods in its history
two of them had been chosen President of the Congress Party. After
independence several held Cabinet or other senior ministerial posts in
the central government and in the states. Well before Indira became
Prime Minister, India had three woman governors—the states they presided over were among the largest in the country and politically the
most volatile—and her own home state of Uttar Pradesh had been
ruled by a woman Chief Minister.

But though few questioned Indira's right to be chosen Prime Minister or her capacity for success in that post for the reason of being a

woman, many in India did entertain certain serious nonsexist doubts about her being adequately equipped and trained to hold that high office. Did a year as Congress President and less than two as Information Minister give her the political wisdom and administrative experience she needed to make even a modest go of her new job? In choosing her as leader had not the party been influenced unduly by its attitude of near veneration for her late father? Was it fair to the country or indeed to Indira to elect her as Prime Minister for the negative reason that that was the only way to keep Desai out of power? Many in India's always vocal press and some even in the party itself agonized over these and other similar questions.

No reassuring answer was available for several months after Indira assumed office. Paradoxically, the initial period of her administration was noted not so much for her strength as for her weakness, not for her decisiveness but for her vacillation, even though during her first year as Prime Minister she was called upon to make several complex decisions and made them with a swiftness and firmness that her father had not been capable of even at his most powerful. Some of these decisions were in fact made with such breathtaking speed that many in India doubted if she had really fully grasped their implications. The problem was that her occasional demonstrations of self-confidence and decisiveness were followed by distressing evidence of a co-existing sense of insecurity and lack of political poise.

The way Indira chose her first Cabinet was perhaps typical of the contrasting, even contradictory, facets of her personality at the time. As the leader of the majority party in Parliament, she had the right to form a Cabinet comprising members of the Congress Parliamentary Party who enjoyed her personal trust. Neither Kamaraj, who headed the organizational wing of the party, nor Dr. Sarvepalli Radhakrishnan, the country's constitutional chief of state, had any authority to interfere with her choice or exert any direct or indirect pressure on her in the matter. After five days of consultations, during which she met Kamaraj several times, Indira made up her mind about the composition of her government. She dropped Law Minister A. K. Sen and Petroleum Minister Humayun Kabir from the Cabinet. Both had been in the central government for a long time, but their contributions were generally agreed to be small. Neither Nehru nor Shastri somehow had been willing to wield the knife, owing, presumably, to long personal association with the two. Indira's own relations with Kabir and Sen had been reasonably cordial but not as close, and she resolved to do what her predecessors had been loath to do. She also decided to bring into the government several persons of her own choice. Some of those she appointed to the Cabinet were not even members of Parliament, and their inclusion created the awkward problem of getting them elected to the central legislature within six months by persuading two of the existing legislators to vacate their seats for them. All this and the cumbersome task of allocating the major portfolios was accomplished quickly and in a businesslike manner. On the afternoon of January 23, 1966, she began the final process of conveying her decisions to the people concerned. All those who were being discarded, included, or elevated were called to her house individually and informed of what she had resolved to do. Kabir was angry and spoke emotionally of his services to the national cause and of the consideration he always received from her father. Indira was unmoved. Sen, surprised at his exclusion, said so bluntly, but Indira did not relent even when he disdainfully declined her offer of a senior ambassadorship.

Yet before the new Prime Minister's task was completed that night, her resoluteness was completely overshadowed by her vulnerability to pressures. Apparently irritated by G. L. Nanda's display of excessive personal ambition and the fact that, because of his close associations with astrologers and *sadhus* he had acquired a rather comical image, Indira had concluded that she should relieve her Home Minister of his portfolio. In this position, Nanda was the central government's link with the states, was responsible for law and order, and controlled all principal cadres of civil servants as well as the department of domestic intelligence. Traditionally, the Home Minister was next in prestige and power only to the Prime Minister, and several others with stronger support in the party than Nanda yearned for the job. Indira decided to attempt to compensate Nanda for his loss of the Home portfolio by letting him retain his highest ranking among ministers, though only as minister without portfolio. Additionally, she offered him the largely honorific post of the Leader of the House in the Lok Sabha. Nanda greeted Indira's decision and accompanying sops with expected agitation and immediately rushed to Kamaraj and, later, to Radhakrishnan to complain about the injustice being done to him. Both intervened on his behalf. After they had made several telephone calls, Indira capitulated and agreed to allow Nanda to continue as Home Minister in her government. Similar parleys also went on between her and Kamaraj over the inclusion of another former senior minister, Jagjiwan Ram. Nehru had dropped Jagjiwan from his government in 1963 under the Kamaraj Plan ostensibly to work for the party but in reality, many suspected, because of persistent allegations of corruption against him. In the contest for party leadership Ram had initially supported Desai and changed sides only at the last moment. Indira now was opposed to including him in her Cabinet and thereby seeming to reward him for his perfidious behavior towards Desai. But Kamaraj prevailed in this as in the matter of Nanda, and Jagjiwan Ram was given a post. Thanks to these outside interventions, Indira's Cabinet-making, which had started as a swift, smooth, impressive operation, acquired a bizarre, chaotic look as the night of January 23 turned into January 24. Instead of driving to Rashtrapati Bhavan in the early evening to formally submit to the President her list of ministers, as was originally planned and traditional, it was almost 3 A.M. when Indira emerged from her study to fulfill the routine obligation. To scores of newsmen and party workers present at her house as that night wore on, her pale, pinched look told a tale of political browbeating, not of a leader's strength and assertiveness.

Some of her other decisions following on the formation of the government, too, were a curious blend of firmness and hesitancy on her part, of aggressiveness offset by a tendency to succumb to pressure. Even her closest party colleagues were often bewildered by her shifts in behavior and did not know exactly what to make of her in the role of national leader. And many of those who applauded her decisiveness —on dividing the border state of Punjab, on devaluing Indian currency, in confronting conservative Hindus over a ban on cow slaughter—also seemed to doubt the quintessential soundness of her judgment or to suspect that she had made her decisions at others' bidding.

The most controversial of her decisions, the devaluation of the rupee, was announced in the beginning of June 1966. The issue had been debated for almost a year. In the public mind the proposed devaluation had come to be associated with U.S. pressure on India exerted indirectly, but nevertheless mercilessly, through the World Bank and International Monetary Fund. Shastri had resisted such devaluation for some time. What was not known generally was that shortly before his death he had begun to recognize the unavoidability of lowering the value of the rupee; many of India's exports were being heavily subsidized by the government and what stood in the way of a formal devaluation were only certain rather intangible political considerations. Indira agreed to end this artificial situation. Less than six months after becoming Prime Minister, she had the daring to announce a whopping 57 per cent reduction in the international value of Indian currency. Her move was influenced by two considerations. First, she reasoned that by ordering devaluation fairly soon after assuming the prime ministership, she would seem to be tackling a problem created by the economic policies of the previous government and as such would not be blamed for the harshness of the remedy. Second, she felt it was better to take one large step towards the solution of the problem than a series of tiny ones. If devaluation was to be accepted, the extent of it, she reasoned, should be adequate.

In her calculations, however, she appeared to overlook the assertiveness of men like Kamaraj, the touchiness of the Indian public, the inadequacies of her economic advisers, and the danger of depending on the monsoon to assure a good crop year. Kamaraj, whose own understanding of economic matters was rather limited, denounced the decision as hasty and foolish. Outside the government as he was, he could not be consulted in advance on a top-secret matter like devaluation, but as the party's "king-maker" he apparently had expected that the woman he thought he had made king would clear important policy matters with him before they were announced. Also, as the ruling party's chief organizer, he considered it political folly for Mrs. Gandhi to take a decision as controversial as that of devaluation on the eve of preparations for the general election due in February 1967. India's vocal opposition parties and press also were distressed and suspected a surrender to U.S. pressure. Had not the Prime Minister visited Washington only two months earlier and been royally feted by President Johnson? they asked suggestively. Nature, too, acted perversely. The rains had failed in 1965; there was no sign of them again in the summer of 1966 in those weeks following devaluation when the monsoon normally breaks. That created a phenomenon that had not been witnessed in a century—two consecutive years of drought. As a result, agricultural production was so sharply reduced as to knock the bottom out of Indian exports. Finally, the Prime Minister's economic experts, who tended to regard devaluation as a complete cure, neglected to visualize and arrange for the various executive decisions that must quickly follow an announcement about devaluation in any country. Indira never acknowledged any faulty judgment in the matter of devaluation. But the extensive criticism—some of it justified—made her wonder if her timing was right.

Her bold decision to divide the state of Punjab, announced within weeks of her appointment as Prime Minister, was, like devaluation, to have its importance obscured by the widespread public belief that it had been taken hastily and under political duress.

After 1959, when Bombay was divided into Marathi- and Gujarati-speaking states, Punjabi was the only one of the fourteen official Indian languages without a home of its own. The Sikhs who inhabit Punjab and speak Punjabi had agitated vigorously for a linguistic state, but unsuccessfully; numerous economic and geographical reasons had been advanced against a Punjabi-speaking state. Behind such arguments was the unstated fear that acceptance of the Sikh demand would create on India's sensitive border with Pakistan a small state inhabited by a community whose religious sentiments might be exploited by Pakistan to generate political turmoil. Many in the government also believed that a Punjabi-speaking state would soon lead to a Sikh demand for secession from India. Indira did not subscribe to these fears —and subsequent developments proved her judgment to be right. But great furor followed the announcement of her government's willingness to demarcate a Punjabi-speaking state. The issue had aroused sharp, often violent, controversy in the area concerned, and the previous governments had clashed many times over it with the Akali Dal, the militant right-wing Sikh party. Indira's decision to concede the demand was wise, but she had neglected to prepare the public for it. The departure from the past governments' stubborn refusal to allow a change was so sudden that many people believed she had acted in panic in the face of an Akali threat of renewed agitation. Few seemed to recall that she had been the one largely instrumental in persuading Jawaharlal in 1959 to concede the linguistic states for Marathi and Gujarati. Even most members of the Cabinet and top leaders of the party did not regard her move as a sagacious one. A panel under Kamaraj at the party level and a Cabinet committee headed by Home Minister Nanda, both set up not long before the decision to study the question, doubted seriously the wisdom of the action and went along with the Prime Minister's view with known reluctance.

In November of that increasingly troublesome year of 1966 Indira dismissed Nanda. The sacking of the Home Minister came in the wake of rather fierce agitation in the country by conservatives among the Hindus for a total ban on cow slaughter. In deference to the religious sentiments of the Hindus, who regard the cow as sacred, the Indian Constitution included protection for the animal among its Directive Principles but left it to the state legislatures to enact the necessary laws to ban cow slaughter. Encouraged by the Prime Minister's seeming vulnerability to pressures, thought to have been demonstrated by her apparent surrender to the Sikhs, certain of the more fanatic groups among the Hindus launched their agitation for an immediate, nationwide ban on cow slaughter. The agitators were undoubtedly emboldened by the fact that *sadhus* (holy men) and other archaic elements in Hinduism held a strange fascination for Nanda. They felt sanguine he would deal with the movement with sympathy and lenience. Guru Shankracharya, the head priest of the famous temple in Orissa at Puri, who is traditionally held in great reverence by the Hindus, started a fast unto death in support of the demand. His fast gave tremendous fillip to the agitation. Should he be allowed to die, his death was expected to cause extensive disorders in the country. While maintaining a firm stance outwardly, Indira watched the situation with considerable nervousness and was dissuaded from making the concession only by a group of senior civil servants who were convinced that the Shankracharya would not let himself die. The high-water mark of the agitation came on November 8, when thousands of *sadhus,* some in saffron robes, some naked, marched on Parliament House. So massive was their invasion that several of them were killed and many injured in a clash with the police. It was that evening that Indira asked for Nanda's resignation. In her view his association with the *sadhus* had hampered him in the performance of his duty as the Home Minister.

Nanda's dismissal had a sobering effect on the Hindu zealots, but it added to Indira's private difficulties with Kamaraj and the Syndicate. The Congress President had close and friendly relations with Nanda and regarded his expulsion as a personal challenge. Shastri in the last few months of his life had greatly reduced Kamaraj's influence in the party and over the government. The Syndicate was determined that it should not suffer the same fate at Indira's hands. Its members, therefore, were assertive and demanding from the start, permitting Indira only a portion of the freedom of action that was rightfully hers as Prime Minister. They frequently gave her subtle—and sometimes not so subtle—reminders that she owed her election as leader to their support and that she needed their continued good will to be able to hold that office. S. K. Patil, a Syndicate member whom Indira had included in the Cabinet as Railway Minister, openly described her government as a "collective leadership" arrangement. He was particularly irked by Nanda's dismissal because the important Home portfolio went to Chavan, who was Patil's detractor in the politics of their home state of Maharashtra.

Besides the Syndicate's Shylockian insistence on its pound of flesh, what contributed heavily to Indira's continued lack of poise and self-assurance throughout most of 1966 were the vicious attacks to which she was subjected in Parliament. She often cut a poor figure in the legislative halls those days, appearing as a shy and indifferent speaker with little capacity for quick repartee or a stern snub as a means of coping with hecklers. Indeed, when heckled—and she often was—she tended to lose the thread of her speech and get confused.

The opposition parties in the Indian Parliament have always participated in all debates more aggressively than their size would seem to justify, but in 1966 there were elements in both chambers that, besides being vocal, lacked all regard for parliamentary decorum and bore a strong personal animosity towards the Nehru family. Dr. Ram Manohar Lohia, leader of the Socialist group, used his considerable histrionic talents to ridicule Indira personally whenever opportunity arose. Some of his associates in the Lok Sabha were sometimes almost vulgar in their attacks on her and the government. In the upper house another Socialist member, Raj Narain Singh, would even disrupt proceedings with his attempts to hurl taunts, abuse, and allegations at Indira. He once alleged that she had accepted a mink coat from the Soviet Government when she accompanied her father to Moscow on a state visit. India's legislature is in session for about eight months in the year, and the Prime Minister is required to face it almost daily. For Indira every appearance in the first year of her prime ministership was a personal ordeal that left her shaky and unnerved.

It was inevitable that India's third Prime Minister, forty-eight years old, a widow, bereft of the father whose advice had always sustained her, conscious of her inadequate experience, harassed by demanding supporters, and badgered by unscrupulous opponents should tend at the beginning of her years at power to lean on a group of trusted friends for solace, self-confidence, and occasional advice. Those who gathered round her were derisively called by the press and the public her "kitchen Cabinet," and most of its members were self-appointed. They changed frequently, and they lacked any common ideological affiliation. The size of the group varied with the fluctuations in Indira's sense of insecurity.

A small number of personal and family friends who had stayed near her during her period of isolation as the Information Minister provided the nucleus of the kitchen Cabinet. Among them were Uma Shankar Dikshit, an Uttar Pradesh MP, a party veteran, and an old friend of the family; Dinesh Singh, another MP with long-standing family connections with the Nehrus; and Inder Gujral, a young Delhi politician. Indira's rise to the prime ministership drew several new members. Into the supposedly privileged circle of her advisers entered C. Subramaniam, Asoka Mehta, Fakhruddin Ali Ahmed, all of whom were appointed to her Cabinet, Nandini Satpathy, a young woman MP from Orissa, and Dwarka Prasad Mishra, the powerful Chief Minister of Madhya Pradesh.

The influence of the kitchen Cabinet was, as is often the case in such situations, grossly exaggerated. The myth of its power over Indira rested largely on propaganda by most of its members. But Indira was, and is, sensitive to the suggestion that any individual has any special power over her. She has always in fact cold-shouldered anyone whose friendship for her appeared to be outweighed by or derived too obviously from personal ambition. Usually those who have stayed near its outer edges and not crowed about their presence in it have remained in Indira's circle the longest. Among such persons in the original kitchen Cabinet were Ahmed, Subramaniam, and Gujral. Though personally closer to her from the start, Dikshit has remained her trusted adviser because his loyalty and father-like affection for her was never in doubt. He was appointed to the government and later given the Home portfolio, but he was always somewhat unenthusiastic about personal power and had to be pressed into accepting it.

Indira early became disenchanted with Mehta because, sour-tempered person that he always was, his attitude towards Cabinet colleagues and party members was marked by unrelieved cantanker-ousness; he quickly became a political liability for her.

Dinesh Singh long enjoyed her trust and thrived in her favor. She admired his competence in facing Parliament and appreciated his ad-vice and occasional help in party matters. His father, a big *zamindar* (landlord) in Uttar Pradesh, had known Indira's grandfather and maintained friendly links with the family; with Indira's benign, almost familial approval, Dinesh Singh rose rapidly from a junior deputy minister to become eventually, in 1969, India's Foreign Minister. He fell from her grace, however, when she became convinced that he was exploiting his association with her for personal advancement and using her name to secure for himself a major role in the party, deliberately trying to create among MPs and even senior Cabinet ministers a highly exaggerated impression of his influence on the Prime Minister. He finally overreached himself in 1969 during the crisis over the appoint-ment of the President that led to the split of the Congress Party. In the United States as a guest of the Nixon Administration when news ar rived of the beginning of the confrontation, he immediately cut short his official visit and rushed home, thereby publicly proclaiming his in-dispensability to Indira during a crisis. On reaching Delhi he started making political deals in the Prime Minister's name but without her authority or even knowledge. A few months later, when an occasion arose for a Cabinet reshuffle, Indira unceremoniously dropped him.

The ideological diversity of the kitchen Cabinet was quite extraor-dinary. Mishra was one of those politicians whose dedication to pur-suit of personal power was so complete that it ruled out any considera-tion of ideology. The political beliefs of Dinesh Singh, Dikshit, and Ahmed were as amorphous as the party to which they belonged. Satpathi and Gujral were acknowledged leftists—Satpathi, in fact, was a former card-carrying Communist. Subramaniam was frequently described as a "pragmatist," a euphemism used at that time for one favoring reason-ably close economic and political links with the United States. Mehta was a "socialist," but one to whom communism was anathema. No decision of Indira's could be said then or later to show ideological characteristics attributable to the influence of any particular member of the inner circle of her friends.

Her first year as Prime Minister not only offered Indira Gandhi a fairly thorough introduction to domestic and to foreign policy but also taught her several lessons, some rather harsh, in both areas. Her moments of triumph as well as of confusion and disenchantment in international affairs echoed those that could be called purely Indian.

Within ten weeks of her election as party leader Indira paid her first official visit to the United States. The visit was planned originally for Shastri, but the invitation was transferred to her when she unexpectedly succeeded him. The assignment was important and delicate. The U.S. Government then was headed by Lyndon Johnson, a man of moods, who had brusquely withdrawn his invitation to Shastri a year earlier in anger over India's criticism of the U.S. bombing of North Vietnam. India itself was always allergic to big-power pressure. A newly elected leader like Indira could ill afford to countenance anything that looked like an attempt on the American President's part to bully her. The problem was further complicated by the continued U.S. involvement in Vietnam and India's economic difficulties owing to the severe drought of 1965 and 1966.

The visit was a smashing success. Johnson almost overwhelmed Indira with his display of courtesy and warmth towards her and his consideration for India. In welcoming her at the White House, he called her "a good and gracious friend." Knowing her deep attachment to her late father, Johnson praised him extravagantly and added that Americans like to think that Nehru "belonged to us, too." Guests at the White House dinner for the Prime Minister were struck by the animation the two leaders showed. Mrs. Gandhi, radiant in purple silk heavily embroidered in gold, her dark hair with its dramatic white streak smartly coiffed, smiled up at an attentive President Johnson as he took her on his arm and beamed down at her. It was clear that the two were pleased with the occasion and with one another. Later during her stay in Washington he attended a cocktail party at the Indian Embassy that was to be followed by a small dinner. In accordance with the rules of protocol the President was not invited to the dinner, but at the cocktail party he expressed a wish to stay on. This unexpected request created a temporary seating problem for the Embassy, quickly solved, but, what was important, pleased Indira immensely. At the dinner that night, in an impromptu toast, Johnson assured the Indian Prime Minister of his Administration's "everlasting friendship and understanding." In concrete terms, during her visit he announced his intention to send a special message to Congress, seeking authority to help India with its food crisis and to set up an educational foundation for work in India financed exclusively by the United States. For good measure, he added to the gifts already selected for her the *Anton Brun,* Harry Truman's old state yacht, which, after some remodeling, could be used by India for oceanic research.

On her part, Indira reciprocated U.S. courtesy and good will with enthusiasm. When she spoke at the National Press Club and addressed the Council on Foreign Relations, she avoided making abrasive remarks or lecturing to the Americans the way her father could seldom resist doing on similar occasions. Apparently, she also said the right things in her private talks with Johnson, for the President told Ambassador to India Chester Bowles that he had been "particularly impressed by the political astuteness she displayed" during those parleys. Indeed, the meetings had been so harmonious that on her way back from Washington when Indira stopped in Moscow for a few hours she reasoned with Kosygin against expecting the United States to leave Vietnam without a suitable face-saving arrangement (to which the Soviet Premier reacted by tartly asking how many Asian lives could be considered an appropriate price for saving U.S. face).

This unexpected and welcome bloom on Indo-U.S. relations was, however, off sooner than even the most pessimistic of observers had foreseen. Within mere weeks of Indira's highly successful visit to Washington, both sides were once again snapping at each other in complete disregard of the promised everlasting friendship.

The educational foundation, whose establishment had been approved by Indian officials before Johnson made the proposal public, was an immediate casualty. The foundation was to have been presided over by an Indian reporting to a board of management comprised of an equal number of Americans and Indians. Besides providing badly needed funds for research, the foundation would have served as a safe outlet for the U.S. PL-480 rupee holdings, paid in local currency by India for U.S. food grains, the enormous size of which by 1966 was causing nervousness among Indian political economists. Officials had advised Indira to accept the proposal, not anticipating the vehemence of the public criticism in India that greeted Johnson's announcement. A majority of educationists, including many with no left-wing predilections, denounced the foundation as a sinister U.S. move to subvert Indian education and gain control of the universities. Bowles, who discussed the matter with her, found Indira jittery about the opposition. The proposal was shelved—to die diplomatically of inattention.

And three months after the Washington meeting Indira herself angered Johnson, perhaps inadvertently. The joint communiqué issued at the end of her official visit to the Soviet Union in July 1966 asked for an end to U.S. bombing in Vietnam and in another part of the document referred critically to "imperialistic powers." The reference was vague and, by all accounts, had remained undetected in the draft shown to Indira at a time when she was preoccupied with something else and had no responsible official near her to caution her. But it was enough to enrage Johnson and prompt his Administration to wish to chastise "these ungrateful Indians."

Actually, Johnson had lost his enthusiasm over Indira well before the Moscow communiqué was issued. On March 30, a few days after Indira's return home, he sent the promised special message to the Congress describing the famine threatening India ("a good and deserving friend") and reminding it that "it is not our nature to drive a hard mathematical bargain where hunger is involved." He followed up the message a few days later with strong personal pleas to senior senators and congressmen whom he invited to the White House especially for the purpose. Yet, soon afterwards, he embarked on what Bowles described as "a foot-dragging performance" (which he, the U.S. Ambassador, failed to understand). The dispatch of food grains was delayed inordinately, and when permitted it was planned that it be in small, intermittent installments. U.S. officials described it as a "short tether" approach; Indians more aptly referred to it as a "ship-to-mouth" arrangement. Bowles was directed to tell the Indian Government to revamp its agriculture program and on one occasion given a message for India's Food Minister that he found so extraordinarily insensitive he declined to deliver it and protested to Washington against it.

For Indira, the sudden change of mind on Johnson's part over promised food came as a bitter but valuable lesson. Thanks to devaluation of the rupee and the failure of the monsoon for the second consecutive season, she was confronted with difficulties that would have unnerved a more experienced and better-established leader. Johnson's tactics, therefore, seemed to her sadistic and also an unforgiveable attempt to "force a change in India's foreign policy." (Her interpretation of the action was not unwarranted. When Bowles remarked to a senior White House official that in asking for an end to U.S. bombing of Vietnam, the Indian Prime Minister was only saying what U Thant and the Pope had said, the official replied, "But the Pope and U Thant do not need our wheat.") Indira's reaction to such pressure was to refuse to bow to it. With cordiality she had been won over to the extent of pleading Johnson's cause in the Kremlin, but she resented his arm-twisting. The delay in the arrival of food ships appeared to have little impact on India's criticism of the U.S. policy in Vietnam. In fact, Indira seldom missed an opportunity of urging an end to U.S. bombing. The big-power tactic was self-defeating. As if to underline her government's independence in the matter, Prime Minister Gandhi took the unusual step of sending warm greetings to Ho Chi Minh on his seventy-seventh birthday.

By that date, roughly a year after she had become Prime Minister, so shy and nervous at the beginning that even in private meetings she would be tongue-tied or give monosyllabic answers to questions, Indira had become quite articulate. At first, she had dumbfounded senior Indian newspaper columnists who were accustomed to hearing the previous two prime ministers discuss their views cogently and at length; her inability to communicate chagrined them as it did her, and many regarded meeting her as a waste of time. A newspaper editor given half an hour for his talk with her would often end the interview in a few minutes because he felt Indira had little to say. Ambassador Bowles recalls how during his early meetings with her, even though they had known one another well earlier when he served his first ambassadorship to India under her father, she would allow long silences to develop. He describes how on some occasions he resolved to say nothing more until "Mrs. Gandhi broke the ice. But after two or three minutes of silence it was always I who capitulated and opened up a new subject." By the year's end, although her answers would not be long drawn out like Shastri's or philosophic like Nehru's, there was little doubt that she knew now what she wanted to say. She was also beginning to get a measure of the politicians and officials she had to deal with. In the party executive she had started speaking up in support of issues and persons she favored and occasionally even challenged a well-entrenched opponent undaunted by fear of a humiliating rebuff.

She was still not excessively confident of her own strength, but she had ceased being overawed by the Syndicate at home and the big powers abroad. In the unexpected elevation to the prime ministership, she had survived.

Somewhat paradoxically, Indira ceased to be a prisoner of her own sense of insecurity just about the time she was at her weakest politically. The beginning of 1967 was a depressing time for her, her friends, and many in the Congress Party. The winter session of Parliament, which had ended in December, had brought forth several sharp attacks on the Prime Minister and her Administration. Many in the opposition and some in the Congress Party itself suggested that she was not in complete control of the government she headed. The allegation hurt more than it should have, because there was much truth in it. The personal attacks on her during the session were particularly distressing. What they lacked in veracity they made up in viciousness and vulgarity. Outside Parliament the situation was even more menacing. The failure of the monsoon for the second successive year threatened more than 100 million people with starvation. The economy was in deep recession—a situation that then appeared to have received so little of the help expected from the devaluation of the rupee that those who had described devaluation as folly seemed to have been proven right. Within the party Indira felt hamstrung by Kamaraj and other members of the Syndicate. Her few attempts at independent action had roused their hostility towards her without noticeably loosening their hold on the party. At the weekly meeting of the executive of the Congress Parliamentary Party, she was frequently challenged and criticized, some of her critics going to the extent of taunting and ridiculing her. Even in the Cabinet, where everyone served at her pleasure, she encountered a measure of resentment and antagonism, especially after her decision to give the Home Affairs portfolio to Chavan following Nanda's dismissal, which accentuated mutual jealousies among ministers.

She was, therefore, in a pessimistic frame of mind when she started her campaign for the 1967 general election. The sense of gloom was deepened by the experts' forecast that the ruling party was heading for a rout. After having voted for the Congress Party in three successive elections, the country, they argued, was ready for a change. Several opposition parties—the right-wing Swatantra, conservative Jana Sangh, and both factions of India's divided Communist Party—seemed to have grown tremendously in popularity and electoral sagacity and were expected to replace the Congress in many states. In the central government, therefore, the Congress was given the prospect of emerging at best as the largest single party, dependent on the good will of some other parties or groups for a possible, rather tenuous, hold on power. As she joined Kamaraj and others in the cumbersome process of choosing the party candidates for the several thousand state and parliamentary constituencies and made ready to embark on her own election travels, Indira had the disconcerting feeling that perhaps she was presiding over the beginning of the end of a remarkable organization that had fought for India's freedom and later held it together during trying times.

The results of the elections in February and March that year largely confirmed predictions about the decline of the Congress Party. It did not suffer a rout, as its opponents had claimed, but an undoubtedly serious setback. It was defeated in eight of the seventeen states by various parties or their coalitions, and in Parliament it all but lost its absolute majority. In the Lok Sabha the party's strength was reduced from 361 to 279 in a house of 525. The margin of majority was small, especially for a party that accommodated within itself warring elements. Headed by an unsure leader, as the Congress Party then was, such a narrow majority could be ominous. It was some solace, but not much, that the forecast about its being reduced to a minority had been disproved.

Yet with all this, Indira began acquiring a new sense of personal strength even before the Lok Sabha results were announced. Within a few days of the start of her election tours, her spirits and self-confidence soared. Like her father, she was always at her best when challenged; in addition, as she traveled to distant parts of the country, speaking to poor, illiterate peasants, she discovered that she had inherited Jawaharlal's capacity to be stimulated by contact with the masses. Nehru often used to wilt and grow sulky at well-organized gatherings of sedate or sophisticated people who were in harmony with him, but after a long day of hectic, dusty travel, talking to enormous, noisy, unruly meetings of Indian masses, he would find himself strangely fresh, almost rejuvenated. The election campaign during

which Indira traveled over 35,000 miles, a large part of it in an open
jeep, speaking to audiences ranging from the slum-dwellers of Bombay
to tribesmen living in the lush Assam hills, was physically exhausting but
emotionally reassuring and bracing. Many years earlier, when she had to
campaign in an area because her father was unable to keep his promise to visit it, Indira had been pleasantly surprised to find that she
could make the people listen to her; in 1967 she was elated to learn
that that innate capacity was not only alive but enlarged. As the word
of her effectiveness spread, her secretariat was inundated by requests
from party organizations in various states for her to visit them. Congress nominees, many of whom were overwhelmed by the seeming
strength of the opposition, sent her frantic pleas for help in their
campaigns.

Wherever she went, she drew large crowds. Often she would be
shouted at by hostile elements in the audience intent upon disturbing
her speech, but she faced them undaunted and the sometimes ugly
confrontations usually ended in her victory. On one occasion, in Orissa,
a group of rowdies pelted the dais with stones. She was hit on the
face, but she went ahead with her speech despite a fairly nasty injury.
The sight of her speaking while stanching the bleeding with her *sari*
shamed her hecklers into silence and awed the crowd.

The 1967 campaign emphasized in Indira's mind an important fact
in Indian politics: It demonstrated that in the post-Nehru period there
were no nationally accepted political leaders except herself. Most
politicians who carried much weight usually did so on the basis of their
hold on their own particular state or, at best, a region. Thus, the senior
Congress leaders such as Kamaraj and Desai received far fewer invita-
tions than she did to campaign outside their own home states, and
when they did the crowds at their meetings were noticeably smaller.
Usually when they were asked to another area, their visit was designed
merely to help maintain the momentum of the campaign, not to rescue
the local organization from a desperate situation. Chavan was powerful
because of his support in Maharashtra, Sanjiva Reddy because he controlled Andhra, Patil because he was the strong man in the Bombay
city Congress, and Atulya Ghosh because he dominated the West
Bengal party machine. But their personal followings outside their
respective areas were negligible. If any of them wielded any influence
in another part of the country, it was through coming to terms with a

local satrap. Three other party leaders—Kamaraj, Desai, and Jagjiwan Ram—each had a somewhat wider political base. But they suffered from other limitations. Even though, thanks to the novel nature of the plan named after him, under which ministers and chief ministers were compelled to renounce office, Kamaraj had come to be nationally known, outside the southern region his personal appeal to the masses was almost nil. As the last of the pre-independence stalwarts, Desai was known almost all over the country, but the sphere of his popularity was circumscribed by the fact that in the public mind he was linked with right-wing, big-business interests. Jagjiwan Ram had spent more years in the central Cabinet than any other leader and was therefore a "name," but support for him was confined largely to India's large Harijan (untouchable) community, to which he belonged. Indira was the only person at the party's top level who, thanks in part to the tremendous advantage of her family background, was singularly free from the kind of cramping, restrictive personal or community or language problems that beset her rivals.

The results of the general election of 1967 more than confirmed the Prime Minister's assessment of her own and others' strength. Most members of the Syndicate not only lost their states to other parties but even failed to get themselves elected to Parliament or their state legislatures. In Tamil Nadu, which was Kamaraj's home state and principal power base, the Congress Party was routed by the Dravida Munnetra Kazahgam (DMK), and Kamaraj himself lost in both constituencies from which he had run for a seat in the Lok Sabha. Patil, long the dominant personality in Bombay city, was defeated by a young trade-union leader. West Bengal was lost to a Communist-dominated coalition, and Atulya Ghosh, the party strong man there, failed to save even his own parliamentary seat. The only two members of the Syndicate who survived the election were Sanjiva Reddy and S. Nijalingappa. As for Indira's rivals outside the Syndicate, Desai was elected to Parliament, but he could not succeed in bringing the party to office in Gujarat. C. B. Gupta, a former Chief Minister, who controlled the Congress Party machine in Uttar Pradesh and who, in the party's factional politics, sided with Desai, not Indira, was similarly defeated. The electorate in her own home state demonstrated what seemed to Indira heartening sophistication. At the same time that the people of Uttar Pradesh voted for Indira and her supporters for various parliamentary seats, they convincingly rejected Gupta's nominees for the state legislature.

When the new Congress Parliamentary Party assembled after the elections to formally choose its leader, there was little doubt in anyone's mind that Indira would be re-elected. Her strength in the party then was nowhere near the awesome proportions it would assume four years later, but it was sufficient to rule out any effective challenge. The Syndicate was left too demoralized by the election results to even think of any one of its members as a possible candidate for prime ministership. Chavan, re-elected to his parliamentary seat, saw greater wisdom in cooperating with Indira than in challenging her. Jagjiwan Ram, also re-elected to Parliament, had briefly declared his candidacy for party leader on two previous occasions, but he realized the pointlessness of making even a ritualistic claim to leadership at this juncture. Desai was the only one who was seemingly undeterred but, as subsequent events suggested, his posture was primarily a tactical move designed to secure his return to Indira's government on the most advantageous terms possible. It would in any case have been out of character for Desai to have acknowledged Indira's supremacy without giving a fight.

As he had done after Shastri's death, Desai claimed that he was the rightful leader of the Congress Party and that given the freedom of choice the majority of its members would readily vote for him. Indira, he sternly declared, was "unfit" for the post. He also told newsmen that there was absolutely no question of his joining a Cabinet headed by her. Unlike past occasions, however, Desai was careful enough not to invite the Syndicate's hostility. Instead of denouncing Kamaraj as a dishonest broker as he had earlier, Desai went to some length to placate him and others around him.

It was no secret that during her first year as Prime Minister, Indira's relations with Kamaraj had acquired a measure of suspicion and tension. Apart from her turning out to be far less amenable than presumed to the Syndicate's influence, she had irritated Kamaraj by her claim during the election campaign that while leaders like him might have support within the party she enjoyed the backing of the Indian masses. "My position among the people is uncontested," she had told an interviewer. Kamaraj's own defeat had demonstrated the validity of Indira's assertion and added to his chagrin. Kamaraj would probably have preferred Desai as the Prime Minister, but a careful head count of party members convinced him that Desai stood little chance of winning the majority. Much of the Syndicate's influence within the party and the government was the result of the shrewdness of its members in backing the winning horse. It could ill afford to make a mistake or even take a chance on a doubtful entry at a time when it lay battered and bruised. Kamaraj, therefore, gave Desai no indication of his willingness to switch sides.

Ultimately, a combination of circumstances, rather than Kamaraj's influence as Congress President and dexterousness as a peacemaker, averted a contest between Indira and Desai and brought the latter into the Cabinet. Indira herself, though conscious of her growing strength, was apparently leery of testing it out at this stage. Some among her supporters, notably Jagjiwan Ram, had a history of shifting loyalties and might, her advisers feared, be induced to change sides by the offer from a rival of a more important portfolio or a senior ranking in the Cabinet. Desai, though stubbornly declaring his resolve to accept nothing but the top position, was assailed by doubts about his prospects and a seemingly consuming desire for ministerial office. He had already been in the wilderness for four years and, if defeated in a contest, he could not expect Indira to accommodate in her Cabinet someone who had publicly refused to accept her as the leader. At seventy-one, he did not hope to get another chance later to return to power. And Kamaraj and the Syndicate had their own reasons for wishing to avert a contest and securing Desai's inclusion in the Cabinet. They regarded him as a possible Trojan horse who, experienced and assertive as he was, might make Indira feel constantly beleaguered and turn to them for succor. As for the Congress MPs, many among them were reluctant to be asked to rise and be counted. They were not sure yet whether Kamaraj's eclipse and Indira's rise to top leadership would be durable. They were therefore unwilling to make precise, clear decisions about party leadership.

Over all these diverse personal and factional considerations hung, like a large ominous cloud, a general sense of anxiety about the party's future. Could the Congress, with its slender majority, ward off the opposition parties' attempts to dislodge it from office? Would it be wise to allow a no-holds-barred contest, which, besides causing much bitterness, would divide the party into two factions? Already there were reports—some not without substance—of opposition parties offering diverse blandishments to Congress MPs to make them cross the floor. According to one report, Jagjiwan Ram was offered the prime ministership should he join the opposition with his followers and help form a non-Congress coalition. The sentiment for unity, not confrontation, was, therefore, strong in the party.

To secure that unity Indira made some concessions. But Desai yielded much more—or at least he appeared to do so. In return for his withdrawal from the contest, thereby making her own election to party leadership unanimous, she agreed to include Desai in the Cabinet with ranking next only to the Prime Minister. Later, when pressed by Kamaraj, she also agreed that Desai be designated as Deputy Prime Minister. These concessions did not seem much of a climb down on her part because, while advancing her claim to be re-elected leader, she had not publicly said that she did not regard Desai as deserving a senior Cabinet post. Desai, however, had repeatedly questioned her competence as leader and categorically stated that it was the prime ministership or nothing for him. He indulged in this type of brinksmanship until the day before the contest was scheduled to take place. When, therefore, he suddenly agreed to serve under her, his decision inevitably gave the appearance of surrender. He, in fact, yielded even more later. As the price for his cooperation he had demanded that besides being designated as Deputy Prime Minister, he be allocated the Home portfolio and given a position of special authority above other ministers. Indira would not even consider taking Home away from Chavan, who had supported her candidacy without any reservations. Desai, she said, must be content with the Finance Ministry that he had held at the time of his exit from her father's Cabinet in 1963. She also firmly declined to elevate him to a special position above other ministers with some kind of overlordship privileges over certain spheres of government in addition to his own portfolio. When Kamaraj pleaded on Desai's behalf, Indira told him firmly that there was no room for "two captains of the team." She said she had agreed to designate Desai as the Deputy Prime Minister in the interest of party harmony and to make the climb down on his part somewhat less embarrassing for him, but she would not give up her right as the Prime Minister to distribute the portfolios according to her own preference and convenience nor accept any arrangement that might restrict her authority or give the impression that Desai had dictated to her the conditions of his entry into her government. The evening before the vote, when an abashed Desai announced his withdrawal from the contest and his readiness to join the Cabinet under Indira, he had no convincing explanation to offer for his capitulation. All he would give the press was the laconic statement that "my friends wanted me to do so."

The next day Indira was elected head of the party unanimously.

9

"The Most Powerful Woman in the World"

I f Indira Nehru Gandhi began her new term as Prime Minister and as Congress Party leader in 1967 in a position of strength, she was still a long way from being what a headline in the London *Sunday Times* six years later would call her: "The Most Powerful Woman in the World."

The combination of circumstances and character that marked her rise in the succeeding years of her prime ministership were quickly foreshadowed, however. The first of the many battles she was forced to fight, and willed herself and outmaneuvered her opponents to win, was political. And her opponents were, unexpectedly, Moraji Desai and the Syndicate.

In the few months following her re-election as leader, Indira had little cause to feel that she had been saddled by an unwanted deputy or that Desai was not giving her the cooperation to which she was entitled. Desai was undoubtedly chagrined by having to work under someone much junior in years and political standing and whom he considered unfit for leadership. But his sense of discipline was stronger than his disgruntlement. (All through his public life Desai's emphasis on discipline has been as fanatical as his faith in prohibition of liquor.) Four years of being out of office and other frustrations had mellowed him somewhat. Additionally, Chavan's unremitting hostility towards him kept him on the defensive. He, therefore, offered Indira unreserved loyalty and support, and she, in turn, seemed almost grateful for his presence by her side at the time. The opposition in the new Parliament was larger and rowdier than before, and Desai with his parliamentary experience and capacity for asperity in repartee was able to cope with it much more effectively than she could have done by herself. In fact, it was Desai's cooperation and moral support during that early period that enabled Indira to accept a rather dramatic challenge from the opposition parties over the election of the country's President. Her success in that confrontation—which, curiously, aroused public in terest far out of proportion to the importance of the issues involved— set her firmly on the path to acquiring the image of an assertive, courageous leader who throve on challenges.

The President of India is elected by an electoral college comprising members of Parliament and the various state legislatures. The presidential election customarily takes place within a few weeks of the parliamentary election. As the country's constitutional head, he is given no executive authority. Like the sovereign in Britain, on whom the office is modeled, the President acts strictly on the advice of the Prime Minister. The definition in the Indian Constitution of his functions and privileges, however, has some twilight areas whereby a President, unmindful of the spirit of the Constitution, could, particularly if the ruling party were weak, browbeat the Prime Minister and even create a constitutional crisis. Until then, the two presidents that India had had were both chosen by the Congress Party. Neither had made any serious attempt to encroach upon the executive's authority.

Though her following in the Lok Sabha had been markedly reduced, Indira was not apprehensive of any challenge that might come from the President. The retiring President, Dr. Radhakrishnan, chosen first to be the country's Vice-President and later President, was a widely known intellectual with no political affiliations with the Congress Party that sponsored him. Indira favored continuance of the tradition of electing a generally respected and politically uninvolved figure to the post. Normally, she would have consulted the principal opposition parties and urged the Congress to choose a candidate who, in addition to the majority party's approval, might enjoy their confidence. What, however, put her back up was the resolve of the opposi-

tion parties, buoyed by the recent election results, to select the candidate
for the Presidency and ask the Congress Party to accept him. According to their calculations the Congress votes in the electoral college had
been reduced to such a narrow margin that it would fight shy of a trial
of strength and its acceptance of an opposition nominee would convincingly demonstrate the weakness of its position. Conscious of the
party's reduced strength and danger of defections though they were,
Indira, Desai, and others were averse to permitting the opposition to
have its way. Acceptance of the opposition nominee did not amount to
any constitutional setback for the government, but the moral defeat
would be unmistakable, and that, they felt, was unacceptable. Additionally, Indira was distressed by the opposition parties' decision to
choose India's Chief Justice, Koka Subba Rao, as their joint candidate.
Rao was due to retire from the bench in less than a year's time, but he
agreed to resign earlier and accept the opposition nomination for the
Presidency. His action was legally permissible, although there was no
precedent of a Supreme Court judge's engaging himself in active politics. As in Britain, judges in India, particularly at the level of the
country's Supreme Court, had jealously guarded their image of political nonpartisanship and even on retirement would usually involve
themselves in nothing but educational and intellectual pursuits. To
Indira, therefore, it seemed highly improper that a functioning Chief
Justice should demonstrate his political preferences so blatantly and be
anxious to join in the rough-and-tumble of a political contest. By acquiescing to the opposition plan to elect Rao, the Congress Party, Indira argued to her aides and advisers, would not only be exposing itself
to a certain degree of mortification but also weakening the long-
established tradition of the judiciary's aloofness from active politics.

Having resolved to accept the opposition challenge, the Congress
Party was faced with the task of choosing a suitable candidate. In that
Indira's role was decisive. Dr. Radhakrishnan, though seventy-nine by
then and in failing health and almost blind, was known to be eager to
serve another term as President. Many in the party were inclined to let
him have his wish, because he was personally popular with them and
because they believed the presence of a South Indian in Rashtrapati
Bhavan would give the government headed by a Northerner a regional
balance. Indira, however, resolved to support Radhakrishnan's deputy,
Dr. Zakir Hussain, for the post. Within the party there was almost as

The Minister of Broadcasting and Information

... with Prime Minister Shastri

Prime Minister Indira Gandhi at the White House, Washington, 1966, with
Mrs. Lyndon B. Johnson, then Ambassador to the United States B. K. Nehru
(a distant cousin), President Johnson, and Mrs. Hubert H. Humphrey

. . . at work aboard her aircraft

. . . addressing a meeting   . . . saluting the *jawans* of the Indian Army

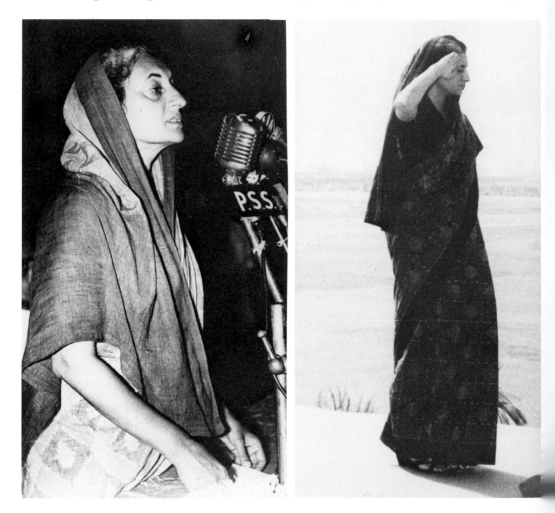

Opposite: . . . inspecting forward positions, Kash-mir, 1971

"A very private person"... with sons Sanjay (left) and Rajiv

... with Rajiv's wife, Sonia, and grandchildren

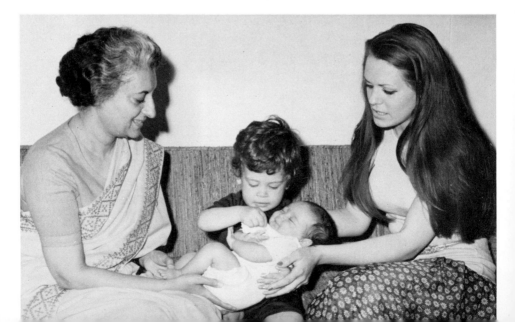

"The most powerful woman in the world"... with Leonid Brezhnev, New Delhi, 1973

... with Richard Nixon, Washington, 1971

"A child of politics," Indira Gandhi tosses a garland
back to the crowd along a campaign route

much reluctance to having Hussain as President as there was support for Radhakrishnan. Hussain's personal credentials were impeccable. He was an educationist and scholar of some eminence and an acknowledged nationalist. Before being elected Vice-President in 1962, he had served as state governor and even earlier as vice-chancellor of a university. Impressive though his background had been, however, many in the ruling party, their supposed commitment to secularism notwithstanding, had reservations about having a Muslim as the country's constitutional head.

Indira worked vigorously to have Hussain accepted as the Congress nominee. Her opposition to Radhakrishnan's continuance was quite firm. He had already had ten years as Vice-President and five as President. His long term in the prestigious positions, combined with the fact of his near blindness—his attempt the previous year to read the President's customary annual address to Parliament was a painful spectacle—made his retirement imperative. She was also unhappy over Radhakrishnan's tendency sometimes to cross the line of constitutional propriety and try to interfere with the process of political decision-making. But beyond that she had positive reasons for endorsing Hussain, several of them, and she stated them in the party councils with much vehemence. Hussain, she pointed out, had a noticeable aura of personal dignity around him. Besides his considerable intellectual attainments, he was a man of sophistication and taste (as Vice-President he had developed at his government house one of the finest rose gardens in the country) who could be relied upon to entertain and perform the other ceremonial functions of the Presidency with poise and grace. But her principal reason for her uncompromising stand in favor of Hussain's candidacy was that five years earlier Radhakrishnan had moved up from the Vice-Presidency, and if that practice was not followed in Hussain's case the Indian Muslims would feel that as a minority they did not enjoy political equality with the Hindus.

Desai, whose own mind has always been free from the taint of religious bias, accepted this reasoning as valid and helped Indira secure Hussain's nomination and get him elected in the contest with the opposition parties' candidate. Both of them pooled their resources in influence and pressure to see that Congress members of the electoral college voted faithfully for the party nominee. Desai and some of his associates set up what was virtually a control room in Delhi from where they contacted almost every party member with a vote to explain to him the importance of the contest and remind him of his duty in the situation. The canvassing lasted more than a fortnight and the pace was hectic, but the sense of common purpose joining Indira and Desai in the effort showed no signs of any strain owing to their mutual wrangling over party leadership only a few weeks earlier. Hussain won by a sizable margin. The result created in the public mind the twofold impression, first, that Indira was developing an assertive, confident personality and, second, that despite differences of age and ideology she and Desai would be able to work in reasonable harmony.

The latter view barely survived the year following the presidential contest. And, ironically, while they achieved the maximum degree of mutual understanding and cooperation over Hussain's election, in the end it was the President's sudden death from heart failure two years later that started a sequence of events culminating in Desai's dismissal from the finance ministership and Indira's break with him and the rest of the Old Guard leadership.

Neither Indira nor Desai consciously acted with the intention of having a showdown. If anything, both saw the advantages of working in consonance with each other. Desai, apparently, had noticed the unattainability of his personal ambition and the vulnerability of his position in the party. In Chavan and Jagjiwan Ram he had committed opponents. His friendship with Kamaraj and the Syndicate was still tenuous. Without Indira's good will he could not expect to last long in the government. At the same time Indira saw in Desai not only someone who could put the opposition hecklers in their place but could also keep the power of Chavan and Ram in some check. Friction between them, however, arose. It came almost imperceptibly and over a wide range of issues from an indirect tax on agriculture to continuance of English as the official national language. Also, true to his right-wing moorings and rigidity of approach in dealing with the Congress Party's opponents, Desai began believing that the Prime Minister was not stern enough in dealing with the various non-Congress ministries in the states.

Desai seemingly held the view that any party or coalition that had defeated the Congress in a particular state and formed the administration there had placed itself in an adversary relationship with the Congress central government and was entitled to no more consideration than what was its minimum entitlement under the Constitution. He was particularly allergic to the left-wing ministries in Kerala and West Bengal, whose rise to power he regarded as an ominous sign for India's democracy. He advocated stern central intervention when the West Bengal government allegedly incited labor unions to create lawlessness in Calcutta's industrial establishments. Indira's dedication to socialism then was not particularly pronounced. During the leadership contest Desai himself had publicly charged that big business had bought support for her. But if she appeared to be unduly indulgent to the left-wing governments in the two states it was because her conception of center-state relationship had undergone a change since her attempt to dislodge the Communist ministry in Kerala in 1959. The prime minister-ship had given her a new perspective in the matter. She also had cordial personal relations with the Communist leaders in West Bengal, some of whom had been her contemporaries when she was a student in Britain. The populist DMK ministry in Tamil Nadu earned her sneaking admiration because its success represented the personal failure of Kamaraj for whom her esteem had diminished greatly by then.

Over and above these factors, however, what shaped her attitude towards the non-Congress state governments was the conviction that in a federal system of government the center must learn to live with states ruled by rival parties. Like Desai, she would have preferred to have her own party rule all the states, but she did not feel inclined to embark on a vendetta against those who had succeeded in defeating the Congress by legitimate, constitutional means. But while she saw wisdom at that stage in avoiding confrontation with the non-Congress state governments if she could get along with them by giving them a long rope, Desai, still an unbending disciplinarian, saw in that stance unpardonable weakness and a vindication of his original claim that she was unfit to be the leader.

The divergence in their thinking on the question of the official language generated even greater distrust between Indira and Desai. Though herself Hindi-speaking, Indira was anxious to amend the Constitution to delay the replacement of English by Hindi as the national official language. This amendment was intended to fulfill a promise to the southern states that had accepted Hindi as the national link language only with the greatest reluctance and regarded the impending change as a form of cultural imperialism by the North over the rest of the country. The offer to permit English to stay as an "associate official language as long as any part of India may want it" was first made by Nehru in 1959, but somehow he never provided the necessary statutory basis for the continuance of English. Indira felt committed to the promise partly out of affection for her father and partly because she had herself reiterated it publicly in Madras in the beginning of 1965 when that state was in turmoil over the issue. Before approaching Parliament for the legislation, she was daunted for a while by the certainty of adverse reaction of the Hindi supporters and its impact on her position in Uttar Pradesh, always a citadel of Hindi fanaticism. But she managed to overcome her nervousness and decided to go ahead with the required legislation because, as she argued with her official advisers then, "someone has to bell that cat sometime."

As the move developed, she was chagrined to find Desai on the other side of the fence. Though himself a Gujarati, Desai unreservedly supported Hindi's claim to be the official national language and, as on various other issues, his attitude allowed for no compromise or accommodation. In the Cabinet and party forums he opposed official language legislation vehemently and seemed to regard it not as an act of statesmanship and magnanimity but, again, weakness and short-sightedness on the part of the central government. The mutual irritation caused by this divergence in their views was deepened by Indira's and Desai's factional association within the party. She suspected him of trying to weaken her position in her home state by pandering to its linguistic fanaticism and demonstrating that he was willing to show greater consideration for its sentiments than she was. He believed that her language policy was intended to discredit C. B. Gupta, the dominant personality in the Uttar Pradesh Congress, and punish him for siding with Desai over the leadership issue. By delaying acceptance of Hindi as the national language, Indira, Desai thought, wanted to demonstrate Gupta's lack of influence as far as the central government was concerned. The Official Language Act was passed towards the end of 1967, Desai concurring with it unenthusiastically. It calmed political suspicions in southern India, and it strengthened personal ones between Indira and her deputy in the government.

Other irritations and suspicions fed the mutual antagonism and widened the rift between the Prime Minister and her Finance Minister. Within months of entering the government Desai traveled to

Washington on an official visit. In the U.S. capital, he was received by Johnson with a considerable show of personal warmth. The press and the Congress, too, appeared to fuss over him. In the cordiality extended to him in Washington, Indira, whose own relations with Johnson had by now turned sour, saw a deliberate U.S. attempt to build Desai as a rival to her and a signal to pro-West elements in Indian politics to rally around him. Later, in his 1968 budget, Desai proposed a small indirect tax on the relatively prosperous segment of Indian farmers and, the proposal causing the expected uproar from amongst agriculturists in the party, Indira bowed to their pressure with what Desai felt was undue readiness on her part. He regarded the eventual abandonment of the tax as a personal humiliation. But what subsequent events turned into a true *cause célèbre* related to the issue of bank nationalization.

Several past attempts by the central government, including some when Nehru was at the height of his authority, to nationalize the banks had been foiled by the right-wing elements in the party. When the question arose again after the 1967 general election, Desai, in his capacity as Finance Minister, suggested a compromise. Instead of acquiring control of the banks and having to pay substantial compensations to their existing owners, the government, he proposed, should seek social control over the institutions. Through its executive authority and, if necessary, some legislation, the government, Desai reasoned, could influence the lending and borrowing policies of the country's banks sufficiently to use their resources to implement official economic and development programs. Indira, whose own background on the subject was limited, accepted this approach despite some "instinctive misgivings." When, however, the question was placed before the party for acceptance as policy, it brought forth a howl of protest from the aggressively vocal Congress left wing. Desai was attacked openly and maliciously for allegedly trying to protect the interests of big business and sabotaging socialism. The attack was led by a "Young Turk" group, most of whose members were believed to be close to the Prime Minister. One of them, Chandra Shekhar, leveled the charge that Desai's son Kantibhai had been peddling influence to the country's business concerns with his father's knowledge and connivance. Desai was convinced—and many in Parliament agreed with him—that Chandra Shekhar had launched the attack with Indira's tacit approval and help. Any doubt he may have felt about the justification of his suspicion was

removed when the party authorized Indira, as the leader, to reprimand
Chandra Shekhar for his lack of discipline and she chose never actually to administer the rebuke.

The problem was, however, that even if Indira's men had not provided Chandra Shekhar with the material for his parliamentary attack
on Desai, it was naive to expect her to discipline him. By then—
midsummer of 1968—Indira had little doubt that the Syndicate was
once again sharpening its sword for her neck and that Desai was an
important factor in its conspiracy to remove her from leadership. The
Syndicate appeared to have recuperated remarkably well from the
setback it had suffered in the elections. Kamaraj and Patil, whose
political clout had declined owing to their defeat in the general election, had succeeded in getting themselves elected to Parliament in the
two by-elections that occurred within a year or so. Both returned to the
Lok Sabha with suspicion bordering on conviction that Indira had
tried unsuccessfully to get them defeated in the by-elections. They
were anxious to cut the Prime Minister down to size and re-establish
their own dominance. By now Desai's ambitions had revived, and he
began wooing them, and Chavan as well, assiduously. S. Nijalingappa,
who was a relatively less assertive Syndicate member and had agreed
to become Congress President at Indira's suggestion, was feeling disenchanted with her and personally neglected. He found her unduly
under the influence of what he described as "noisy radicals" like
Chandra Shekhar or politically inconsequential individuals like Dinesh
Singh. In his personal diary on August 24, 1968, he wrote: "I am convinced that this lady should remove herself from the baneful influence
of fellows like Dinesh."

But the lady was not prepared to abandon fellows like Dinesh to
make peace with the Syndicate and Desai. Apparently, on a signal
from her, the Young Turks embarked on a denunciation of the Old
Guard leadership and its right-wing ideological moorings. Indira and
the Syndicate had found it impossible to co-exist. They spent the latter
part of 1968 and the first few months of the following year sparring
with each other, each side convinced of the other's hostile intentions
but unsure of its own strength and lacking a suitable strategy. Nijalingappa wrote in his diary on March 12, 1969, that "I am not sure
if she deserves to continue as Prime Minister. Possibly soon there
may be a show-down." A few weeks later he recorded in the same

journal that Desai discussed with him "the necessity of the P.M. being removed."

In this situation of intense but passive mutual animosities President Zakir Hussain's sudden death on May 3 from a heart attack came as a cataclysmic agent. In the unexpected vacancy at the top and the need to fill it, the Syndicate saw an opportunity to humiliate Indira publicly, to demonstrate to her and the country the extent of its own power, and to create circumstances in which she could be eliminated when necessary. Indira was acutely conscious of the threat to her future and in the following months fought them hard—sometimes with her back to the wall.

The Vice-President, V. V. Giri, was promoted to take Hussain's place temporarily. (By the Indian Constitution a new President must be formally elected should a vacancy occur unexpectedly.) Various names were briefly mentioned for the post. Nijalingappa sounded out Desai on whether he would be interested. Desai had little doubt about his entitlement to that position of national honor and said so unhampered by any sense of modesty, but he also reasoned that his continuance in the government was important for, as he reportedly put it, truly embittered by now, without him that "woman will sell the country to the communists." Indira herself vaguely suggested Jagjiwan Ram for the Presidency but did not press when it was pointed out to her that only recently her nominee had been found to have failed to pay income tax for the previous ten years. The disclosure had, to say the least, strengthened public doubts about his personal integrity, she was reminded.

Kamaraj and his associates finally decided to sponsor Sanjiva Reddy for the post. Reddy, then the Speaker of the Lok Sabha, had been one of the original members of the Syndicate whose antipathy to Indira was deepened by the grievance that she had tried surreptitiously to thwart his election to the Speaker's post. If elected President—and the Syndicate had no doubt that he would be—Reddy, a strong, assertive person with considerable expertise in political manipulation, could be relied upon to keep the Prime Minister in a weak, defensive position. Should she continue to ignore the Syndicate's wishes, Reddy, his sponsors hoped, would use certain verbal imprecisions in the Constitution about the President's authority to bring about Indira's ouster from prime ministership.

Indira was aware of the implications of Reddy's selection by the Syndicate. If there was any tendency on her part to be sanguine, it was dispelled by Dinesh Singh and others among her friends who presented to her an exaggerated picture of her opponents' intentions. But for some time after it was proposed that Reddy be the Congress nominee, she seemed to revert to a state of confusion and befuddlement. How could she stop Reddy's nomination? Who was there among her friends whose candidacy she could sponsor convincingly and with the hope of defeating the Syndicate's game plan? She looked around and found none. She then suggested to Nijalingappa that the choice of the party candidate be left to her as it was she, as Prime Minister, who would be in constant touch with the President. This was turned down with expected firmness and with the terse reminder that in the past on all occasions the party nominee was chosen by the party's top executive and not the Prime Minister. Later, she hoped against hope that the 8-member Parliamentary Board, which would take the final decision in the matter, would be divided over Reddy's nomination. She finally made up her mind to support Jagjiwan Ram against Reddy and plead personally for his selection. According to her calculations, besides Fakhruddin Ali Ahmed, Chavan would vote on her side, which should produce four votes against Reddy. Nijalingappa, she hoped, would not decide a matter as important as choosing the country's President with his casting vote. But when the meeting was actually held in Bangalore in the middle of July, Indira found that she had miscalculated in almost all respects. When she proposed Ram against Reddy, Desai, backed by Nijalingappa, to her chagrin, prevented her from arguing her case. There was no need, Desai told her with his customary brusqueness, to praise one whom all of them knew well and who was present at the meeting as a member. She got an even bigger shock when Chavan voted for Reddy, thereby giving the latter's nomination the clear majority and obviating the need for Nijalingappa's casting vote.

The humiliation she suffered at the Parliamentary Board that day did something to Indira Gandhi. As those who met her after the meeting recall, she was like a wounded tiger. Apparently, it was then that she resolved to take the battle into her opponents' own camp. Reporters who talked to her later that evening found her speaking threateningly about her antagonists—something she had seldom done before. Those who had chosen Reddy against her wishes "will have to face the consequences," she declared. In an attempt to mollify her the Congress Party President decided to withhold formal announcement of Reddy's selection. Perhaps when she cooled down, Indira, he hoped, would join him in making the decision public and thus preserve at least the appearance of organizational unity. But she was too distressed to contemplate cooperation with the victors. For a while she even declined Nijalingappa's suggestion for a meeting and later, after agreeing to receive him, curtly refused to discuss the issue. She regarded the conflict with her opponents as unavoidable and saw no point in making temporary compromises to gain time that she did not need.

Within hours of suffering the rebuff at the Parliamentary Board meeting, Indira gathered her close friends and advisers. Ahmed, Gujral, and several others were there, but the principal strategist was D. P. Mishra, Chief Minister of Madhya Pradesh. In planning factional battles Mishra was as experienced and shrewd as any member of the Syndicate. His age, temperament, ideology, and desire for personal power could have rendered him an almost typical member of the Syndicate—but circumstances had placed him on Indira's side. It was Indira's intervention with her father some years earlier that had enabled Mishra to return to the Congress after having been expelled from it for indiscipline. Besides wanting to repay the favor, he had been drawn to Indira's camp since her election as Prime Minister because her spells of seeming helplessness and vulnerability offered irresistible opportunities for political influence.

The plan that Indira devised with Mishra's help was to continue to try provoking Kamaraj and others into an open fight before Reddy's election and to give the battle an ideological slant by presenting the Syndicate as a reactionary element determined to thwart socialism. The presidential election provided the deadline. She and her supporters were convinced that with Reddy in the President's House, the Syndicate would endeavor to bring about her downfall. Mrs. Tarkeshwari Sinha, a flamboyant young Bihar MP (often called "the glamour girl of Parliament") who was closely associated with Desai, had virtually said so in an article she wrote for a Bombay weekly. The Syndicate, conscious of the relative weakness of its position then and the considerable strength that Reddy's installation as President would bring it, determined not to be provoked into a fight prematurely.

Already at the meeting at which Reddy was chosen as the party candidate, Indira had presented a note on economic issues entitled "Stray Thoughts." The note, which proposed nationalization of banks and several other radical measures, failed to irk the Syndicate into a fight over it. Instead, the Syndicate accepted it, biding its time and conscious that, in securing Reddy's nomination, it had won a valuable advantage over a Prime Minister who, as Nijalingappa put it in his diary on July 15, seemed "to be taking too much for granted and is so over-bearing and haughty" but who "has been taught a lesson now." The Old Guard did not wish to fritter away that gain by joining battle before the right moment. Having failed to rile her opponents on economic ideology, Indira now tried personal provocation. She used her prerogative as Prime Minister to strip Desai of his Finance portfolio on the plea that his known conservatism and personal association with big business disqualified him from being entrusted with the implementation of the radical policies she wished to pursue.

Her dramatic action had some part of the effect she intended. It focused nationwide attention on the conflict and gave it, at least in the public mind, an ideological basis. Instead of seeming another factional fight for personal power, all too familiar in Indian politics, Indira's challenge began to look like a strong-minded and brave attempt to dislodge obscurantists. It also brought Desai's resignation from the government, for, as was expected, he refused to accept the slur on his integrity and continue to serve as Minister without portfolio. But she still had failed to draw the Syndicate out of its lair.

Neither Chavan, who had sided with the Syndicate over Reddy's selection and who was supposed to be with it in ousting the Prime Minister, nor even close associates of Desai chose at that stage to precipitate a crisis by resigning from the Cabinet and creating a full-scale crisis. If anything, members of the Syndicate endeavored to deflect Indira from the path of direct confrontation by publicly assuring her of their good faith towards her. Nijalingappa wrote to her vehemently denying "rumors about toppling the present Congress government . . . ," and Reddy himself issued a press statement vowing to act, if elected, only as the constitutional head with no policy or program of his own. He even wrote a personal letter to the Prime Minister seeking her good will and support.

In the plan of action that she had been executing with the precision of an experienced chess player, Indira made one false move. In a moment of weakness, when her resolve for a showdown had not hardened sufficiently and her strategy had apparently not taken precise shape, she had allowed herself to be persuaded to endorse Reddy's selection after the fact and to sign his formal nomination papers before the Election Commission as a proposer. Her action, probably also taken when she still hoped that the Syndicate would be drawn into the open before the poll, now hung round her neck like a moral albatross. How could she work for the defeat of one who was the party's choice and whom she had herself formally endorsed?

A way out of this curious dilemma was provided by a tactical blunder that Nijalingappa made a few days before the poll was scheduled to be held. He met with leaders of the Jana Sangh, a right-wing Hindu-dominated political organization, and the Swatantra, an avowedly conservative party, to seek their support in Reddy's election. Although the Congress Party itself had always abounded in communal or religious as well as conservative elements, it had in the past regarded the Jana Sangh and Swatantra with unconcealed disdain and dismissed any proposal for cooperation with either of them as ideologically abhorrent. Nijalingappa's action in holding private talks with the two parties was immediately denounced by Indira's followers as an unpardonable sin. This made it impossible for the supposedly socialistic wing of the party to cooperate with the Syndicate. When Nijalingappa protested that it was merely his anxiety to ensure the success of the party nominee that prompted his initiative, the other side hurled at him the accusation that his meetings were really part of the conspiracy to topple Indira's government and make Desai the Prime Minister—with the help, if necessary, of the opposition parties. Indira, who had until then declined to issue to the party members the customary directive instructing them to vote for Reddy, argued that Nijalingappa's "perfidious" activities left her with no option but to advise members to exercise "the freedom of conscience" in voting for their choice among various presidential nominees.

Giri, who as acting President had earlier put forward his claim to being elected in his own right, was virtually adopted by Indira's supporters as their nominee. The Young Turks announced their resolve to vote for him. Indira's efforts to defeat the official nominee of her own party suffered from no sense of self-consciousness on her part or any doubts about their propriety. A nervous Syndicate made some peace over-tures at that late stage in the hope of saving Reddy's candidacy. Kamaraj and Nijalingappa sent Indira messages offering her their solemn prom-ises that her leadership would be assured until the next general election if she would stop working for Reddy's defeat. But it was too late in the conflict for such compromise offers to be taken seriously. Peace feelers were followed by threats of disciplinary action, including even expul-sion from the party. Those, too, failed to impress Indira and her sup-porters.

Backing Giri against Reddy, particularly when the poll was due to take place in less than a fortnight, was a gamble. Indira and some of her associates in Delhi undoubtedly were convinced they had no option except to fight the Old Guard. But would legislators in the various state assemblies who constituted the bulk of the electorate in the presi-dential poll share their sense of desperation? This was no ordinary election in which Indira with her charismatic family associations could appeal to the masses over the heads of the party bosses. Also, Giri was not a particularly strong or appealing candidate. It was inevitable that he would be compared with his three distinguished predecessors, and he fared poorly in such a comparison. He had neither the political eminence of Rajendra Prasad, the reputation for scholarship of Sarve-palli Radhakrishnan, or the graciousness of Zakir Hussain. However, circumstances were such that Indira had to back him. She did so unreservedly. She contacted the chief ministers of all states, including those who did not belong to the Congress Party or were closely affili-ated to the Syndicate. She also personally appealed to a large number of prominent legislators in the states. That her camp had denounced Nijalingappa for negotiating with the Jana Sangh and Swatantra for their support for Reddy did not stop the Prime Minister from making similar overtures to various opposition groups to gather support for Giri: in fact, Giri won narrowly and primarily on the strength of the votes she secured for him from the Communists, right-wing Akalis, the DMK of Tamil Nadu, some Socialists, and some former members of the Congress. Almost two-thirds of her own party in the central govern-ment and in the states would not flout party discipline or the Syndi-cate's wishes and dutifully voted for Reddy.

Once the gamble over the President's election was won, events began to happen strictly in accordance with the pattern Indira and Mishra had envisaged at their strategy meeting in Bangalore. With Reddy defeated, Desai and the Syndicate humbled, and the Damoclean sword that had hung over her government at least moved aside, MPs and state legislators began shifting their loyalty with tremendous speed. The Syndicate hastened to pick up the pieces and salvage as much of its hold over the organization as it could, but the inevitable split in the ruling party occurred, only ten weeks after the presidential poll. When the time came to choose sides, a large number of those who had voted against Giri decided to stay with Indira, giving her the support of 204 of the ruling party's 279 members in the Lok Sabha. In the All-India Congress Committee, the main council of the organizational wing of the party, Indira got no more than about 25 per cent of the members. But that did not worry her, for, as she told her friends at the time, in a parliamentary democracy the organizational wing of a party derives its sustenance from the executive and legislative section. She was confident that in time the AICC segment that had gone with the Syndicate would begin to shrivel up.

The Old Guard leadership had lost much more than it seemed to realize at the time. Besides being deprived of the bulk of the parliamentary wing of the party and the usual source of its political strength, it had been routed in the propaganda war. The public image of the Syndicate, never very attractive, was tarnished further. Though it was undeniably a quarrel involving personal power, Indira had succeeded in presenting it to the public as a classical struggle between good and evil. By moving to nationalize banks, to cancel the large privy purses still given (under the promise made at the time of independence) annually to former princely rulers, and by forcing a reputedly right-wing leader like Desai out of the government, Indira had not only turned a personal fight into an ideological one but in the process had acquired for herself the image of a leader who felt deeply for the poor but whose efforts to promote their interest were being thwarted by a power-hungry, corrupt clique of aging leaders.

In the days following the nationalization of banks, thousands of the capital's poor—rickshaw pullers, petty traders, junior clerks, unemployed young graduates—thronged to her house daily to congratulate her and express their faith in her leadership by offering her garlands of marigolds and tuberoses and shouting for her victory. Wherever she went—and she traveled extensively those days—hundreds of thousands of middle-class and poor Indians would turn up to welcome her at every stop and hear her speak of her crusade against vested interests and those who represented them in the party. All the while the Syndicate members spoke defensively and self-consciously. When they pointed out that they had no objection to nationalization of banks, they sounded unconvincing. The links that some among them had always maintained with big business were widely known. When they spoke of the importance of party discipline and bemoaned Indira's disregard of it, it appeared as if they were trying to use that perfectly legitimate issue merely to browbeat Indira into submission and maintain their avaricious hold on power. So successful was Indira in presenting what a newspaper writer at the time described as "a two-tone" picture of herself and her opponents that the public willingly overlooked the fact that in the first year of her prime ministership she herself had rejected the proposal for bank nationalization and that among her opponents were men like Kamaraj and Nijalingappa, both widely respected for their unquestioned honesty and integrity and their liberal approach to public issues during their long terms as chief ministers of their states.

The impact on the public mind of Indira's actions and words was also apparently much greater than most political writers and analysts guessed at the time, and this was to be demonstrated by the results of the parliamentary elections held in the beginning of 1971. The voters that spring were to place in Indira's hands even greater power than what her father had been entrusted with at any time during his seventeen years as Prime Minister.

The parliamentary elections were called a year ahead of time—they were normally due to be held in the spring of 1972—ostensibly because Indira found heading a minority government irksome and frustrating. The real reason for her using her prerogative as Prime Minister to advance the poll was her anxiety to translate into parliamentary strength the public approval her conflict with the Syndicate had generated. The party split had left her with the support of only a little over 200 members in a house of 525. She entered into no formal coalition with any other groups in the Lok Sabha to secure the majority backing, and, normally, under the rules of parliamentary government, she should have tendered her resignation. But she was able to carry on her Administration because, as proved in the voting for President, she enjoyed the tacit backing of the Communists, some Socialists, and parliamentary representatives of certain regional parties like the Akali Dal of Punjab and the DMK of Tamil Nadu. The arrangement, however, was awkward and restrictive. The informal and implied nature of the support her party enjoyed from certain opposition groups invested them with undue strength and the situation with greater insecurity than would usually be experienced in a regular open coalition. To retain that support it was necessary for Indira's government to see that nothing it did offended either the left-wing susceptibilities of the Communists and the Socialists or the conservative predilections of the Akali Dal and the DMK. Her government, she realized, might manage to live precariously in this necessarily self-contradictory and hamstrung manner until 1972, but by then its seeming helplessness and enforced inaction would inevitably have deprived it of much of the popular support she had won in 1969.

But though it was the logical, and obvious, thing for her to do, her decision towards the end of 1970 to call the elections ahead of schedule took her opponents totally by surprise. The reports that she contemplated advancing the elections were frequently published in newspapers. Their appearance was invariably immediately followed, however, by vehement official denials. After a while her opponents tended to believe the denials more than the press reports. She had won her gamble over the presidential election narrowly. Why should she test her luck again so soon? they asked. To stay in power she had made compromises with the Syndicate for nearly three years. Why should she now be averse to entering into political accommodation with the opposition groups if that would keep her in office for another two years? In persuading themselves that she would not risk the earlier election, the seceding Congress faction and others were also influenced by the general verdict of the Indian press that parliamentary elections, whenever held, would not give the ruling party a clear majority. What was not appreciated at that stage of Indira's political career was her reluctance to compromise—she does so only when there is no choice —and her readiness—much greater than Jawaharlal's—to take a chance.

In the elections the Congress Party wing headed by the Prime Minister hit the jackpot. It won 350 seats in a house of 525, thus ending its embarrassing dependence on ill-matched, raffish allies and regaining for the party the type of majority that it had won in the earlier years when its role in the freedom fight was fresh in memory. The rival faction of the Congress, which at the time of the 1969 split carried over 70 members in the Lok Sabha, contested 238 seats and won only 16 of them—this despite the grand alliance that the Syndicate leaders had formed with certain opposition parties in an endeavor to avoid splintering of votes against Indira's party. Perhaps owing to their association with the Syndicate faction of the Congress, both the Jana Sangh and Swatantra parties, long regarded as potential rivals to the ruling party, declined noticeably in the 1971 election. The Swatantra following, for example, was reduced from forty-four in 1967 to a mere eight. Almost all political parties, on the Left as well as the Right, lost votes to the ruling party.

For Indira personally it was a time of unprecedented political satisfaction. She now headed a party with more than enough strength to form a stable government. Her detractors had been completely routed. The country's constitutional head was beholden to her for his election. Within her party none—not even Chavan nor Jagjiwan Ram—had the temerity any longer to think of himself as a possible rival. And outside the government and Parliament the Indian masses looked to her with the kind of hope and faith that they had previously reposed only in Nehru and the Mahatma. They had turned out as voters have never before turned out in a free and open election.

In choosing her Cabinet and allocating the various portfolios among its members she exercised unrestricted freedom. None of the ministers had any doubt that he or she was in office at Indira's pleasure. Even the Young Turks in her party, noted for their brashness and arrogance, seemed overawed by her and, after the election, had little role to play. A leading Indian columnist writing about her rise to top leadership described her self-confidence and power as "formidable, almost frightening." The Information and Broadcasting Minister who had felt lost and vulnerable after her father's death, who was sometimes driven close to tears by the rough cuts from the opposition, who complained bitterly of being neglected by Shastri, had come a long way.

Many in India and abroad were baffled by the suddenness of Indira's enormous success, perhaps because they underestimated her personality and perspicacity. It is possible that they misjudged the country's mood and had as well a somewhat overblown view of the Syndicate's strength and political dexterity.

Kamaraj and Nijalingappa and one or two others aside, most members of the Syndicate were widely thought to be personally corrupt. They had allegedly amassed enormous fortunes by peddling influence and serving the interests of big business—and then used a portion of their wealth to preserve their hold on the party machine and executive power. Atulya Ghosh in West Bengal, Patil in Bombay, and Sanjiva Reddy in Andhra had run their state politics like Tammany Hall bosses, and their disregard of ordinary political proprieties had disgusted the people. Indians, curiously, as many observers of other nationalities have noted, accept corruption and even nepotism calmly and even as if it must be taken for granted up to a point. But when some unseen but strongly sensed line is crossed, they tend to get very angry very swiftly. Also, while they do not object to concentration of power in a few hands, they like to believe that that power is used for benevolent purposes and not merely for the self-aggrandizement of those who have it. It was ironic that Kamaraj, who in 1963 had initiated that novel experiment in renunciation of power that bore his name, only nine years later had come to be associated in the public mind with a brazen desire to dominate the government. People were convinced that the Syndicate was anxious to retain power and had lost its sense of moral purpose: Defeating it at the polls was not the Herculean task that had been imagined.

Considerably more significant than the disrepute into which the Syndicate had fallen was the change in the country's temper. The leadership that had emerged as a result of the independence movement had grown old and lost its appeal. That a particular leader had spent many years in a British prison or had worked under the Mahatma had by 1971 ceased to be important. The country was ready for a new generation of leaders, and in Indira's challenge to the Old Guard it saw the change whose time had come.

The trial of strength with the Syndicate was largely thrust upon her by her opponents, but Indira can (and does) claim credit for judging the country's mood correctly. She took advantage of it to enlarge and consolidate the gains she had won in the party split. Most of those who sided with her in the party struggle were apprehensive of facing the electorate and advised her against calling the general election ahead of time. In the 1967 election the Congress Party had with difficulty managed to secure a bare majority; in its divided state the party, her supporters argued, would be committing political *hara-kiri* if it were to seek a new mandate. Indira was unimpressed. For obvious reasons of strategy she publicly always denied any intention of advancing the election date. But to close associates and friends she expressed the view that they were being unduly pessimistic and excessively cautious. She was confident that her faction of the party would win the majority in Parliament in a fresh election, because, as she argued, by discarding the Syndicate, it had burnished its public image and that would be reflected at the polls. Her final argument, and the one that more than any other brought many of her advisers around to her way of thinking, was that the risks involved for the party were negligible, for, as even the most pessimistic among them acknowledged, it was certain at least to re-emerge as the single largest party in Parliament. The ruling faction, she said, had nothing to lose except its irritating dependence on the Communists and certain other opposition groups.

In transforming the party's minority status into an overwhelming majority, Indira was undoubtedly helped by her family and cultural background. As Nehru's daughter she commanded a degree of attention and even indulgence from the Indian people not given to anybody else. Crowds came to her election meetings at least in part because they wished to see the only child of a beloved, dead leader. Moreover, when they heard her, they were drawn to her not merely because she invoked her father's name and professed to share his love for the Indian people but also because she, unlike him, spoke to them in a typically Hindu idiom. Indira's commitment to a nonreligious, secular society is beyond question as sincere as Nehru's was. However, his cultural orientation was, for a Brahmin, peculiarly British-Muslim, while she was brought up in an atmosphere in which Hinduism was the principal ingredient. Of her parents, her mother, who was a devout Hindu, exerted the greater influence on her during her early childhood. Moreover, Indira's basic language was Hindi, not Urdu which Jawaharlal and Motilal loved. Thus, the Hindi she speaks today is genuine, and not, as was the case with her father, simple Urdu laced with Hindustani words to give it a spurious Hindi character. Coupling her easy use of the official national language with analogies drawn mostly from Hindu scriptures,

Indira, once she found her voice before crowds, was better able than her father had ever been to communicate with the masses of India—nearly 85 per cent of whom, whichever one of the fourteen regional languages they speak, are Hindus.

In no small measure, however, Indira's success must also be attributed to her willingness to play politics with few holds barred. She often describes herself as "a child of politics." This not very original description is intended to emphasize her family's deep involvement in politics and also to point out that as a politician she is different from her father. Her father, she says, "was a saint who strayed into politics. . . . but I am not of the same stuff." She suffers from none of the inhibitions and self-imposed restrictions of the type her father's saintliness imposed on him. She plays politics by the customary rules and, when necessary, makes rules of her own. (One reason why many forecasts about her success were wrong was that observers assumed that in dealing with her opponents and devising strategy she would be bound by Jawaharlal's rather stern sense of propriety. She was not.)

Her way of dealing with Chavan is a good example. Once the confrontation with the Syndicate had ended in her victory, Indira proceeded to cut Home Minister Chavan down to a size that suited her. In the summer of 1969 she had been distressed by reports, which she knew to be correct, of Chavan's hobnobbing with the Syndicate in the hope presumably of becoming Prime Minister with their help. But when she resolved to precipitate the conflict with her opponents, Indira had attacked Desai, not Chavan, although sacking Chavan at that time would have given her greater satisfaction and would also have served the purpose of bringing the Syndicate into the open. Apparently she resisted the temptation because Desai, thanks to his son's alleged misdeeds, could be attacked more convincingly and because his dismissal would give the conflict a suitable ideological basis.

Since his appointment as Home Minister in November 1966, Chavan had grown steadily in importance. Traditionally, the Home Minister had been the most important member of the government after the Prime Minister, serving not only as the central government's link with the states but also watching over law and order, controlling the country's principal administrative services and intelligence agencies, and even choosing judges for appointment to the Supreme Court and various state high courts. Often in the past it had been suggested that excessive power was concentrated in the hands of the Home Minister. But moves to limit the ministry's authority had not led to meaningful action. After the battle with the Syndicate was over, Indira revived the proposal. She transferred to the Cabinet secretariat the general control of the civil services and the Home Ministry's functions relating to the filling of the top posts in the central bureaucracy. A few weeks later the Central Bureau of Investigation, India's equivalent of the FBI and the Scotland Yard, was split in two, and the relatively more important and politically sensitive aspects of its functions were placed with a bureau in the Cabinet secretariat. The moves not only curtailed Chavan's authority but also had the effect of increasing that of Indira, as the Cabinet secretariat is administered directly by the Prime Minister. Chavan's chastisement, however, was not complete. In April 1970 Indira reshuffled the Cabinet and took the prestigious Home portfolio away from him and instead gave him Finance, a field in which he felt unsure and distinctly uncomfortable. Although Chavan was unhappy over the change in his portfolio and the obvious diminution of his position in the government, he had no option but to accept. Had he displeased Shastri or Nehru similarly, his punishment almost certainly would not have been as harsh and as obvious.

Erring or unduly ambitious politicians are not the only ones to feel Indira's rap on their knuckles. In the beginning of 1971 it was disclosed that the government was contemplating legislation designed to "diversify" newspaper ownership in the country. The measure was officially claimed as a move towards socialism, but many in the press, particularly the more powerful and influential sections of it, saw it correctly as arm-twisting. Most of India's principal newspapers—in English as well as in Indian languages—belong to chains owned by the various big business houses. They tend to dominate the field, present what is ideologically a limited and at times slanted viewpoint, and offer the smaller and more independent journals unequal competition. The need for some kind of "antitrust" move against them seems as valid as the effort to curtail the Home Ministry's authority and responsibilities. But, perhaps coincidentally, it was initiated just when the leading newspapers were criticizing Indira's government consistently and vociferously. Several of them had supported the Syndicate, and others opposed Indira in the 1971 parliamentary elections. Some were unimpressed by Indira's triumph and continued their criticism of her government's listing towards what they regarded as too much socialism. The proposed legislation aroused the expected storm of protest. It was never formally introduced in Parliament, and the move towards diversification of ownership was gradually allowed to recede into the background but, perhaps again coincidentally, only when most of the former newspaper critics had clearly learned the virtue of adopting a more temperate tone.

The long article on Indira Gandhi that the *Sunday Times* carried under the title "The Most Powerful Woman in the World" described the Prime Minister as "the supreme and silken autocrat" who had taken, almost imperiously, decisions that her own father would not have dared take. Other writers have similarly acknowledged the vast reach of Indira's authority and her readiness to exercise it without seeming hesitation. Many have noted the fact with admiration; some have done so with a touch of derision or apprehension. The day she was due to arrive in Canada on a state visit, a dispatch in the *Toronto Star* referred to her (with awe or irony?) as the "Empress of India," an expression earlier also used by the *Economist* to describe Indira. In the summer of 1973 the *Illustrated Weekly* of India, a widely read journal, wrote worrisomely about excessive concentration of power in Indira's hands. Morarji Desai, by now one of her most outspoken political opponents, remarked in the same period to a visiting journalist that "she is not a communist, she is a fascist." Various assessments of her power are influenced obviously by the angle from which it is viewed, but there is little doubt that Indira has long lived down her days of insecurity in 1968 when she was nicknamed by Delhi newsmen *Goongi Gudiya*—the "Dumb Doll," whose movements were manipulated by the not-so-invisible strings attached to the deft fingers of the puppeteer behind the screen.

Indira herself vehemently denies that she has more authority than what her party's overwhelming majority in a parliamentary system of government entitles her to or that she exercises it capriciously. She reacts with irritation to suggestions in Indian newspapers and legislatures that her commitment to preservation of democratic institutions lacks her father's earnestness and that her actions ill conceal dictatorial tendencies on her part. In what way, she angrily asks, has her exercise of authority been different from that of her father?

It is true that a great deal of what Indira has done since becoming an effective national leader bears a noticeable similarity to the way Jawaharlal ran the government and the party. But there are differences. Many of them trouble thoughtful people in and out of India.

Few Indians had begun seriously to question them, however, before events in 1971 in the remote capital city of what was then East Pakistan catapulted the nation into its third war with Pakistan since independence and made Indira for a period seem in truth the Joan of Arc she had dreamed of being in her youthful fantasies played out in her grandfather's house in Allahabad.

10

Pakistan and the Bangladesh War

T REMENDOUS though it was at the time, Indira's power did not attain its peak with the unexpected and overwhelming electoral victory she won for her party in the beginning of 1971. In the following twelve months she was to face a challenge much bigger than the one the Congress party "Old Guard" had posed, and her remarkable success in tackling it was to impress the world and turn the substantial but fairly routine political support of her own people into what was for many months real, if sometimes frenzied, adulation. The threat to India's security came from its neighbor and old adversary, Pakistan, but because of the way the situation developed in the subcontinent the United States and the Soviet Union, particularly the former, also got deeply involved, politically and diplomatically, in the conflict.

About the time Indira and her supporters in India were jubilantly watching the announcement of the parliamentary election results, Yahya Khan, Pakistan's military dictator, and other leaders in that country were confronted with an unnerving situation that threatened to split their country governmentally as drastically as it was already split geographically. Yahya Khan had come to power in Islamabad in March 1969, following a coup against his predecessor Ayub Khan. Yahya Khan had promised to hold elections and restore normal political institutions—some, including free elections and an uncontrolled press, abolished as far back as 1958. The general elections held in fulfillment of that promise gave the majority in the Pakistan National Assembly to the Awami League, the dominant party in the country's distant eastern wing, 1,000 miles away across the intervening territory belonging to India. This party, led by Sheikh Mujibur Rahman, was committed to securing maximum autonomy for East Pakistan. Not surprisingly, the prospects of a national government headed by Sheikh Mujib and autonomy for East Pakistan deeply agitated the ruling groups in West Pakistan, which had until then enjoyed power and economic benefits almost exclusively.

Plainly, Yahya Khan and those who supported the junta had not visualized such a development. (While visiting Islamabad, Henry Kissinger, was asked by a half-drunk Yahya Khan at a banquet, "Do you think I am a dictator?" Reportedly, the U.S. national security adviser quipped, "Mr. President, for a dictator you run a lousy general election.") Efforts at a compromise between the Awami League and Zulfikar Ali Bhutto, who had emerged as the principal leader of the western wing, failed. Yahya then sent several divisions of Punjabi troops to Dacca, the capital city of East Pakistan. There ensued a barbaric attempt to put down the largely Bengali, protesting citizenry, Hindu and Muslim alike.

As all those who understood the Bengali mind knew might be expected, but as Yahya Khan apparently did not, the brutal use of force by their countrymen, instead of overawing the East Pakistanis, stiffened East Pakistan's resolve to end the western wing's dominance. Mujib and some other Bengali leaders were arrested. Many others eluded Yahya Khan's police, however, and went underground in East Pakistan or across the border in India. And as a ragged but fiercely determined guerrilla force came into being, the Awami League's ultimate objective changed from autonomy within Pakistan to complete independence for the 75 million people in a country that now tentatively adopted for itself the name Bangladesh.

Mrs. Gandhi vehemently denies the Pakistani charge that the Bengali uprising drew its inspiration from and was later sustained by India. "India had no part in the internal development of Pakistan—West or East," she says. The sympathy of the Indian Government, however, as well as of the public undoubtedly was with Sheikh Mujib. Pakistan's Western wing leaders had trod on Indian toes so frequently since the partition of the subcontinent that to see them discomfited and to consider the possibility of Pakistan's breakup as a nation caused widespread satisfaction in India. Furthermore, at a later stage of the liberation movement, the Mukti Behini, or Freedom Fighters, received considerable help from India in training and equipment. But in March 1971, when the conflict began, India was distinctly not involved in what Indira described as the "battle that Pakistan was waging against its own citizens." Those close to Indira testify that there was no link —direct or otherwise—at that time between Indira or any of her authorized representatives and Sheikh Mujib—if for no other reason than that she was too deeply engrossed in her own political survival to mastermind a revolt in a neighboring country. She was then still fighting her political opponents at home with grim earnestness, and so complete was her involvement in that battle that she deferred attention to all other matters, however pressing. While the political drama in Dacca was moving to its bloody second act, Indira was engaged in the hectic election campaign during which she traveled over 40,000 miles. On many days she was at places deep in the interior of the country where news of what was happening in East Pakistan often did not even reach her.

The Pakistani Army's vicious crackdown in Dacca began as Indira, after celebrating her victory in the elections, was getting her new government in Delhi on the rails. Most of the Western newsmen who congregated in Dacca to watch Pakistan's constitutional tussle work itself out were forcibly prevented from witnessing the atrocities that the West Pakistani troops were ordered to commit in the hope of terrorizing the Bengali populace into submission. But before the Military Governor of East Pakistan summarily debarred the press—no exception was made even in the case of correspondents from traditionally pro-Pakistani conservative papers in Britain and the United States—many visiting newsmen had seen enough of what was beginning to occur or evidence of the earliest atrocities to write dispatches that made their readers' stomachs turn. In the organized burning of villages, destruction of crops, mass shooting of innocent people (whose bodies were left to be devoured by vultures), and the rape of tens of thousands of Bengali women, many Western reporters saw terror equaling, perhaps surpassing, that which the Jews had suffered in Hitler's Germany.

It was inevitable that Indians would be much more deeply affected by the gory developments in and around Dacca than were people living continents away. Dispatches from British and American newspapers were reproduced in the Indian press, but Indians had even more graphic and moving accounts of what was happening from those East Pakistanis who began crossing into India by the thousands before the Pakistani Army's "campaign" was a month old. Despite the barrier that partition had erected between them, Indian and Pakistani Bengalis had maintained strong cultural and emotional ties over the years. The Hindus in East Pakistan constituted a defenseless minority and were the special target of the Pakistani Army's venom. Most of those who now fled to India were, therefore, Hindus. Many Indians believed that the Pakistani Army repression was designed primarily to rid East Pakistan completely of its non-Muslim population, and the anger aroused was widespread. In Parliament and in the press there were some who from the start seriously advocated war with Pakistan to stop the terror and the influx of refugees. Indira, deeply affected by the tragedy, later wrote in *Foreign Affairs:*

> We would normally have welcomed the attainment of freedom by any victim of colonial oppression but usually it would have little direct impact on us. Bangladesh, however, was a part of our subcontinent. How could we ignore a conflict which took place on our very border and overflowed into our own territory?

It was only a short time before the conflict between the two wings of Pakistan spread into India. Since the partition of the two countries in 1947, Pakistan had driven out several million of its Hindu citizens, who had crossed into India in periodic waves. Thus, East Pakistani Hindus seeking refuge in the Indian state of Bengal were by no means an uncommon phenomenon. They arrived, destitute and in a state of shock following sudden, inexplicable outbursts of religious hatred or equally inexplicable acts of official highhandedness in their homeland. In the decade following independence, nearly 4 million Hindus from East Pakistan had been reluctantly absorbed into India—their expulsion viewed as an unfortunate extension of the communal frenzy that had seized people in both countries at the time of partition. But over the years the pace had slowed almost to a trickle and by now, twenty-four years after independence, official as well as public attitudes towards having to offer them permanent refuge had changed. In March 1971 over 10 million Hindus were still in East Pakistan. They were citizens of Pakistan. India considered the lengthy chapter in the subcontinent's history devoted to exchange of persons finally closed. Not that Indians would shut the door in the face of the terror-stricken. Poor in the world's terms as their country was, they would look after these new refugees from Pakistan as best they could—but it had to be understood that the refugees' stay must be short. They were East Pakistanis and in time they must return home.

Indira Gandhi wondered if Pakistan was trying to solve one of its problems by driving out the 10 million people whose presence as citizens it found "inconvenient." As April gave way to May and June, another aspect of the steadily rising influx that worried her was its possible impact on the area in India into which refugees were streaming. West Bengal bordering East Pakistan was—and still is—among the most thickly populated and politically restive parts of India. The state had a history of administrative instability, and sizable sections of its volatile people had earlier tried to seek power through Maoist attempts at organized violence. The arrival of a large number of refugees was liable to strain the area's limited economic resources, and the ensuing frustration might well encourage further violence. From the very start, therefore, Indira was quite clear in her mind that irrespective of the fact that the majority of them were Hindus the East Pakistani refugees must return home. And in the beginning of October 1971, by which time a staggering 9 million refugees had entered India, she told the BBC, "We have no intention of absorbing these people here—no matter what. I am absolutely determined about it."

When, during that terrible summer and early autumn, Yahya Khan protested that what his army was doing in East Pakistan was the country's internal matter and many abroad appeared to agree with him, Indira, through Indian and international news media, reacted strongly. The problem in East Pakistan was not of India's making: "We have never interfered in any way in the politics of Pakistan," she said. "But Pakistan can no longer pretend that this is its internal problem." With millions of helpless Pakistani citizens entering India, "it has become an internal problem for us and it has become a major problem of humanity, a question of conscience and of the protection of people's lives and rights," she asserted. India's Foreign Minister Swaran Singh, whom she dispatched that summer to London, Washington, Moscow, and other major capitals to explain the implications of the refugee influx, told various heads of governments that what India was experiencing was "a civilian invasion." As the verbal battle mounted, Yahya Khan, equally angry but less decorous, told a correspondent of *Le Figaro* in August that Indira "is neither a woman nor a head of state by wanting to be both at once." Should he come face to face with her, he would say to her, "Shut up, woman; leave me alone and let my refugees come back," he declared.

Not many even among Yahya Khan's friends abroad seriously believed that India had any interest in deliberately holding back Pakistani refugees from returning home, as Yahya Khan was now claiming. For one thing, the overwhelming nature of the strain on India's resources was obvious. Several special taxes, including a substantial surcharge on the postal rates, were levied temporarily to raise additional revenue burdening an already weak economy. India was then spending $5 to $6 million daily to feed the refugees and provide them with some improvised shelter and basic medical care (an outbreak of cholera in epidemic form was narrowly averted). When torrential rains hit West Bengal, the refugee camps turned into vast marshy lakes. The more fortunate among the residents were those who had had the initiative to establish squatting rights in large concrete sewer pipes awaiting installation. U.N. observers, volunteers of numerous international relief organizations, visiting U.S. senators and congressmen, British MPs, and scores of reporters from all over the world wrote or spoke of the miserable conditions in which the refugees had to live and the sacrifice that India was required to make to keep them there at all and alive, even if in misery. Despite these reports there were those who sometimes inquired in apparent innocence why India did not "let the refugees return home" as Yahya Khan had suggested. Snappishly, Indira pointed out the absurdity of the return-home "invitation." How could any refugees be persuaded to go back when tens of thousands more of their countrymen were arriving every day with new horror stories to tell and with evidence in their blank eyes and scarred bodies of the continuance of the terror from which they had fled?

Even those who expressed admiration for India for the way it offered succor to the terror-stricken did not always please Indira. After a while, in fact, such expressions of praise became, she said, "a bit of an irritant." India's efforts, she believed, were being dismissed with flattering words. Meanwhile, Pakistan was continuing to get material help from the United States and China. The world, she often said with exasperation, even bitterness, as the situation steadily worsened, was not doing its moral duty towards the people of Bangladesh. Instead of condemning Pakistan for the "callous, inhuman, and intemperate butchery" that its military apparatus had organized, most countries were merely appeasing their consciences or their isolated groups of outraged citizens by praising India or offering some food, clothing, and medicines for the refugees. There could be "only one solution," she told an Italian journalist:

> Conditions must be created in East Pakistan, Bangladesh as it is called, in which there is not military terror but normal democratic functioning of the people's will, so that the refugees are enabled to return to their homes and their safety is guaranteed. The rulers of Pakistan must be made to see that there is no other way. It is the duty of every country which has any influence with Pakistan to impress the truth upon them.

But Indira's hope that the world community would exert the required pressure on Pakistan's military junta was, and all along had been, slender. Fairly early during the conflict in East Pakistan, she had come to feel reasonably certain that the Western wing's repressive hand would not be withdrawn until too late, and that East Pakistanis, particularly Hindus, would continue to flee from terror in massive numbers while the world held back from action to end the tragic situation. Armed conflict with Pakistan, she and her advisers had begun to reason, might become unavoidable if her resolve to send back the refugees was to be fulfilled.

As early as the beginning of April 1971, soon after she had formed her new Cabinet, Indira had issued formal directions to India's army chief, General S. H. F. J. Manekshaw, to prepare for the eventuality of a war. As he told an interviewer, Manekshaw (who has since been promoted to be India's first field marshal) was impressed by the "clarity of the briefing issued to me by my political command." The influx of refugees, he was told, was expected to continue and was creating economic, social, and psychological burdens that India could bear for no more than ten months to a year. If the government's efforts to find a peaceful solution of the problem did not succeed during that period, the armed forces would be ordered to achieve "the specific objective of opening the door" for the refugees to return home. While preparing for the task, he must keep in view the fact that the international situation and the political pressures that India was likely to invite upon itself in the event of a war with Pakistan would permit the army only "three to four weeks" to achieve the objective. Besides allowing herself time to search for a peaceful solution, Indira's ten-month deadline for the refugees' return presumably took into account the time that Manekshaw must need to prepare the army for the conflict and the fact that from June until September the monsoon would make any swift military operation almost impossible.

At the same time that they were helping her make the necessary preparations for a war, the Prime Minister's advisers also warned her against getting the country involved in battle at a time and place of Pakistan's choosing. Pakistan could be expected to launch an attack from its Western wing, where its military power was considerable, and to occupy a certain amount of Indian territory before responding to the almost certain Security Council plea for a cease-fire. If that happened, India would find itself in an embarrassing predicament: It would have to pull back its troops from East Pakistan in order to have its own territory in the western area surrendered by Yahya Khan's troops. Also the Bangladesh problem would then be internationalized, which would give Islamabad all the time it would need to put down the Bengali uprising. The Political Affairs Committee of the Cabinet, over which Indira presided, therefore considered that India must be strong enough to deliver a quick, effective blow in the East while defending its borders in the West. It must also acquire some kind of a shield against big-power pressure for halting the conflict before the return of the refugees to their homeland was secured.

The shield that India acquired was the Indo-Soviet Treaty of Friendship concluded in Delhi on August 9, 1971. The treaty, which many Americans and Europeans tended to see as a virtual abandonment of India's policy of nonalignment, had originally been proposed by Moscow and discussed by the two countries in considerable detail in 1969. That was the year when Soviet leadership was beginning to shed some of its suspicions about Indira's ideological moorings originally fostered by her swift move to devalue Indian currency in 1966 under seeming

World Bank pressure and by the warm welcome that President Johnson had accorded Mrs. Gandhi during her visit to Washington soon after she became Prime Minister. Not only had Brezhnev and Kosygin seen indications of India's moving closer to the United States under Indira's leadership, but Indira in her turn had her own reasons to be wary of Soviet intentions. It was about that time that Moscow endeavored to adopt a nonaligned posture in the affairs of the subcontinent and started for the first time supplying arms to Pakistan in the hope of gaining certain political leverage with its military rulers. The quantities of arms given to Pakistan were limited, but they were enough to distress India. Also, during a visit to New Delhi in the beginning of 1968, Kosygin offered Indira advice about affairs in Kashmir and management of various Soviet-collaboration industrial projects that to Indira's sensitive ears sounded not like friendly counsel but unwarranted interference. By the middle of 1969, however, both sides had overcome much of their suspicion and realized the fruitlessness of drifting apart. Indira's confrontation with the Congress Party Old Guard and her close association with the Communist Party of India, the Moscow-affiliated section of Indian Communists, in her temporary tacit coalition government, brightened her image in Brezhnev's eyes. Additionally, Moscow by then had found that its decision to supply arms to Pakistan was yielding no noticeable dividends and, much to India's satisfaction, had resolved not to make any fresh commitments.

The suggestion that India and the Soviet Union should sign a friendship treaty was, however, greeted by many Indian leaders with hesitation and a marked lack of enthusiasm in 1969. Indira's advisers were divided among themselves over its political implications. The treaty, some argued, would bind India too closely with the Soviet Union for it to function with complete independence—and would needlessly antagonize its Western friends. If the bear could hug, it could also bite, they pointed out. Others held that fears about impairment of India's independence and nonalignment were exaggerated and that India had gathered sufficient self-confidence and political stability to be able to join a partnership even with a superior power without limiting its freedom of action. This group among her advisers argued that any misunderstandings the treaty might cause in India's relations with Western powers would be temporary and outweighed by the enormous political, psychological, and even military gains that the arrangement would of-

Kosygin wrote Yahya Khan a personal letter protesting against the bloodthirstiness of his troops. The Soviet leaders were disturbed, moreover, by the unreserved support that Peking had offered the Pakistan Government. When, therefore, Dhar suggested that the treaty be concluded, they responded with alacrity. (Few reports could be farther off the mark than the one in the *New York Times* four days after the signing of the treaty, suggesting on the authority of a secret CIA informant in the Indian Government that Indira had extracted the Soviet signatures as the price for deferring formal recognition of Bangladesh. At stake on both sides was much more than the recognition issue.)

The move to resurrect the document and sign it publicly was one of the best-kept secrets in the Indian capital. Besides Indira, not half a dozen persons knew about the last-minute exchanges with Moscow. The Indian Cabinet was informed of the Prime Minister's decision to enter into a treaty arrangement with Moscow just half an hour before the accord was due to be signed by Foreign Ministers Gromyko and Swaran Singh.

The announcement about the conclusion of the Indo-Soviet Friendship Treaty had the expected impact on the morale of the Indian public. A few brief expressions of skepticism apart, people received it exuberantly. In their view, it meant that in the affairs of the subcontinent the Soviet Union at least was no longer sitting on the fence. Through the treaty, the Russians promised India support in the war with Pakistan that by then seemed almost certain to come. The treaty also issued to the United States and China an implicit warning that they would intervene in the conflict on Pakistan's side only at the risk of elevating it into something much bigger than a limited war between two relatively backward countries. Most Indians were grateful for this assurance and praised Indira for her adroitness in securing it for them.

In sharp contrast to her success with Moscow, Indira's attempt to persuade Nixon to exert pressure on Yahya Khan to stop the killing and come to terms with Mujib was a singular failure. Yet in the protracted confrontation between them over the issue, Nixon, not Indira, appeared the real loser. In the view of much of the world—and, indeed, of many Americans—the Nixon Administration seemed to be supporting Pakistan and courting Peking at the expense of the freedom-seeking people of Bangladesh.

Neither in their assessment of the real nature of the problem in East Pakistan nor over the correct way to resolve it did the U.S. President and Indian Prime Minister see eye to eye. From the time when the military crackdown began in East Pakistan until the end of the war that established the new state of Bangladesh, the two leaders held a lengthy dialogue through public pronouncements as well as private communication. The whole time, however, they seemed to be talking at cross-purposes. The stubbornness with which Nixon refused to take what Indira regarded as effective action in Pakistan puzzled legislators and political writers in both countries. Perhaps, as some reasoned, Nixon felt morally obliged to stand by a friendly country in the time of its crisis and prevent its disintegration. Perhaps he was irked more than his predecessors in the White House had been by India's continuing policy of nonalignment, its seeming partiality to Moscow, and its often arrogant posture in world politics. However, it is reasonably certain that personality factors also counted for much in the lack of rapport between him and Indira.

Between India and Pakistan, Nixon was known to have feelings of much greater warmth towards the latter. When he visited Pakistan soon after his defeat in the 1960 election, Nixon was accorded a hero's welcome. Pakistanis remembered his role in the conclusion of a mutual security pact in 1954 and the accompanying supply of U.S. arms that had been part of John Foster Dulles's policy of containing communism. That Nixon was no longer in the U.S. Government had seemed scarcely to matter to his Pakistani hosts. In the spring of 1967 he had a similarly heartwarming reception when he returned, again as a private citizen, to the subcontinent. By the summer of 1969, when, as U.S. President, he passed through the region, an element of slight chill had entered the two countries' relationship owing to Pakistan's acceptance of arms from Moscow. Yahya Khan, who had by then displaced Ayub Khan as the country's military dictator, was also personally unknown to Nixon. However, during the single day that the American visitor spent in Lahore—he had expressed his inability to go up to Pakistan's capital in Islamabad—the two reportedly developed a strong sense of personal affinity. The bond grew in strength and warmth in 1971 when Yahya Khan's government agreed to provide the line of communication with Peking as the Nixon Administration sought to reestablish relations with the Communist Chinese Government and enabled Henry Kissinger to take off from a Pakistani military airport on his historic secret mission to China's capital. Earlier that year, when heads of governments from all over the world assembled in New York to celebrate the twenty-fifth anniversary of the founding of the United Nations, Yahya Khan was among those who readily responded to Nixon's invitation to travel to Washington for dinner in the White House. At the dinner other guests noticed that when a noticeably tipsy Yahya Khan indulged in some buffoonery, Nixon, his own normally puritanical ways notwithstanding, looked on with amused indulgence.

Nixon's experience with India has been totally different. During his 1961 visit to the subcontinent he was almost ignored in New Delhi. The only official function in his honor was a lunch by the then Finance Minister, Morarji Desai, who served him an indifferently cooked vegetarian meal and also some blunt, biting comments about the United States and its alliance with Pakistan. During his 1967 global tour his stop in New Delhi brought him a meeting with Indira, who had just been re-elected Prime Minister. But the meeting held at her house was brief, and Indira had little to say to him. She could, in fact, scarcely conceal her boredom with her visitor. After about twenty minutes or so of desultory chat, she inquired of the Indian Foreign Office official escorting Nixon how much longer the interview would last. The question was asked in Hindi, but its tone indicated its purport. In 1970 Indira, also visiting New York for the U.N. celebrations, declined Nixon's invitation to dinner without offering any really plausible reason for her inability to accept.

Perhaps inevitably, therefore, as 1971 progressed and the Bangladesh tragedy grew in dimension, the dialogue between Nixon and Indira acquired an increasingly shrill, abrasive character. Both looked at the same happenings. But what each saw was quite different from what appeared important to the other. Both claimed and doubtless believed that they were striving to keep peace on the subcontinent and to minimize human suffering. Both felt and behaved self-righteously about the way they were tackling the problem. As the gulf between them widened steadily with every passing month, their mutual dislike and distrust was evident to all.

At the outset Nixon acted with noticeable promptitude in expressing his disapproval of Yahya Khan's policy of repression. In the beginning of April the Administration stopped issuing and renewing licenses for military equipment for Pakistan and suspended the processing of a special $80 million arms sale to Pakistan to which the United States had committed itself the previous autumn over strong Indian protest. Economic aid was also stopped. On May 28, when the suspension of U.S. arms supplies appeared to have had little impact on the Pakistani Government, Nixon wrote to Yahya Khan urging him to end "civil strife and restore peaceful conditions in East Pakistan." He also expressed his "deep concern" over the possibility that events might lead to "international conflict" in the subcontinent. To avert such an occurrence he suggested that Yahya Khan create "conditions in East Pakistan conducive to the return of refugees from Indian territory as quickly as possible."

As the American President analyzed it and explained later in his State-of-the-World Message to the U.S. Congress, the Bangladesh problem had three aspects—the humanitarian, the political, and the threat of war it posed to the subcontinent. Of these, he regarded the humanitarian problem involving the care of the refugees who had fled to India as "monumental and immediate." A political settlement between the Yahya Khan regime and Sheikh Mujib's followers, he felt, would take time. His administration, Nixon claimed in the message, had obtained assurances from Yahya Khan that Sheikh Mujib would not be executed and that the Military Governor of East Pakistan would be replaced by a civilian. He said that:

> In August we established contact with Bengali representatives in Calcutta. By early November, President Yahya told us he was prepared to begin negotiations with any representative of this group not charged with high crimes in Pakistan.

Indira showed no interest in the U.S. efforts. She regarded them as totally inadequate and liable to strengthen Yahya's brutal hold on East Pakistan. Nixon's action in suspending military and economic aid to Pakistan seemed to her no expression of a sense of moral outrage at the inhuman way Yahya Khan was "pacifying" East Pakistan but merely the compulsion to respond to pressures from the U.S. Congress, many of whose prominent members were shocked at what was happening. Indira was also irritated by the fact that a few days after William Rogers, the then Secretary of State, had solemnly assured her Foreign Minister that no U.S. arms were being supplied to Yahya Khan, the

New York Times disclosed that several million dollars' worth of spare parts, some meant for lethal military equipment, were on their way to Pakistan. She found Nixon's priorities concerning the Bangladesh problem topsy-turvy. By assigning top priority to refugee relief, the administration was merely shifting attention away from the basic malady, she contended. Unless there was a satisfactory political settlement in East Pakistan the flow of refugees into India would not and could not stop—and none of the millions who had already entered India could be induced to return home. In any case it was preposterous, as she saw it, for the U.S. Government to advise Yahya Khan, as it apparently did, to grant amnesty for the refugees, instead of asking him to atone for his army's crimes against them.

Indira was also unimpressed by Nixon's claim that as part of his quiet diplomacy U.S. officials had established contact with Bengali leaders in Calcutta and that he was hopeful of useful negotiations' beginning soon between Yahya Khan and Mujib's men. From India's own intelligence sources she learned that the individuals contacted were of very low political status and could neither speak on behalf of their imprisoned leader nor even influence the course of the Bangladesh freedom movement. By insisting on talking only to those Bengali leaders who were not accused of "crimes," Yahya had debarred from such parleys almost all Bengali leaders of any political consequence. Nixon was seen to be knowingly exaggerating Yahya Khan's willingness to negotiate with East Pakistani leaders or respond to U.S. initiatives. Despite his close personal friendship with the Pakistani dictator, the U.S. Ambassador in Pakistan, Joseph Farland, had been refused permission to meet Mujib in jail. While the White House publicly proclaimed that the U.S. Embassy had been allowed to establish contact with Mujib, all that Farland had in fact been permitted was to talk to Mujib's lawyer. Even that privilege was rendered useless by the lawyer's refusal to meet any U.S. Embassy official. But Nixon quietly disregarded the lawyer's curt no and continued to give the impression that a major political break-through had been secured—one that India, he implied, lamentably chose to ignore. Nixon's own Ambassador in India, Kenneth Keating, who knew about the lawyer's refusal, was puzzled by the White House claim and in a cable to the State Department protested against the seeming distortion of facts.

What distressed Indira and many others in the country more than anything else was Nixon's attempt to equate India with Pakistan. It was Pakistan's military rulers who were responsible for tragedy and turmoil in the subcontinent. India was the indirect victim of their tyrannical actions. Why should the U.S. Government treat India as one of the culprits in the situation and deliver it periodic sermons on the importance of keeping peace? it was asked. About the same time Nixon wrote to Yahya, he sent a personal letter to Indira that "the problems involved in this [Bangladesh] situation can and should be solved peacefully." He said he was deeply concerned that the situation not develop into a war between India and Pakistan "either as a result of the refugee flow or through actions which might escalate the insurgency which may be developing in East Pakistan." Rogers was less circumspect in warning India when he met the Indian Ambassador in Washington on August 11. The United States, he bluntly told the envoy, would stop all economic aid to India should India precipitate a war with Pakistan. To Indians such warnings appeared totally unmerited and unjust and a clear indication of the Nixon Administration's strong bias in favor of Pakistan and its President.

Irritations, exasperations, and suspicions apart, Indira's attitude remained determined by one basic consideration: The East Pakistani refugees must go back. She pressed for Mujib's release, because she was convinced only he could negotiate a settlement acceptable to Bangladesh and create the climate of peace and confidence essential for the refugees' return. She objected to the timetable for the restoration of civilian rule in East Pakistan that Nixon proposed, because it was so slow-moving that it would take years before any solution to the refugee problem could be found. With passage of time the refugees' inclination to return to East Pakistan would subside, for they would have begun to grow social, cultural, and economic roots in India. Indira Gandhi told a Cabinet colleague in the autumn of 1971 that "if the refugees do not go back soon they will never go."

Having to feed, clothe, and house 9 to 10 million Pakistanis for an indefinite period of time was a burden heavier than that of going to war to secure their return. India was dedicated to peace, but it was not committed to preserving peace at all costs. Economic and political stability was more precious than peace, and that is precisely what Indira told Nixon when she met him in Washington in the beginning of November in a final effort to persuade him to use his influence with his friend in Pakistan for a quick and effective solution of the East Pakistan problem.

The meeting got off to an inauspicious start. At the customary reception on the White House lawn Nixon went out of his way to refer to
a news report that morning about monsoon floods in the state of Bihar
and to offer Prime Minister Gandhi his sympathy over the hardship
that that must have caused a portion of her countrymen. However, he
pointedly omitted any mention of the Pakistani refugees who had endured much deeper suffering for a considerably longer period than the
flood victims in Bihar. To Indira, it seemed a calculated political affront
combined with a measure of personal callousness to mention a relatively minor and routine calamity—floods in certain parts of India
are an annual occurrence—while ignoring the bigger tragedy. Even
though the reception was strictly a protocol function, Indira was not
about to let her host get away with it. In a speech quickly redrafted
minutes before the ceremony, she pointedly admonished Nixon for referring to a natural disaster while ignoring a "man-made tragedy of vast
proportions." She had come to Washington, she told him, "in search
of some wise impulse, which, as history tells us, has sometimes worked
to save humanity from despair."

At other public functions in her honor, too, pleasantries and compliments hid an occasional political barb. The private talks, as the Columbia Broadcasting System reported at the end of her visit, "had many
tense moments." Contrary to the impression given to newsmen at
White House briefings, the Indian Prime Minister never gave Nixon
an assurance that India would not resort to war if peaceful efforts
failed to give the country relief from the refugee problem. If anything,
she told the U.S. President that, should a war start, it would not be a
limited one, by which she meant that hostilities would not be confined
to the eastern wing of Pakistan or merely to the use of ground
forces. She refused to accept the U.S. plea for withdrawal of forces
from India's borders with Pakistan. That Pakistan had accepted the
suggestion did not impress her. Having been attacked thrice by Pakistan since independence, India, she pointed out, had no faith in Islamabad's promises or in any assurance that its friends might offer on its
behalf. India was not interested in Pakistan's breakup, but it was also
not committed to the preservation of Pakistan's territorial integrity, she
said. Nixon was equally firm in expressing his disagreement with her
views. He was not convinced that Mujib alone could negotiate a po-

litical settlement with Yahya Khan. Much useful ground, he argued, could be covered by any of his nominees. He repeatedly urged her to order Indian troops to pull back from the border and to use her influence with the Bengali guerrilla forces to end their insurgency. On her return home, Indira claimed she was satisfied with her reception in Washington and that she had had a sympathetic hearing. But much of that was just polite talk. Both Indians and Americans who had followed the course of her talks had little doubt about the failure of her mission.

In London, Bonn, and Paris, cities she visited as part of the same mission that had taken her to Washington, Indira received much greater sympathy and understanding. But in these capitals, too, she sensed little desire to exert any pressure on Yahya Khan. She returned home convinced that a major conflict with Pakistan was unavoidable and that should that war come the Nixon Administration would try its utmost to prevent India from attaining its objective. Those who met her at that juncture noticed little evidence of trepidation or sense of despair on her part. Some recall even an air of buoyancy around her, as if she had been rid of the enormous burden of making a difficult decision. Militarily, the situation had changed in India's favor in the preceding months. Manekshaw had finalized his plans and had received all he asked for to prepare his men for the war. The monsoon had ended and a quick, decisive action was possible. India had collected extensive intelligence about deployment of Pakistani troops and the Mukti Behini, the Bengali Freedom Fighters, had attained some measure of strength, training, and confidence. The West Pakistani troops, conversely, were physically fatigued by their own excesses and demoralized by the sea of venom and hatred that surrounded them. Pakistani aircraft and naval ships had to travel 3,000 miles to bring supplies and replacements from West to East Pakistan. An Indian plan for Bengali insurgency had been in operation for some months, and guerrillas trained and equipped on Indian soil—Indira had made no secret of her government's support for them—had been committing increasingly daring acts of sabotage. Harrassed Pakistani soldiers would often cross the border into India chasing them or shell their hide-outs and camps, only to invite upon themselves sharp Indian reprisals. There was no better time for the inevitable trial of strength.

The question, however, that remained, and the one over which Indira and her four Cabinet colleagues on the Political Affairs Committee agonized almost daily was: How and at what point should India intervene militarily in the Bangladesh situation? Manekshaw, who was usually invited to attend the committee's meetings, was quite sanguine. He told them, "Do not worry. . . . Yahya Khan will give us what we want without his knowing it. . . . He would at any moment commit an obvious folly. Then we would move."

Yahya Khan committed the expected act of foolishness on December 3, nearly three weeks after the Prime Minister's return home following her unsuccessful diplomatic endeavor. Pakistani Air Force planes suddenly struck at Indian Air Force stations at Srinagar, Amritsar, Agra, Ambala, Pathankot, and three other points near the western border. Pakistani artillery also began heavy shelling of several strategically important points along the Indian border. Yahya Khan had not only offered the justification India needed for its military intervention but had even given an advance warning of his action. On November 23 he had publicly announced that war with India would begin in ten days.

Though all precautions had been taken against any sudden Pakistani attack—the damage to Indian Air Force stations was negligible—Indira apparently had not regarded Yahya Khan's war timetable too seriously. On the day of the Pakistani air attack she was nearly 1,000 miles away from the capital delivering a speech in Calcutta. The Defense Minister and almost all other members of the Political Affairs Committee, the body supposed to deal with emergency situations, were either abroad or touring different parts of the country. Indira was in the midst of her speech when the news of the Pakistani air attack was conveyed to her. She wound up her address rather abruptly and returned to Delhi, by then shrouded in total darkness as a precaution against further Pakistani air raids. When someone in her party expressed concern about her security and pointed out that the Pakistani Air Force might attack her aircraft, she reportedly snapped back, "Well, if it does, what is the Indian Air Force for?" At about ten o'clock that night she went on the air to announce to the country that it was at war with Pakistan and that a state of emergency had been declared. In the course of her brief broadcast she said:

Since last March, we have borne the heaviest burden and withstood the greatest pressure in a tremendous effort to urge the world to help in bringing about a peaceful solution and preventing the annihilation of an entire people. . . . But the world ignored the basic causes and concerned itself only with certain repercussions. . . . Today the war in Bangladesh has become a war on India. . . . We have no other option but to put our country on a war footing.

The war, as Manekshaw had predicted, was "short and bloody—quick and decisive." It ended in India's victory. Pakistani soldiers fought stubbornly, almost ferociously, but the superiority of Indian strength and diverse advantages Manekshaw had over his adversary overwhelmed them.

The Indian Army chief knew the terrain in East Pakistan like the palm of his hand. Before his appointment as the head of the Indian Army, Manekshaw had held the Eastern Command. There he was entrusted with the task of watching over the security of the entire eastern region from West Bengal and Sikkim to Assam and the region bordering with Tibet and Burma. In that post "I had nothing to do except read maps," he said, and he never ceased to think of what might need to be done in the event of a war between India and Pakistan. "Sometimes I used to shut my eyes and recall, even in the dark, the map of East Pakistan—its plains, rivers, and cities. The picture was vivid in my mind all the time and in full detail," he told a visiting editor. He also knew and understood the person against whom he was pitched. Two years before India's partition Yahya had been a major in the British Indian Army unit that Manekshaw commanded. He knew the Pakistani dictator to be "a very stupid man" who could "not control his nerves." What was more, his study of the power structure in Pakistan convinced him that at the top "the Pakistani political and military mind was confused." As a result, their armed forces' faith in it was shaken. The control of the political and military leadership "was weak and its lines [of communication] were feeble," he said.

On the Indian side there was no evidence of any confusion in thinking or inadequacy of communication between the political leaders and military commanders. Indira claims that her relations with the chiefs of the Indian Army, Air Force, and Navy were marked by complete mutual trust. She respected their judgment and advice in tactical and technical matters, and they retained confidence in her assessment of the political aspects of the situation. Manekshaw, for example, decided to avoid capturing big cities as the Indian Army moved into East Pakistan, for he felt the control of big urban areas placed an unusually heavy strain on the army's resources; Indira promptly accepted his reasoning, even though the psychological and political advantages of capturing well-known towns and cities were tremendous. Similarly, when it was decided to deploy the air force to attack targets not only in the East but also in the West, and that the navy should shell the Karachi harbor, the service chiefs readily accepted her directive against "terror-bombing" or hitting civilian population. In any event, the Indian forces moved forward so steadily and the war ended so quickly that there was scarcely a situation that might require extraordinary "control over nerves" or bring to the surface elements of "confusion in the political and military mind" in New Delhi.

Curiously, it was left to President Nixon to introduce into the conflict the only element of high drama. Four days after the beginning of the war he ordered part of the U.S. Seventh Fleet to sail into the Bay of Bengal. For many this was a startling development, immediately raising the specter of a wider and protracted war. Indian officials and the press angrily denounced the U.S. Government for employing gunboat techniques of a bygone era. The public was in an uproar. But Indira says the news that the U.S.S. *Enterprise* was heading towards Dacca caused her "amusement," not worry. What was it that the fleet could have done? she asks. All that its dispatch demonstrated, she recalls, was how little Nixon understood the situation in the subcontinent. She did not give this assessment at the meeting of the Political Affairs Committee summoned urgently late that evening to study the development, but, as those present remember, she was cool and unflustered. At the meeting Manekshaw said the most that the Seventh Fleet would attempt would be to establish a beachhead to evacuate some of the top Pakistani civilians. Some argued that the U.S. act was nothing but sabre-rattling on Nixon's part. There was, however, a touch of nervousness and worry in their demeanor even as they said that. Despite the widespread indignation in the country, Indira adjourned the meeting ("we have a busy day ahead of us") after directing that the conduct of war should remain unaffected by the impending arrival of the U.S. nuclear-armed ship. Perhaps it was an empty threat, or perhaps Washington was impressed by India's angry response or belatedly noted the hazardous implications of its move, but the fleet was ordered to sail back long before it could come anywhere near Indian or Bangladesh waters.

Indira was not amused by some other American actions. As was expected, the United States moved to ask the U.N. Security Council for an immediate cease-fire and withdrawal of troops. While urging this course of action, the U.S. chief delegate at the United Nations, George Bush, accused India, bluntly and repeatedly, of being the aggressor. He not only ignored the fact that Pakistan had taken the first major military step towards war by bombing Indian airfields but also charged that India was anxious to annex territory in the Western wing and was conspiring to bring about Pakistan's total disintegration. As days passed and the U.S. efforts to secure withdrawal of Indian forces from East Pakistan were thwarted by the Soviet veto, Bush's diatribe against Indira and Indian leaders acquired a sharper, more wounding tone. In Washington, in the meantime, the administration had summarily adjudged India the aggressor and stopped all economic aid. It even froze the $88 million in assistance for which commitments had already been made and formal contracts signed. Through Kissinger, Nixon also ordered all departments of the government to follow the policy of a "tilt" against India. Kissinger went to the extent of directing that "henceforth we show a certain coolness to the Indians, the Indian Ambassador is not to be treated at too high a level." Of the Indian Prime Minister, Kissinger said at a secret White House meeting, "the lady is cold-blooded and tough."

On December 15 Indira reacted to the administration's anti-India stance and in a letter to Nixon asked sorrowfully if he as "President of the great American people will at least let me know where precisely we have gone wrong before your representatives or spokesmen deal with us with such harshness of language." She told him that "we are deeply hurt by the innuendos and insinuations that it was we who have precipitated the crisis and have in any way thwarted the emergence of solutions." The letter was not merely a sentimental plea for greater sympathy. Indira also bluntly told Nixon how his administration had failed the people of Bangladesh and must share the responsibility for the tragedy. War between India and Pakistan, she said, could have been avoided "if the power, influence and authority of all the

States and above all the United States, had got Sheikh Mujibur Rahman released. . . . Lip service was paid to the need for a political solution, but not a single worthwhile step was taken to bring this about."

Nixon, obviously chagrined by the U.S. failure to prevent the breakup of Pakistan and embarrassed by the naïveté of his Seventh Fleet move, refused to accept Indira's criticism of his role. In a confidential letter he sent her on December 18 he rebuked India for having "spurned" efforts and proposals that the United States had been making to find a peaceful solution to the Pakistan problem and instead having chosen war as an instrument of policy. His administration, he wrote, was not against India. What it opposed was the resort to military means when political resources for a solution had not been fully explored. To Indira's remark in her letter that "there are moments in history when brooding tragedy and its dark shadows can be lightened by recalling great moments of the past," Nixon responded by remarking curtly that "there are times when statesmanship could turn the course of history away from war."

That Nixon was unmollified scarcely worried the Indian people. Under Indira's leadership their country had won a war that, apart · from being more decisive than the three earlier military conflicts with Pakistan, had led to the breakup of an intensely hated neighbor and secured the creation of a new nation, Bangladesh. Pakistan, as an Indian columnist tritely wrote in a Delhi newspaper, had been "cut to size." The victory washed away the humiliation the Indian people had nursed for almost a decade since the border war with China. Their adoration of Indira—no other word can be used to describe the public attitude towards her in the beginning of 1972—was heightened by the fact that she could twit a world leader of Nixon's stature. Throughout the country, as the refugees began to go home to Bangladesh, hopes were high that now at last India under Prime Minister Gandhi would be recognized as a power of consequence—a role that many Indians had yearned for in the twenty-five years since independence.

11

"A Very Private Person"

INDIRA Gandhi's toughness and resoluteness and the success of her charismatic leadership in the war with Pakistan brought her to a pinnacle of popularity so high it probably could not have been expected to last. Even those countries and individuals at home and abroad who opposed or questioned her actions saw her as a woman endowed with uncommon practical sense and capacity for purposeful —and, when necessary in her eyes, ruthless—action. Writing in the *New York Times* Sunday magazine December 31, 1972, Aubrey Menen called her "sort of the De Gaulle of India."

Well into 1972 her power remained total and largely unresented by any large segment of the Indian people. They offered her their love and trust with the enthusiasm and generosity they had once shown her father, and they extended these feelings to her party, returning it to office in almost all states where elections were held in the period shortly after the end of the war. In fact, as the refugees from Bangladesh began to move back across the border in the flood-devastated low-lying lands northeast of Calcutta, the veneration in which Indira was held by her countrymen eclipsed that accorded her late father. Jawaharlal, people in Delhi and elsewhere were often heard to remark in the weeks following the swift defeat of the Pakistani forces, would never have had the nerve to go to war as she had done. Had he been Prime Minister in 1971, it was said, he would have hesitated and procrastinated in the face of the military threat, and India might have been permanently saddled with 10 million homeless and unwanted citizens.

January 26, 1972, saw a quarter-century of Indian independence and the just-won, heady victory over Pakistan celebrated with a Republic Day parade that revived in full measure the old pageantry learned from Moghul rulers and their successors in the British Raj. Extravagant parades on Republic Day had been usual in the earlier years, especially in the 1950s when they were seen as necessary pomp to focus pride in national achievement. But even before Nehru's death they had been scaled down quite drastically. Now austerity was cast aside. Once again Raj Path, the broad avenue leading from Rashtrapatli Bhavan past the great red sandstone office blocks built to house the British Government, for twenty-five years now occupied by the Indian bureaucracy, and on down the grassy mall past fountains and reflecting pools, echoed to the sound of military bands playing Indianized marches, the tramp of boots and horses' hooves, the rumble of tanks and trucks and flamboyantly decorated motorized floats. Military camels, their noses cocked snootily, elephants painted and caparisoned as in ancient times, troops of vividly dressed folk dancers, and schoolboys and -girls in their varicolored uniforms streamed past the reviewing stand where Prime Minister Gandhi and other officials stood at attention. On the final day of the week-long celebration, towards sunset, the vast crowds preparing to start home before the winter's evening chill got into their bones paused in silence for the traditional day's end "Beating of Retreat." From the tall tower of the South Block of the Secretariat a lone bugler sounded the anachronistic, still sweetly moving notes of "Abide with Me." It was a day of joy and triumph.

But not many months after the Republic Day banners and pennants had been folded away, and the elephant droppings swept from the streets, a change began to be apparent in the nation's mood. The euphoria faded, and as it did Indira's popularity was swiftly eroded.

At the time in late 1971, when the Nixon White House regarded Indira Gandhi, in the words of a British journalist, as "a potential Lady Macbeth," there was probably not a person in all of India, whatever his private doubts or long-standing opposition to her policies may have been, who would not have spoken up hotly in the Prime Minister's defense. But once the threat to India's security was behind them, press and Parliament both began to find fault with their leader. Comparisons of her qualities with those of her father, Jawaharlal, continued, except that with the passing months Indira was more and more often pronounced wanting in certain of his remembered virtues. She lacked the humility and benevolence that Indians traditionally expect in one entrusted with power, it was said in the coffeehouses of downtown Delhi. She seemed to seek power too voraciously. Madame was resentful of any criticism and especially of attempts to limit her exercise of authority. (A visitor from Europe in the winter of 1972–73 noted the curious way in which the Prime Minister was referred to simply as "she" or "her" or, less frequently, but with sarcastic stress, "Madame." There was clearly never any question who was meant.)

During most of his seventeen years in office Prime Minister Jawaharlal Nehru's personal power was as extensive as Indira's had become by 1972. He dominated the Congress Party as well as the government apparatus in Delhi and in the states. In 1951, when his opponents were rash enough to challenge him openly, the conflict resulted in their rout. Most ministers in the central Cabinet served at his pleasure, and in the states the Congress Party often called upon him to choose the Chief Minister. Whenever the party was divided on a matter of ideology or administrative policy, Nehru was inevitably entrusted with the power to take the final decision. What, however, saved him from being accused of authoritarianism were certain restraints that he imposed upon himself. In choosing his Cabinet colleagues Nehru always ensured the presence of a few individuals who had a political base of their own and who were capable of offering him independent, often unpalatable advice. He even accommodated in senior positions in government men whose politics he thoroughly distrusted. When he was invited to intervene in a factional dispute in a state and decide who might be chosen leader, he usually picked someone with strong roots in the state and a very firm base in the party. If circumstances produced a state leader whom he personally disliked he tried to work with him, not topple him. In the Congress Party in Parliament, where he had no rival for leadership at any time during his prime ministership, he imposed his will usually only in minor, routine matters and gave way when he sensed genuine opposition to any of his ideas. At weekly meetings of the Parliamentary Party Executive members occasionally disagreed with him without fear of inviting his ire. The opposition parties in Parliament, small and divided, received from Jawaharlal respect and attention far in excess of their strength. India's press lashed out against him frequently, sometimes with needless harshness, without running afoul of him. In Indira's years, increasingly, the constraints on personal power implicit and customary in a democracy appear markedly less conspicuous than many might wish.

Her prime ministership has witnessed a rapid decline in the assertiveness of individual members of the central Cabinet and Parliamentary Party, as well as of the press. There is none now in the Cabinet who disagrees openly with or stubbornly argues for the acceptance of a viewpoint she does not favor. Such senior ministers as Jagjiwan Ram and Y. B. Chavan, who ceased to be her rivals only in 1969 when she successfully brought about a split in the party, accept her lead in all administrative and political matters with baffling meekness. Through successive reshuffles Indira has removed from her government all those who were considered capable of expressing themselves with some degree of fearlessness or who had earned her displeasure for some reason. Moreover, barring Ram and Chavan, who still claim to retain a political base of their own, others in the government are entirely beholden to the Prime Minister for their positions. In the choice of a minister and an allocation of a portfolio the principal consideration is Indira's attitude towards an individual rather than his status in the party or the country. The Home portfolio, which, even after being divested of some of its traditional functions, remains the hub of the country's administration and which Indira herself held after Chavan was made to part with it, was given in 1972 to Uma Shankar Dikshit whose experience in government was limited and status in politics unimpressive but who is an old and trusted friend of the Nehru family. Similarly, in the choice of chief ministers in states where the Congress was victorious in the 1972 elections, Indira tried as far as possible to install her own friends. Later, when factional fights offered the opportunity she sent some more of her confidants from Delhi to head certain state governments. She nominated Mrs. Nandini Satpathi, her junior minister in the Information Ministry, to become Chief Minister of Orissa. P. C. Sethi, another junior minister, was named Chief Minister of Madhya Pradesh, India's largest and perhaps politically most backward state. For Bihar, also faction-ridden and ill-administered, she nominated Kedar Panday. Rajasthan, Gujarat, and Mysore were similarly brought under the control of her nominees. In choosing chief ministers, the Prime Minister seemingly paid little regard to whether those she favored enjoyed any personal backing in the states they were supposed to govern; certainly she has not made the type of concession Nehru always made to local political realities. When her nominees' essential rootlessness in one state after another has made their continuance in office untenable, Indira Gandhi has imposed President's rule (a euphemism for central government administration) and assumed temporarily the responsibility of administering the state. This authority is provided in the Constitution to ensure stability in states in which parties in the legislature may be so hopelessly divided or splintered as to be unable to form a stable ministry, and is not in any sense illegal. But that it has been used almost as often since the beginning of 1971 as during the preceding twenty-one years has caused some discomfort among observers.

Both the Congress Parliamentary Party, which has a long established tradition of outspokenness, and the press have behaved since the last general election with noticeable timorousness. At the periodic party meetings members either listen silently to what Indira, as the leader, might have to say on a particular issue or express their views only on subjects in which they know she is not deeply interested. The Young Turks and other groups anxious to keep the government on the straight and narrow through fearless exposure of its failures and inadequacies have all gone into oblivion. The press bemoans the government's inability to tackle certain economic issues and offers general criticism about administrative inefficiency, but it appears to keep clear of the issues about which the Prime Minister is known to be personally sensitive.

Indira angrily denies any suggestion of rapaciousness in her exercise of power. The charge is an attempt to blacken her name by those who were routed at the polls, she says. As for the quick change in the public mood so soon after the successful conclusion of the war with Pakistan in 1971, she regards it merely as a temporary phase caused by certain unavoidable economic hardships—hardships that she complains her opponents have exploited relentlessly.

Economically, 1972–73 has undoubtedly been the worst period for the Indian nation since independence. Apart from the impact of the enormous expenditure on the war and care of the refugees from Bangladesh, India experienced widespread drought during 1972. So severe and extensive was the drought that it affected to varying degrees nearly 180 million people. Hurriedly organized relief projects employed over 9 million persons, but many other millions were reduced to utter destitution. In parts of Gujarat and Maharashtra even drinking water was not available, and tens of thousands of persons had to be fed daily in free kitchens opened by private philanthropic organizations. The drought also caused a crippling shortage of hydro-electric power, which in turn markedly reduced the production of steel, fertilizers, cement, and textiles. Indira claimed with some pride that though 1972 involved serious hardships "we have been able to avert a calamity." And in an obvious reference to the various opposition parties that have been flaying her mercilessly, she complains that "instead of people getting together to meet a very genuine crisis, some merely want to take advantage of the difficulties by making the utmost demands."

The resentment of her critics, not all of whom are politically motivated, is however based on much wider grounds than economic problems. Indira, they say, has failed the country in many more ways than her response to the economic disasters wrought by war and capricious monsoons. Her years of power have witnessed a distressing debasement of political values, they claim, a staggering increase in corruption at all levels including the top, callous misuse of authority, and a sharp decline in administrative efficiency. In a letter to the *Hindustan Times* in July 1973 a reader warmly applauded the Indian press for its extensive coverage of the Watergate hearings in Washington and then went on to chide it for doing nothing about the "numerous Watergates right under its own nose."

This reference, which must have been obvious to most readers of Indian newspapers, was to two matters in particular. First, there is the widespread concern over the enormous amounts of "black money" that two of Indira's senior ministers and close associates allegedly collected for the party election fund in 1971 and 1972 from industrial houses, big and small, either by promising favorable changes in government policies concerning them or by unabashed arm-twisting. Second, there is the troublesome affair involving the help and favors that various government departments are supposed to have offered Indira's younger son, Sanjay, in building a factory near Delhi to produce the Maruti ("son of the wind god"), a small car that he has been designing.

Collection of contributions to the election chests of political parties is not new in India. In Nehru's time, too, big business houses were frequently approached for donations. Those who gave money undoubtedly hoped for and sometimes received dividends in the form of official help. But the contributions were comparatively small and were usually collected by one or two individuals especially authorized to do so. Much of the money was in the form of checks and was thus accounted for in the books of the party and tax agencies. The law governing commercial companies permitted such financial assistance, and most donors gave to the ruling party as well as some opposition party of their preference. Since 1970, however, such "donations" have reportedly been more like extortions: The money that Indira's senior Cabinet colleagues collected for the parliamentary elections in 1971 and state elections the following year allegedly amounted to tens of millions of rupees and usually changed hands on the basis of a clear *quid pro quo*. At times ministers deliberately talked publicly about nonexistent government plans to nationalize or regulate a particular industry or trade with the intention of creating nervousness among the people concerned. This naturally encouraged the flow of contributions, especially as the apparent threat ceased once the interests concerned had paid up.

What lifts this fund-raising to the level of a national scandal, however, is the widespread belief among Indians of all classes that the ruling party has accepted large amounts in cash in full knowledge of the fact that the donations were made in so-called black money on which the donors had evaded various taxes. The volume of black money or undeclared assets is so large in India today that even government economists refer to it as a parallel economy. Unearthing such untaxed, hoarded money has been the government's avowed endeavor for over a decade, with various commissions recommending drastic measures to eradicate the evil. The reputed acceptance by central Cabinet ministers of this black money is seen as the virtual legitimization by Indira's government of illegally hoarded assets. And allegedly the ruling Congress Party itself has become one of the biggest hoarders in the country of undeclared cash.

The second scandal, that over the activities of Indira's second son, Sanjay, the official favors he has allegedly received, and the wild, sometimes shocking, rumors and gossip that surround him have done even more than the black money affair to rob Indira's name of the luster with which it shone in late 1971 and early 1972.

Both her sons live with Indira in her official residence, as she herself
—and the boys as children—lived with her father. Temperamentally,
the two men are strikingly dissimilar. Rajiv, who married an Italian
girl whom he met when he was a student in Europe, works as a senior
pilot with the state-owned Indian Airlines Corporation. He is a somewhat withdrawn, quiet individual seldom in public view. Sanjay, a
bachelor, is much more outgoing and aggressive (some say unduly) fun-
loving and fiercely independent. After studying automobile engineer-
ing in Britain, he could have had a lucrative job as an executive in any
of India's three automobile manufacturing companies. Instead, he
chose to produce a small "people's car" in a factory of his own. He, in
fact, claimed that he himself could and would design a small car especially suited to Indian needs and conditions and for this set up a con-
sultancy firm of his own in addition to the factory.

By the time Sanjay came forward with his plan the question of producing an indigenous small car had already been hanging fire in India
for almost fifteen years. At various times committees of experts appointed by the central government had studied the issue, examined the
economic and technical feasibility of various projects and even held
preliminary negotiations with leading European manufacturers for possible collaboration in establishing a state-owned factory. The proposal
was, however, always shelved, owing partly to the political pressure of
the existing private-sector car manufacturers who did not want competition and partly to the government's hesitancy over allocating scarce
capital to the production of a motor car in a poor country where as yet
not even the need for bicycles had been adequately met.

The Prime Minister's opponents and many others, including ordinary citizens, noted with chagrin that this question of priorities was
completely ignored when Sanjay decided to set up his factory. The
economic and ideological objections previously considered valid were
quickly brushed aside. Not only was the production of a cheap motor
car suddenly considered a desirable undertaking but it was transferred
from the hitherto favored public sector to the private sector without any
explanation. Sanjay was able to raise the necessary capital, obtain the
government's formal approval, and acquire a large tract of land near
Delhi (extremely scarce by 1972) with a speed and facility not commonly associated with India's notoriously red-tape-ridden administration. Later, as is not unusual in such circumstances, Sanjay's ventures

spawned a large number of exaggerated, sometimes totally unfounded, tales of the young man's use of official machinery to help those who invested in his factory and of his browbeating people who stood in his way.

To the charge that special favors were shown to her son in the establishment of the Maruti factory, Indira reacts with heat. She says she has investigated the accusations and studied the growth of the factory with meticulous care and she is convinced that nothing illegal or irregular has been done. Must a young man be debarred from pursuing a profession of his choice merely because he happens to be the Prime Minister's son? she asks rhetorically. "What must I do if my son does not happen to be a professor-type?" No objection is raised if an established tycoon expands his industrial empire, but if a young man wishes to build something from scratch, it is regarded with suspicion and hostility, she complains.

The opposition raises the issue in Parliament with unfailing regularity and counters Indira's argument with a couple of rhetorical questions of its own: In today's India, with its officially regulated industry, would a young man with only minimal technical credentials be permitted by the government to embark on an ambitious car-manufacturing project if he were not the Prime Minister's son? How could an inexperienced person with almost no capital acquire precious land near Delhi and set up a multimillion rupee industry without the active help and connivance of various official agencies? The charge of flagrant nepotism is hurled at Indira during every session of Parliament. Most political observers believe that the Maruti issue is causing Indira Gandhi greater harm than she seems to realize.

Few in the country seriously believe that Indira herself is guilty of corruption. But many are convinced that she is not averse to coming to terms with corrupt elements and at times even shielding them should that serve her political ends. A commission headed by a senior judge found Harekrushna Mahatab, a former member of the central Cabinet under Nehru and often Chief Minister of Orissa, guilty of having accepted a bribe of 600,000 rupees from an industry. No action was taken against Mahatab, presumably because Indira needed his cooperation in getting Nandini Satpathy, her nominee for the state chief ministership, elected to the legislature. Later, Mahatab was expelled from the Congress, not for the acts of corruption he had committed but for having worked against Mrs. Satpathi.

Mounting economic difficulties—prices rose by 22 per cent during 1972–73—combined with the Indian public's growing doubts about the personal integrity of many central and state ministers had, by the end of 1973, created among the people a feeling of contempt for the political leadership. This disenchantment in turn led to more corruption and callousness at various bureaucratic levels and caused widespread unrest among working people. It also created a general public mood of defiance of authority. Bombay alone, according to the *Illustrated Weekly of India*, witnessed 12,089 strikes, sit-in protests, and demonstrations during the eighteen months following the end of the Bangladesh war. Delhi, Calcutta, Madras, and other big cities had their proportionate share of displays of public anger, and there were police charges on crowds and vicious religious riots in many parts of the country. In Gujarat students rioted for almost three weeks in January 1974 over food prices and political corruption. Many were killed by police fire. In Lucknow, capital of Uttar Pradesh, even the police themselves mutinied and clashed with the army, causing over forty lives to be lost in the exchange of gunfire. A new spirit of violence seemed to pervade the nation born of Mahatma Gandhi's nonviolence movement.

In dealing with all this Indira has appeared curiously ineffective. Government at all levels seemed to reflect her mood, if mood is what it was. In the country's capital, where street traffic had been reasonably well-regulated, even government-owned buses would drive through the red lights at busy crossings, while policemen looked carelessly on. Adulteration of food and medicines was officially acknowledged to be widespread, but the authorities appeared to have no means to prevent it. In August 1973 the engineers on Indian railways went on strike, causing the country's economy a loss of hundreds of millions of rupees. Moreover, they beat up their superior officers without inviting any punishment. Technicians at the power-generating units serving the city of Delhi deliberately sabotaged units under their care and subjected the public to what the *Statesman* editorially denounced as "blackmail by black-out." No action was taken against them. Shortages of such essential items of daily use as bread, butter, cooking oil, and fuel would develop suddenly, and the government would be unable to do anything about them. Even the government-run Delhi Milk Supply scheme was turning away regular customers because, it said, not enough milk was available—at the same time private grocery shops were openly selling bottles of milk, with the official DMS seal intact, at twice the normal price.

Why is it that a leader who acted so determinedly and appeared to take the right decisions almost intuitively during the Bangladesh crisis seemed baffled and helpless against petty hoarders, profiteers, and irresponsible trade unions? Many political analysts attribute Indira's inaction and vacillation as her popularity and her government's strength faltered to the fact that her understanding of economic matters, like her father's before her, is exceedingly limited. She is credited with having a sixth sense in playing at power politics, be it at the party level or the international level, but it is believed that coping with economic problems of the magnitude and complexity facing India in the 1970s is beyond her. Some hold that her lack of precise ideological moorings is to blame for her helplessness. They say that her pragmatism, adequate to the crises of war and politics but not to long-range leadership, shows in the way she shouts socialistic slogans to get the popular vote but accepts vast contributions from big business to spend in elections. Plainly, she is often pulled in opposite directions. In the beginning of 1973, for example, Indira nationalized the food-grain trade in fulfillment of one of her socialist election pledges and fixed a low price for the procurement of wheat, but she would not compel farmers to part with their produce at the unprofitable price because the big landowners, who alone had the excess grain to sell, were among the party's principal financiers and supporters.

Perhaps the simple truth is that Indira is a politician who came to the top and to incredible personal power through a process of party infighting and that she is now finding herself out of her depth in administering a chaotic, anarchical country of India's size. Perhaps she is the kind of leader, great but limited, like Churchill and De Gaulle, who functions well only in the face of grim, dramatic challenge. The truth was not clear as Indira in 1974, approaching her fifty-seventh birthday, marked her eighth year as Prime Minister of India.

A part of the answer to the problem of deciphering the truth of Prime Minister Gandhi's present capacities and character may lie in her own assessment of herself. When a visiting Italian journalist asked her to describe Indira Gandhi, the woman, the Prime Minister was reported as saying: "In spite of always living in the public glare, she has remained a very private person. Her life has been hard. This has made her self-reliant but has not hardened her."

Such descriptions of a personality, particularly one as complex as that of Indira, can seldom be complete or entirely accurate—perhaps particularly when they are self-assessments. Various descriptions of the "real Indira" tend to diverge enormously. Many of them doubtless reflect, as did Henry Kissinger's observation that the lady is cold-blooded, the predilections of the viewer himself. Others catch but one or two facets of her complex mind and heart. Most people who have known her reasonably well or interviewed her often have noted, with varying emphasis, her aloofness. To some she has seemed self-conscious and uncomfortable in the presence of others. To others she has appeared calculatedly arrogant and indifferent.

Soon after she first became Prime Minister, an article about her in the *New York Times* by Anthony Lukas, then the resident correspondent in India, portrayed Indira as a "profoundly lonely person." It stressed the point, in fact, stating that "by upbringing and circumstances she stands remarkably—almost frighteningly—alone." Possibly, as this statement suggests, Indira does remain even now as lonesome as she felt as a child in Anand Bhavan, even though over the years she has converted loneliness into a strange capacity to draw upon her own resources rather than to depend on others. Her seeming aloofness can be seen largely as a combination of shyness never entirely overcome and her determination to limit her need of or reliance on others to the absolute minimum. As a child in her grandfather's mansion she had watched with apparent helplessness the unhappiness of her mother in the Nehru household, and she confessed to a woman reporter, "I saw her being hurt and I was determined not to be hurt."

This is not a resolve in which anyone can hope to succeed, but on occasions when she has been hurt she has managed to an almost unbelievable degree to keep her sorrow entirely to herself. The last few years of her marriage are a case in point. Her prolonged bouts of marital unhappiness came when she was constantly in the public gaze. Yet few people caught even a glimpse of what passed in her mind. As far as one knows, Indira confided to no one in the matter. In this period Satish Gujral, a young and sensitive Delhi artist, did a brilliant semi-abstract portrait of Indira depicting her as a soul on the cross. His painting was greeted with a storm of protest. He had portrayed emotional anguish that was not Indira's, critics said. But Nehru, who liked the painting, assured Gujral that those who attacked it "do not know Indira."

This is not to suggest that India's Prime Minister is a woman who has built an emotional moat around herself that none may cross or that the childhood damage of watching her mother's unhappiness rendered her incapable of giving deep love. Recipients of her affection may be few, but the warmth of her feelings for them is never in doubt. The constancy of her affection for her father remains almost legendary. Even after she had a family of her own, Jawaharlal remained the principal object of her devotion. When she first married, she was, from all accounts, much in love with Feroze. As for her two sons, she has always doted on them. It is in fact the uncritical quality of her affection for the younger son, some feel, that has obscured from her otherwise very sharp view the political hazards involved in his Maruti project. She is also deeply attached to her beautiful Italian daughter-in-law, Sonia, who is now described in Delhi as her best friend. On her hurried visit to the United States in 1971 she asked her driver in New York to make an unscheduled stop at Saks Fifth Avenue so she could do some shopping. The New York papers reported that she bought lingerie and "very feminine" negligees for herself and for Rajiv's wife. The two are said to share concerns not only over Sonia's children but also hairdressers and the choice of clothes. (Sonia generally dresses in Western style. Indira wears quiet, but always modish and becoming *saris* of hand-spun cotton yarn and Kashmiri shawls of simple design but expensive workmanship and quality when traveling in the country or facing India's Old Guard parliamentarians. Abroad or when entertaining dignitaries, she dresses fastidiously and fashionably in heavy, usually Bangalore, silk *saris* with gold or silver embroidered borders, often topped by a cape in cold weather.)

Her two grandchildren, Rahul and Priyanka, both still small, seem to have become the focus of much of Indira's love. When she rushes home in the middle of the day it is not so much for rest or for lunch— she is a committed weight-watcher and often gladly skips that meal— but largely to get a brief period of play with her grandchildren. Many an evening, when she sits in her study attending to urgent papers and no other person dare disturb her, Rahul is privileged to set up a small table of his own next to hers where he pores over his papers in earnest imitation of Dadi Amman ("Grandma") as he calls her.

Her relations with her in-laws are proper, cordial, and by no means devoid of affection. Her mother-in-law Rattimai died many years ago, her sister-in-law Tehmina only recently. But to other relatives of Feroze's who live in Bombay, Indira writes regularly. She meets them every time she is in that city and makes certain of their presence at all important family events. When her eldest son, Rajiv, was to be married in 1968, she set the wedding date to suit their convenience. Indira's antipathy towards her eldest aunt, Vijayalakshmi Pandit, is no secret and has persisted over the years. But there is no evidence that any of that is extended to Madame Pandit's three daughters, two of whom are married to senior officials of India's diplomatic service. These three, whom Indira often looked after in the stressful days before independence, are frequent and welcome visitors with their families to the Prime Minister's house. Her second aunt, Krishna Hutheesing, of whom Indira was particularly fond, died rather suddenly in 1967 in London, and Indira has maintained a close personal contact with both of Krishna's sons and sees them often. During her November 1971 visit to the United States Indira, the hectic and sensitive nature of her mission notwithstanding, insisted on spending a quiet afternoon with one of Krishna's sons, who works for the World Bank in Washington, and his family.

Those who might be described as Indira's personal friends are singularly few, and all of them are women. Probably the oldest friend is Padmaja Naidu, former Governor of West Bengal and daughter of the poetess Sarojini Naidu, who at Indira's birth declared her the symbol of India's "new soul" and later recalled her at six months of age as "the proudest looking baby I have seen." Another good friend is Pupul Jayakar, a Delhi woman, somewhat older than Indira, whose active participation in social welfare projects and cultural and art movements has won her much public notice. Of all her circle, Teji Bachhan, wife of a well-known Hindi poet, is probably the closest to her. When Sonia arrived in India from Italy, she stayed for the few weeks before her wedding to Rajiv in the Bachhan home.

To her household staff, members of her official secretariat, and her top advisers, Indira is unusually kind and considerate. In her relations with them she is, in fact, entirely free from that element of brusqueness often detected in her dealings not only with political adversaries but some associates as well. She keeps herself informed of the personal affairs of those in her household or inner circle and assists and advises them in resolving problems that they or their families encounter. Like her father, who often wrote frantic notes from his prison cell urging the Nehru family to look after the welfare of their domestic staff, Indira is particularly mindful of the interests of the family servants— especially those who have served the Nehrus over a long period. She is not unduly demanding of service and appreciates merit and loyalty. Whenever a difficult task is accomplished—even at times when things have not gone quite the way she wished they would—Indira scribbles brief notes of thanks and appreciation to various members of her staff, domestic or official. All told, in seeming contradiction to her general reputation for aloofness, Indira has also always maintained a relationship of informality bordering on real friendship with those who work for her. In her secretariat she frequently walks unannounced into the room of some relatively junior official whom she might not have seen for a few days to inquire if there is anything he wishes to discuss with her. When she has some suggestion for a subordinate she does not send for him or convey the thought through her secretary. Instead she quickly writes a brief note in her own hand.

She is an inveterate scribbler of notes. Her office in the Central Secretariat as well as another in Parliament House, the room where she presides over the weekly Cabinet meeting, the car she rides in, and every nook and corner of her house, including her bathroom, are always kept equipped with a memo pad and pencil. She promptly jots down all ideas that come to her or instructions that she may issue. The basis for her talks with Nixon during the Bangladesh crisis came from a number of points she had noted down on stray scraps of paper at various times during the preceding weeks. In the course of a meeting in Delhi with the Prime Minister of Sri Lanka (formerly Ceylon), Mrs. Sirimavo Bandaranaike, she suddenly thought of her own impending visit to Canada and scribbled a note to remind the Foreign Office that a portion of her address to Parliament in Ottawa should be in French. During Cabinet meetings she has been known to hurriedly send a scribbled note out to her secretary asking him, for instance, to telephone her house and remind the cook that some of the guests for dinner are foreigners who might not fancy the tissue-thin silver paper often used to decorate fancy Indian deserts. Not all that she records on her memo pads relates to affairs of state or management of her house. She often writes down something funny or sarcastic she would have liked to say in a particular situation but did not for fear of causing offense or misunderstanding. Sometimes it may be something personal she suddenly wants to share with someone: During a helicopter ride in the course of her extensive election tour in the beginning of 1971, she passed a note to her press secretary captioned as "Important News Bulletin" announcing that her grandson Rahul had cut his first tooth that morning.

Indira's enormous capacity for work, as great as her father's, has puzzled all those who believed her frail constitution and long history of indifferent health would make it impossible for her to bear for long the physical strain of the prime ministership. On the day of her election as the party leader, Vijayalakshmi sneered about her poor health, but far from breaking under the strain, Indira, eight years later, is fitter than she has ever been. The unduly long hours and the tensions that the office involve seem to become her and even to have bred stamina in her. The adulation that the high office brings, the sight of large crowds turning out for her, refreshes Indira as it does politicians all over the world.

Indira also appears to have inherited her father's amazing ability to cast off in a few moments fatigue accumulated over many hours of hectic travel or demanding work. She is capable of recouping her energy in almost no time by doing something briefly that she really enjoys or by establishing contact, as she describes it, with a near and dear one. During her term as Congress President, it has been reported, she once arrived in Bombay late in the afternoon after nearly ten hours of travel in an uncomfortable jeep and addressing numerous rural audiences in the interior of the state. In the city the party organizers had arranged and publicly announced an extensive program of political meetings and talks extending well into the night. Totally exhausted though she was, she regarded the canceling of any of those engagements as unthinkable. Instead, Indira begged her hosts to allow her fifteen minutes for rest before embarking on the crowded schedule. She used that brief time not to lie down or have a refreshing shower but to write to her father whom she had left in Delhi only that morning and was due to see again before her letter would reach him. As soon as the envelope was handed over to a person for posting, those present recall, she appeared as fresh as if she were starting a new day.

Fairly soon after being chosen Prime Minister, Indira learned the importance of organizing her time with particular care. When in Delhi she follows a fairly strict routine, with only rare and brief deviations. She wakes at 6 A.M., and the first two hours after she gets up in the morning are strictly private, devoted to yoga and other general fitness exercises and routine personal chores. During this time she also glances through six of the capital's seven English-language dailies—the exception being the official organ of the Jana Sangh, the sectarian political organization to whose views she is particularly averse. At 8 A.M. her seniormost private secretary, N. K. Seshan, who worked with her father in a similar capacity, meets her at her house with important documents requiring her immediate attention. Half an hour later she emerges from her study to meet the large—often very large—number of unscheduled callers who since the early years of independence have traditionally thronged to the Indian Prime Minister's residence. Among such morning visitors are often many groups with grievances as diverse as the lack of a well in their village and the alleged highhandedness of a state Chief Minister. Individual callers usually get no more than a couple of minutes of her time during these interviews. Later, she moves by car to her elegant office in the southern wing of the massive red sandstone Secretariat that the famous British architect Sir Edwin Luytens designed to serve the imperial needs of the Raj. Indira does not live in the Luytens-designed house her father occupied, which she ran for him when he was Prime Minister, but in the Secretariat she has retained for herself the room in which he sat for so many years.

One of her principal engagements on most mornings is a fairly lengthy meeting with her secretary and a couple of other top officials of her secretariat. The discussion covers a wide range of important administrative and political matters and usually produces more decisions than the weekly Cabinet meeting. When Parliament is in session —which is almost seven months in the year—she functions from an office in the circular Parliament House not far from the Secretariat. On an average she spends two to three hours daily in either of the two chambers of Parliament. The rest of the time she remains within call and rushes to her seat in the house should the quorum bell ring or a situation requiring her intervention develop. When not attending

Parliament she receives from a dozen to twenty visitors every day in her office. During such interviews she is more of a listener than a talker. (Even at Cabinet meetings she speaks very little and is often seen doodling while ministers explain their respective proposals and anxiously await her reaction to them.) Her callers usually include state chief ministers, senior civil servants, diplomats, and visiting foreign newsmen who find her one of the most easily accessible heads of government in the world. When Parliament is meeting, MPs form a sizable proportion of her daily visitors. An MP, whatever his party affiliation, is seldom refused an appointment with her.

On returning home in the evening—almost never before 7 P.M.— Indira spends another hour or so in unavoidable telephone talks with Cabinet ministers or party functionaries. Before dining at about 9 she briefly relaxes with her family, occasionally has a romp with her grandchildren in the garden as twilight deepens and before they are sent off to bed, discusses household chores and problems with her staff, looks through some women's journals, and sometimes tries her hand at arranging flowers. Every once in a while she is seized by a strong desire to move around the furniture in her house or rid the storeroom of unwanted articles and then everybody available gets involved. She eats alone with her sons and Sonia more often than not. Very seldom does she see visitors who are not really close friends at her house, preferring to keep it as private as possible, except when she must entertain officially. Soon after the meal she closets herself in her study to pore over official documents and to read.

Her taste in reading is catholic. She can read the *Ladies' Home Journal* with enough attention to spot a recipe for her cook to try or an idea for something the tailor might copy for her grandchildren, but she also reads with great interest and care Norman Cousin's *Saturday Review World*, the *Atlantic*, and *Harper's*. Her subscription list to various newspapers and magazines is enormous. Other well-known American journals she gets are *Newsweek, Time,* and the *New Yorker*. From Britain she receives the *Sunday Times,* the *Observer,* the *Economist,* and the *Guardian*. From Paris come *Le Figaro, Réalités,* and *Paris Match*. She even likes occasionally to look through some German newspapers and magazines, though her knowledge of German is so limited that she is able to understand only the main headlines and captions to photographs. Her choice of books suggests that there is no set pattern in her lifelong habit of reading. One day she may pick up a new book of poetry—she reads a lot of poetry, mostly English, some French—and the next day she may take up a book on film-making. Nonconformist writers particularly interest her. In recent years she has read a number of books on problems of the environment, including Rene Dubos's and Barbara Ward Jackson's *Only One Earth.* Alvin Toffler's *Future Shock,* Dee Brown's *Bury My Heart at Wounded Knee,* Joseph Lash's biography of Eleanor Roosevelt, and, curiously, a recent book on the life of the last of the powerful Manchu empresses are some of the things she was reading in the troubled summer of 1973.

Important news received after she has retired is usually kept for the morning unless there is something unusually urgent and pressing. She was, for example, not awakened to be told of the sudden death of Egyptian President Nasser, news of which reached her secretariat at 3:30 A.M. (Jawaharlal would have been given that news immediately.) Among the few occasions when an exception was made to this rigid rule was the night the King of Bhutan died while on a visit to Kenya and the Crown Prince was anxious to speak to her as soon as possible on the telephone from the capital of his Himalayan kingdom.

When Indira travels, her routine is varied and less precise, but she is always anxious to make the best use of her time. Except during an election campaign, when it is unavoidable that she go about extensively by jeep and car, much of her traveling is done in a rather modestly equipped aircraft of the Indian Air Force. Her advisers and personal staff usually accompany her during such journeys, and while in flight she spends much of her time consulting them or studying official files. She scoffs at devoting a great deal of time to getting dressed, and when necessary she can, she claims, bathe and dress in 4½ minutes. She has more than once terminated an in-flight conference with her staff just as the aircraft touched down at its destination and emerged from her cabin in a fresh *sari* with her hair brushed and smart-looking by the time the plane taxied to the terminal and the door was about to be opened. During visits to a state capital when she customarily stays in the governor's palace, she prefers to have her meals quietly in her own suite. That is partly due to her shyness and partly because she finds formal lunches and dinners needlessly time-consuming and possibly fattening.

Indira eats carefully but not fussily. She neither smokes nor drinks (consumption of alcohol by women is generally uncommon in India, but Indira additionally belongs to a generation and class of women who regard it with social disdain.) At state banquets, when formal toasts are exchanged, she usually asks for fruit juice instead of wine. Because of anxiety about her weight—she has visibly succeeded in keeping it under check so far—she gladly skips breakfast altogether on most mornings, and a ound 11 A.M. has a cup of soup served to her at her desk out of a thermos flask. Lunch is simple—usually a light European-style dish accompanied by boiled vegetables. Dinner is somewhat more elaborate and is often cooked in Indian style. She likes Kashmirian and other north-Indian dishes but when traveling in different parts of the country partakes of meals prepared in the local or regional style. The only demand she makes of her hosts is that the food not be unduly hot or excessively spiced.

For all that she reads and reads, and for all the notes she scribbles, Indira Gandhi is no spinner of original or complex political concepts. Her father loved propounding his ideas on diverse national and inter-national issues and wrote millions of words in personal letters and official notes to record his thinking. To Krishna Menon, the keenness of whose intellect stimulated him, Nehru, for example, wrote nearly 400 letters in a period of about five years. Indira has little if any desire to enter into elaborate philosophical discussions with anyone or to polish phrases. Her speeches to the Indian masses as well as to more formal audiences are so matter of fact as to be often pedestrian. Her answers to interviewers, though freely given, are short and suggest a distinct disinclination on her part to be drawn into an argument or to have to identify those factors and considerations that might have influenced her mind on a particular issue. In the end she gives to most people the impression of being first and foremost a hardheaded politi-cian who reaches her objective by the shortest possible route and has little patience for moral or intellectual justifications for what she does.

Surprisingly, however, she courts intellectuals, writers, and artists with zest. During her visit to New York in 1970 to attend the twenty-fifth anniversary celebrations of the United Nations, she invited a group of American writers to meet her in her hotel suite. And so ab-sorbed did Prime Minister Indira Gandhi become in their talk that the then U.S. Secretary of State, William Rogers, who was due to meet her later, was obliged at her request to put off his visit. Visiting Canada three years later, she asked her hosts to arrange for her to meet some of the country's leading film-makers. Over the years she has acquired many personal friends in the field of arts and letters and keeps in touch with them. Letters from Buckminster Fuller and Yehudi Menuhin, or a brief note from a French poet accompanying his latest collection of poems, delight Indira immensely.

Who is she then, this strong woman with unexpected periods of weakness and inaction in her exercise of authority, this intelligent woman who resists rigorous thought in conversation and letters but is attracted to intellectuals far more than to the political animals with whom she daily thrusts and parries? Questions have always been asked and will continue to be:

Is she a committed socialist in the Fabian sense, or do her overtures to the Russians in 1973, like her father's before her to the Russian and Chinese communists, suggest a more Marxist commitment? For a socialist, does she flirt and compromise too much with the capitalists of her own country and the world? As one who was so close to Gandhi, and is now leader of a country that proclaims peace as an article of faith, how could she so easily use the final violence of war against Pakistan?

Is she plainly and simply a power broker, but one whose dedication to Indian nationalism explains her every action? Is she a convinced parliamentary democrat? A potential dictator? As a devoted mother, is she blind to the threat that private loyalties can pose to the public loyalties that are her first duty as the chosen leader of 560 million people.

Was she emotionally scarred to the point of being always dangerously subject to unpredictable vacillation and overweening need for power by the insecurity she suffered as a child? Or did that childhood of luxury and loneliness in a city at a confluence of sacred rivers, in a time of confluence in the histories of the Western and Asian worlds, make her perhaps the only person who in the years immediately ahead can preserve India's freedom—and with it a necessary balance in world politics?

To no one of these questions is there as yet a definitive answer. The final fascination of the most powerful woman in the world—and that

Indira Gandhi remains despite the falling off in her personal popularity in India—is that the secrets of her personality and dreams are locked even now within that very private person she has been since she was a girl in Allahabad.

Bibliography

Books

ABBAS, KHAWJA AHMAD. *Indira Gandhi: Return of the Red Rose.* Bombay: Popular Prakashan, 1966.
ALEXANDER, M. K. *Madame Gandhi: A Political Biography.* North Quincy, Mass.: Christopher Publishing House, 1969.
BHATIA, KRISHAN. *The Ordeal of Nationhood.* New York: Atheneum, 1971.
BOWLES, CHESTER. *Ambassador's Report.* New York: Harper & Row, 1954.
———. *Promises to Keep.* New York: Harper & Row, 1972.
BRANDON, HENRY. *The Retreat of American Power.* New York: Doubleday, 1973.
BRECHER, MICHAEL. *Nehru: A Political Biography.* London: Oxford University Press, 1959.
CHATTERJEE, BASANT. *The Congress Splits.* New Delhi: S. Chand, n.d.
DAS, DURGA. *India from Curzon to Nehru and After.* New York: John Day, 1970.
GHANDI, INDIRA. *Selected Speeches of Indira Gandhi.* New Delhi: Publications Division, 1971.
HANGEN, WELLES. *After Nehru Who?* London: Rupert Hart Davis, 1963.
HUTHEESING, KRISHNA NEHRU. *Dear to Behold: An Intimate Portrait of Indira Gandhi.* New York: Macmillan, 1969.
HUTHEESING, KRISHNA NEHRU, ed. *Nehru's Letters to His Sister.* London: Faber & Faber, 1963.
HUTHEESING, KRISHNA NEHRU, and ALDEN HATCH. *We Nehrus.* New York: Holt, Reinhart, & Winston, 1967.
MENON, K. P. S. *The Flying Troika: The Political Diary of India's Ambassador to Russia, 1952–61.* New York: Oxford University Press, 1963.
MOHAN, ANAND. *Indira Gandhi.* New York: Hawthorn Books, 1967.
MORAES, FRANK. *Indira Gandhi.* New Delhi: Directorate of Advertising and Visual Publicity, 1966.
NANDA, B. R. *The Nehrus: Motilal and Jawaharlal.* London: Allen & Unwin, 1962.

————. *Mahatma Gandhi: A Biography.* New York: Baron, 1965.
NAYAR, KULDIP. *India: The Critical Years.* New Delhi: Vikas Publications, 1971.
NEHRU, JAWAHARLAL. *Glimpses of World History.* New York: John Day, 1942.
————. *The Discovery of India.* New York: John Day, 1946.
————. *Toward Freedom.* Boston: Beacon Press, 1958.
————. *A Bunch of Old Letters.* New York: Asia Publishing House, 1960.
————. *Autobiography.* New York: Paragon, 1965.
PANDIT, VIJAYALAKSHMI. *Prison Days.* Calcutta: Signet Press, 1945.
RAU, M. CHALAPATHI, UMA PARASHER, INDER MALHOTRA, KRISHAN BHATIA, K. M. AGARWALA, and "RANGA." *Indira Priyadarshini.* Mystic, Conn.: Lawrence Verry, 1966.
SAHGAL, NAYANTARA. *Prison and Chocolate Cake.* New York: Alfred A. Knopf, 1954.
WILLCOXEN, HARRIET. *First Lady of India: The Story of Indira Gandhi.* New York: Doubleday, 1969.
WIRSING, GISELHER. *The Indian Experiment.* New Delhi: Orient Longman, 1972.

Speeches and Articles

ATTWOOD, WILLIAM. "A Frank Talk with a Powerful Woman," *Look,* April 30, 1968.
CAMERON, JAMES. "India's First Lady: Indira," *Envoy* (London), June 1966.
CHALFONT, LORD. "Indira Gandhi of India," interview broadcast on BBC, October 26, 1971.
FRIEDAN, BETTY. "How Mrs. Gandhi Shattered the Feminine Mystique," *Ladies' Home Journal,* May 1966.
GRIGG, JOHN. "A Woman with a Heart of a King," *Sunday Times* (London), March 7, 1971.
LUKAS, J. ANTHONY. "She Stands Remarkably Alone," *New York Times,* May 27, 1966.
MENEN, AUBREY. "Indira Gandhi Is Sort of the De Gaulle of India," *New York Times Magazine,* December 31, 1972.
MICHAELIS, ARNOLD. "An Interview with Indira Gandhi," *McCall's,* April 1966.
MORAES, DOM. "The Indian PM," *New York Times,* February 14, 1971.

Index

Index